Confucianism, Discipline, and Competitiveness

CDC offers a new perspective on education and competitiveness.
—Professor Eric Hanushek, Stanford University, USA

CDC book shows that rules and etiquette governing school discipline has farther-reaching benefits in the economic arena.
—Professor Wujin Chu, Seoul National University (SNU), Seoul, South Korea

A must read for all policy makers.
—Professor Rosalie L Tung, Simon Fraser University (SFU), Vancouver BC, Canada

The clear message from the research reported in this book is that the Confucian heritage provides a context in which teenagers are capable of some of the world's best measured performances derived from school teaching.
— Professor Gordon Redding, INSEAD & University of Hong Kong

The importance of competitiveness has increased rapidly in recent years, where a fresh look at the different forms in which competitiveness manifests is needed. Though the exceptional growth of East Asian economies has been hypothesised previously from a sociocultural perspective, links have often been vague with little empirical evidence to support them. This book proposes that a unique paradigm of competitiveness has developed in the East as a result of the cultural traditions and social values influenced by Confucianism, and extends this hypothesis by exploring a critical missing link: the role of discipline.

Based on data from the Programme for International Student Assessment (PISA) and World Economic Forum (WEF), this book sheds light on important insights, through empirical evidence, that culture and discipline play an important role toward a country's academic performance, and ultimately, competitiveness. In comparing six geographical clusters, this book analyses data by applying the 'Inter-Ocular Test (IOT)'—visualisation of data distributions—to supplement traditional statistical mean comparisons.

The findings advance the discourse on culture and performance, by drawing attention to the significant impact that improving discipline can have for a nation's productivity—not only those of Confucian East Asia. Written with the evolving global economy in mind, this book highlights the relevance of discipline for shaping individual productivity for the future workforce, and offers new perspectives on how this can be achieved for all societies through three key contributions: taxonomy of discipline dimensions, Parent-Engagement-School-Discipline taxonomy (PESD), and wheel of competitiveness.

Building on the authors' prior works, this book offers a comprehensive look at three interrelated concepts: Confucianism, Discipline, and Competitiveness, and how they relate to performance in East Asia. Written in an accessible style, this book will be a valuable guide for students, educators, practitioners, and policy makers who seek to further understand the valuable role of discipline in shaping the success of societies, present and future.

Chris Baumann is an Associate Professor at Macquarie University, Sydney, a Visiting Professor at Seoul National University (SNU) in South Korea, and a Visiting Associate Professor at Osaka University in Japan; formerly also at Aarhus University in Denmark.

Hume Winzar is an Associate Professor at Macquarie University, Sydney, and director of the degree in Business Analytics.

Doris Viengkham completed her doctoral thesis in the Faculty of Business and Economics at Macquarie University, Sydney.

Routledge Studies in International Business and the World Economy

Managing Culture and Interspace in Cross-border Investments
Building a Global Company
Edited by Martina Fuchs, Sebastian Henn, Martin Franz, and Ram Mudambi

Venture Capital and Firm Performance
The Korean Experience in a Global Perspective
Jaeho Lee

Expatriate Managers
The Paradoxes of Living and Working Abroad
Anna Spiegel, Ursula Mense-Petermann, and Bastian Bredenkötter

The International Business Environment and National Identity
Tatiana Gladkikh

European Born Globals
Job creation in young international businesses
Edited by Irene Mandl and Valentina Patrini

Management Research
European Perspectives
Edited by Sabina Siebert

Global Business Intelligence
Edited by J. Mark Munoz

Confucianism, Discipline, and Competitiveness
Chris Baumann, Hume Winzar, and Doris Viengkham

For a full list of titles in this series, visit www.routledge.com/Routledge-Studies-in-International-Business-and-the-World-Economy/book-series/SE0358

Confucianism, Discipline, and Competitiveness

Chris Baumann, Hume Winzar, and Doris Viengkham

Routledge
Taylor & Francis Group

LONDON AND NEW YORK

First published 2020 by Routledge

2 Park Square, Milton Park, Abingdon, Oxon, OX14 4RN

605 Third Avenue, New York, NY 10017

Routledge is an imprint of the Taylor & Francis Group, an informa business

First issued in paperback 2020

Library of Congress Cataloging-in-Publication Data
Names: Baumann, Chris, author. | Winzar, Hume, author. |
    Viengkham, Doris, author.
Title: Confucianism, discipline and competitiveness / Chris Baumann,
    Hume Winzar, and Doris Viengkham.
Description: NewYork, NY : Routledge, 2020. | Series: Routledge
    studies in international business and the world economy | Includes
    bibliographical references.
Identifiers: LCCN 2019015399 | ISBN 9780815378617 (hardback) |
    ISBN 9781351062220 (ebook)
Subjects: LCSH: Competition. | Economic development. | Confucianism. |
    Academic achievement.
Classification: LCC HB238 .B38 2020 | DDC 658.4/01—dc23
LC record available at https://lccn.loc.gov/2019015399

ISBN: 978-0-8153-7861-7 (hbk)
ISBN: 978-0-367-78586-4 (pbk)

Typeset in Sabon
by Apex CoVantage, LLC

Contents

Tables and Figures

Tables

Figures

Endorsements

The literature has long aspired to better understand how education relates, yes 'drives', a nation's economic performance. Baumann, Winzar, and Viengkham's work labelled CDC (Confucianism, Discipline, and Competitiveness) adds to this debate the dimension of 'discipline' as a driver of performance and competitiveness. East Asia has long stood out as a peak performer in academic performance, but it was not well understood 'why'.

CDC provides evidence that indeed a Confucian approach to pedagogy contributes to strong performance. This book offers a new understanding of pedagogy, contrasting East Asia to other parts of the world. In addition, their 'wheel of competitiveness' showcases the complexity for developing markets to become more competitive. Ultimately, the proposed new taxonomy of discipline dimensions and Parent-Engagement-School-Discipline taxonomy (PESD) should be inspiring for policy makers in education and economic strategy around the globe.

—**Professor Eric Hanushek**, *Stanford University, USA*

In "The Protestant Ethic and the Spirit of Capitalism", Max Weber analysed how the economies of Western and Northern Europe managed to develop rapidly based on the Protestant ethic. In particular, the influence of the Protestant ethic on accumulation and use of capital in these countries is well documented. This book on CDC is an ambitious effort to carry out an analogous investigation for the rapid economic development of East Asian societies in the modern era. The authors show through intuition and data that Confucian values of education, hard work, and discipline have led to the successful economic development of 'Confucian Orbit' societies.

The CDC book shows that rules and etiquette governing school discipline has farther-reaching benefits in the economic arena. Such norms and etiquette—Confucian value of "li"—have been a strong influence in the formation of business relations and company cultures in Asia. High-performing Asian firms are characterized by harmonious worker-management relationships and equitable relations between suppliers and OEMs (Original Equipment Manufacturers).

This book promises to be an important platform for further study on Confucian ethic and competitiveness. It is a must read for those who want to obtain a deeper understanding of Asian business and the Confucian approach to education.

—**Professor Wujin Chu,** *Seoul National University (SNU),*
Seoul, South Korea

Prologue

Competitiveness has long been the 'Holy Grail' for nations in a highly interconnected world economy. Baumann, Winzar, and Viengkham in their work on Confucianism, Discipline, and Competitiveness, or CDC, have focussed on the important role that cultural attributes—emphasis on education, discipline, and hard work—can play toward a country's academic performance and competitiveness. CDC fills a gap in the literature with its new and unique focus on discipline as link between culture and performance/competitiveness. Amy Chua's book *Battle Hymn of the Tiger Mother* (2011) offered insights into Asian parenting, with this book on CDC now extending this perspective to 'East Asian schooling', or how schools are run and perform in global comparison.

This book sheds light on important insights, supported by evidence, how countries can enhance their performance and competitiveness in the global arena, not least by maintaining or enhancing discipline standards in their education systems. The authors offer new perspectives:

- Taxonomy of discipline dimensions;
- Parent-Engagement-School-Discipline taxonomy, or PESD;
- Wheel of competitiveness.

The Programme for International Student Assessment (PISA) data on student performance has been analysed extensively in the literature, but this book is new by applying 'Inter-Ocular Testing (IOT)': distributions of discipline, academic performance, and competitiveness are plotted for geographic clusters. This approach allows for visual comparison that goes beyond traditional statistical mean comparison.

CDC is thought provoking with its outlook on education for the future. The authors offer two scenarios where students are viewed and 'treated' as learner or as customer, each with its own pedagogical approach, and as the authors demonstrate, diverging performance. The jury has long been out on which pedagogical approach will ultimately assist developed nations to maintain their economic standard and competitiveness, and how emerging and developing markets can enhance their standing. This book makes an important, evidence-based contribution to this debate. Should education be a business, or should it be part of a "country's overall objectives and aspirations, and national culture is also instilled in students"?

Baumann, Winzar, and Viengkham's book on Confucianism, Discipline, and Competitiveness (CDC) is a must read for all policy makers in the private and public sectors who are concerned with performance and competitiveness at different levels of analysis. Education policy makers, teachers, and professors will benefit from reading CDC, with educators in the Confucian Orbit offered a better understanding of what is at stake if they deviate from their traditional Confucian approach to education, and for Western educators, this book could serve as a wake-up call that academic performance and competitiveness should not be taken for granted.

—Professor Rosalie L. Tung
Simon Fraser University (SFU), Vancouver BC, Canada

PhD, MBA (UBC); BA (York); Ming & Stella Wong Professor of International Business, FRS(C), Fellow of the Academy of Management (AoM), Fellow of the Academy of International Business (AIB), Fellow of the British Academy of Management. She has published 11 books and over 90 articles and has served as the 2003–2004 President of the Academy of Management (AoM) and the 2015–2016 President of the Academy of International Business (AIB).

1 Setting the Scene for CDC

Introducing CDC

We are introducing the idea of combining three seemingly unrelated dimensions from three different areas of study:

- *Confucianism* from cultural studies;
- *Discipline* from the fields of education and pedagogy; and
- *Competitiveness* from the sphere of business and economics;

or in short: CDC. "Competitiveness is not that bad . . . at least in the east, and also the west", concluded Baumann and Harvey (2018, p. 198), pointing at competitiveness as a factor in the seismic changes in global economic (and other) power shifting to East Asia. Combining such well-researched areas with extensive literature each in their own right is not a trivial exercise. But then again, developing 'something' new, linking seemingly unrelated or disassociated constructs, and recommending a new way of looking at things is perhaps not meant to be easy.

We are novel in linking these three areas in one empirical study reported in this book, such a combination being the confluence of two fundamental questions that we aspire to answer in our research:

1. Could discipline be a driver of performance and competitiveness?
2. Could it be that under Confucianism, discipline is stronger, and therefore drives performance and competitiveness?

The literature has explored Confucianism and competitiveness, separately, and in great detail—we will summarise some key literature in the chapters to come. There are also numerous books (e.g. Yao, 2000; Tu, 1996; Moon, 2000; Porter, 2011). Nonetheless, the domain of discipline applied and passed on in a country's education system has not previously been explored as a 'link' between Confucianism and competitiveness as we aspire to in the next four chapters of this book—this shall be our contribution offered here, i.e. a better understanding of how discipline drives performance and competitiveness.

Discipline has been studied in the context of parenting (Baumrind, 1991a; Dornbusch, Ritter, Leiderman, Roberts and Fraleigh, 1987) and education (Pellerin, 2005a), generally pointing towards a positive correlation with some performance indicators, but empirical work testing discipline as a driver of academic performance and competitiveness has only recently emerged, and this book contributes to this debate—does discipline drive performance and competitiveness?

The premise for our research is that human capital and talent has equal and normal distribution by nature across ethnic and racial groups, i.e. from a biological perspective, no group is really better than the other, but the differentiation factor we anticipate is culture such as Confucianism. In other words, culture determines how education systems 'work', how schools are run, what type of school policy applies to which area (e.g. dress code), the curriculum and pedagogy, and ultimately it is these educational institutions and their style that result in higher (or lower) academic performance in global comparison. Again, there would be a normal distribution in terms of innate talent and intelligence (IQ) for each society, but we argue that the way education 'works' (i.e. the passing on of knowledge and values) is ultimately culturally driven, and a matter of self-discipline (Duckworth and Seligman, 2005). Our study is designed to explore precisely these issues—how does discipline drive performance, whether there is a difference between cultures, and to what extent does it drive national competitiveness?

We use international student data as measurement for discipline and academic performance, namely data from the Programme for International Student Assessment (PISA), a worldwide project by the Organisation for Economic Co-operation and Development (OECD). PISA started in 2000 and is conducted every three years. In the last few testing rounds we saw Confucian societies (China, Japan, Korea, Singapore, Taiwan, and Vietnam) peak perform, outperforming the West and other Asian societies, indeed outperforming the majority of the world (Figure 1.1). This begs the question: in what way is education done differently in Confucian societies than in the West, other Asian countries, and other parts of the world?

As previously alluded to, discipline stands out as a key candidate for differentiation with evidence in the literature (Baumann and Krskova, 2016) that education in the Confucian Orbit follows strict principals with a focus on respect, punctuality, and performance orientation. Given the very nature of these Confucian 'traits', we anticipate that a Confucian approach to education should drive academic performance and ultimately also drive competitiveness.

In sum, this book explores the mechanisms, the empirical associations among the three dimensions Confucianism, Discipline, and Competitiveness (CDC). Conceptually, our framework is anticipated to work as follows (Figure 1.2).

PISA Science 2015			PISA Math 2015			PISA Reading 2015		
Rank	Country	Mean	Rank	Country	Mean	Rank	Country	Mean
1	**Singapore**	556	1	**Singapore**	564	1	**Singapore**	535
2	**Japan**	538	2	**Hong Kong**	548	2	**Hong Kong**	527
3	Estonia	534	3	**Macao**	544	3	Canada	527
4	**Taiwan**	532	4	**Taiwan**	542	4	Finland	526
5	Finland	531	5	**Japan**	532	5	Ireland	521
6	**Macao**	529	6	**China**	531	6	Estonia	519
7	Canada	528	7	**South Korea**	524	7	**Korea**	517
8	**Vietnam**	525	8	Switzerland	521	8	**Japan**	516
9	**Hong Kong**	523	9	Estonia	520	9	Norway	513
10	**China**	518	10	Canada	516	10	New Zealand	509
11	**South Korea**	516	11	Netherlands	512	12	**Macao**	509
12	New Zealand	513	12	Denmark	511	16	Australia	503
14	Australia	510	21	New Zealand	495	22	United Kingdom	498
15	United Kingdom	509	22	**Vietnam**	495	23	**Taiwan**	497
16	Germany	509	25	Australia	494	24	United States	497
35	United States	496	40	United States	470	27	**China**	494
	OECD Average	493		**OECD Average**	490		**OECD Average**	493

Figure 1.1 PISA 2015 Rankings Across Academic Performance

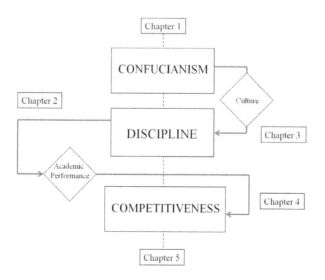

Figure 1.2 Roadmap Structure of CDC

Structure of This Book

In short, we offer a new way of looking at culture and how it drives performance/competitiveness through discipline. Our key argument is that discipline drives performance and competitiveness, and that there would be differences around the world based on how cultural values determine the types of discipline imposed, and their degree of importance.

We have structured this book along the way we make our argument with subsequent empirical evidence. Each chapter is centred on a fundamental question we seek to answer, which, when taken together, contributes to our overall understanding of how the Confucianism-Discipline-Competitiveness (CDC) model operates.

Chapter 2—The Confucianism-Discipline-Competitiveness (CDC) Model

In Chapter 2 we explore the relationships among CDC dimensions. Essentially we use Structural Equation Modelling (SEM) to probe to what degree discipline dimensions associate with competitiveness, and we contrast our model findings across six geographic clusters. Special focus is placed on a comparison of the Confucian Orbit to other areas with comparable economic circumstances, namely Anglo-Saxon and Western European nations. This testing shows how associations in the CDC model work, in general, but it does not demonstrate a direct comparison of CDC dimensions (mean, median, spread/distribution). In this chapter, we aim to answer the following: *could school discipline be a driver of academic performance?*

Chapter 3—Discipline and Academic Performance Under the Microscope

In this chapter, we pose the question of whether school discipline is stronger under Confucianism. We offer the results of our Inter-Ocular Testing (IOT) (Baumann, Winzar and Fang, 2018) where we explore differences among geographic clusters and cultures for each CDC dimension. Here we offer mean and median statistics. However, rather than simply concluding on cultural differences on statistical significance alone (i.e. a p-value), where with the large PISA data set means almost all would be significantly different to each other just due to the sheer size of students involved in testing, we offer comprehensive charts that plot the distribution for each dimension. This allows for a more realistic comparison of how the differences and similarities across the geographic clusters really play out.

Chapter 4—CDC Over Time: A Simulation Approach

In this chapter, we apply a temporal lens to examine the effect of academic performance on national competitiveness, with PISA data from 2000 to 2015, and World Economic Forum data from 2000 to 2018. Drawing on data from over two decades, we ultimately demonstrate that the discipline passed on in schools, at one in point in time, has a positive effect on a nation's competitiveness in half a generation (approximately 15 years). We plot the data to illustrate the temporal developments of CDC dimensions, and establish a direct association between individual (micro) student performance, and national (macro) competitiveness rankings. We further dissect the data by segmenting students' academic performance into 'low' and 'elite' (top 15 percent) performers, and present a number of simulated effects to account for changes in global competitiveness if discipline—at the school level—were increased, decreased, or simply maintained.

Chapter 5—Conclusions and Outlook on CDC

In our last chapter we look back on the results of our study, and offer theoretical, practical, and research implications. We also reflect on CDC from a broader perspective, including previous debates about the *Battle Hymn of the Tiger Mother*, Amy Chua's bestselling book on Asian-heritage parenting, but also why a case can be made that discipline is an important factor for future generations working in the gig economy. Importantly, we do recommend that CDC be incorporated in future work and research on education, and that discipline specifically should be explored more in various contexts. For practitioners, we offer a call to maintain or indeed improve discipline standards in classrooms since that is associated with better performance. We offer a practical typology of discipline dimensions, areas that trigger consequences for non-compliance, e.g. poor behaviour, disrespect, bad manners, unpunctuality, and—crucially and novel—also underperformance.

Spotlights

Throughout this book we include 'Spotlight' sections based on academic literature and popular press detailing the approaches of East Asian societies on a number of discipline/performance issues. This is a practical and easy-to-comprehend way to showcase how CDC elements have been enacted/construed/perceived across cultures and contexts.

In sum, we aspire to showcase a novel approach to a current topic discussed in the media, by experts and parents around the globe, and ask: how can we better prepare future generations for an increasingly competitive workforce? Our focus on discipline as a driver of performance

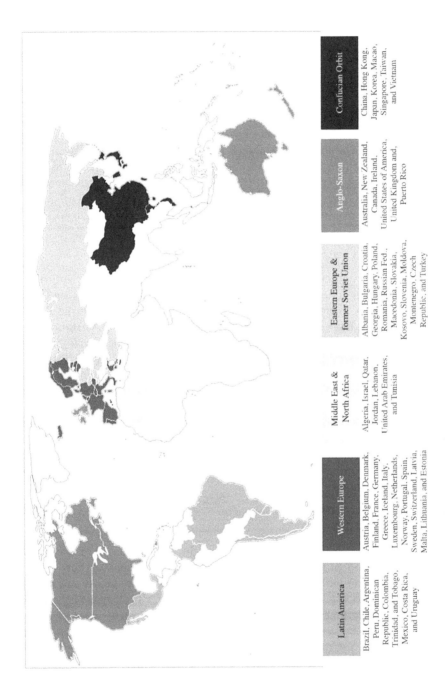

Figure 1.3 Visualisation of Cluster Groups by Country

Latin America	Western Europe	Middle East & North Africa	Eastern Europe & former Soviet Union	Anglo-Saxon	Confucian Orbit
Brazil, Chile, Argentina, Peru, Dominican Republic, Colombia, Trinidad, and Tobago, Mexico, Costa Rica, and Uruguay	Austria, Belgium, Denmark, Finland, France, Germany, Greece, Iceland, Italy, Luxembourg, Netherlands, Norway, Portugal, Spain, Sweden, Switzerland, Latvia, Malta, Lithuania, and Estonia	Algeria, Israel, Qatar, Jordan, Lebanon, United Arab Emirates, and Tunisia	Albania, Bulgaria, Croatia, Georgia, Hungary, Poland, Romania, Russian Fed., Macedonia, Slovakia, Kosovo, Slovenia, Moldova, Montenegro, Czech Republic, and Turkey	Australia, New Zealand, Canada, Ireland, United States of America, United Kingdom and, Puerto Rico	China, Hong Kong, Japan, Korea, Macao, Singapore, Taiwan, and Vietnam

and competitiveness is new, since this dimension of education systems has been largely overlooked in the literature to date (at least in the context we explore in this book), and our focus on cultural differences as driver of competitiveness may also to contribute to the literature on what really drives competitiveness (e.g. Confucianism through a disciplined approach in education).

All three CDC dimensions are dynamic—i.e. they change over time, and are different in different parts of the world. Our analysis focusses on the most recent wave of PISA data collection in 2015, with a temporal analysis over time for the simulation part of our book (Chapter 4).

In order to test for differences on the CDC dimensions, we have categorised the PISA data along the following geographical clusters, following Baumann and Winzar (2016), where countries have been organised on the basis of similar economies and that the educational systems operate in similar manner;[1] we use alphabetical sorting below, and we show these clusters in the world map in Figure 1.3.

- Anglo-Saxon;[2]
- Confucian Orbit;
- Eastern Europe and Former Soviet Union;
- Latin America;
- North Africa and the Middle East;
- Western Europe.

Introducing Confucianism

A Foundation for CDC

The role of culture (Confucianism) in driving (or hindering) economic progress remains unclear—although this has been the subject of many theses and criticisms, not least since culture and economic development are not always measured at the same level, or unit of analysis. Such discussions often operate at the macro level with broad theorisations and unclear (or non-supported) linkages. During slow economic growth in the first half of the twentieth century, Confucianism was identified as hindering progress ("they *do not* develop their economies because they are so Confucian"), whereas during the second half of that same century, Confucianism was then identified as a driver of strong(er) economic growth ("they *do* develop their economies because they are so Confucian"). Our research presented in this book subscribes to the latter narrative, i.e. Confucianism acts as a driver of performance, not least through discipline in the education system.

The way Confucianism is relevant to any narrative is dependent on which perspective is taken of the ancient tradition. For *our* narrative, we see Confucianism as the cornerstone of modes of behaviour and ways of

Figure 1.4 Confucius 551–479 BC

Photo credit: Dr Chris Baumann (2015).

Photo taken at the birthplace of Confucius temple/conference facility near Mountain Ni, 25 kilometres southeast of Qufu city, Shandong Province.

thinking within East Asian societies, so deeply ingrained through centuries of tradition, that its effect is tacit. If you were to ask most people from these societies if they considered themselves to be Confucians, or even adherents of Confucianism, you would probably be met with a surprised 'what?'; because they 'live' Confucianism every day, they do not think about it nor 'see' it that way in the first place. Yet many of the values that are shared within these societies, from their views on education, to how they define their social roles, and observe traditions, represent hallmarks of the ancient scholar's wisdom.

We take Confucianism as the starting point for our CDC model because the philosophy[3] continues to have a pervasive influence over the region.

A Brief History

Confucianism was born approximately 2,500 years ago, and is attributed to the great scholar named Kong Fuzi (551–479 BCE) during the Spring and Autumn period of the Zhou Dynasty (Figure 1.4). Also known as *Ruism*, the philosophy emerged against the backdrop of a feudal state of chaos and disorder in ancient China. Many great thinkers of the time aspired to pioneer a 'solution' to the weakening state which was defined by military conflict between states and power, the destruction of the order of social life, and suffering and misery (Legge, 1992). Kong Fuzi, or Latinised as Confucius, was one of the most prominent scholars of his time (notwithstanding that his true 'fame' came post-mortem), and believed that such corruptions in society were the result of the abuse and misuse of ritual and propriety (*li*). From this, he embarked on a lifelong mission to restoring the value of these rituals and rules of propriety within society, which would be made possible through education:

> In order to set up guidelines for good family and social life, Confucius reinterpreted the meaning and methods of learning and education of the *ru* tradition, and believed that the promotion of the tradition had great leverage on improving the quality of social life, was the key to overcoming present problems, and would lead the people to a refined and redefined world of goodness and harmony.
>
> (Yao, 2000, p. 23)

The main concern for Confucius was with the nature of human beings, and the fundamental principles of humanity, which he believed could be cultivated and improved with learning. While he is acknowledged as the innovator of Confucianism, he had well over 3,000 students—and somewhere around 72 intimate disciples—who transmitted his teachings, which is available today as the *Analects of Confucius* (*Lunyu*, literally translated to 'Edited Conversations').[4] The ancient text has drawn much debate and opinion among Western and Eastern scholars, with no agreed upon evaluation on his works; despite this, the centrality of the following tenets is often cited and understood to be associated with the Confucian tradition:

Confucian Tenet	Description
Five Cardinal Relationships	The relationship between the ruler and minister, father and son, husband and wife, older and younger, brother and friend. In essence, the 'junior' member of each dyad "owes strong duty of service and reverence" to the senior, and the senior owes a "duty of care and benevolence" (Sun, 2008, p. 12; Phillipson, 2013).
Filial Piety	Primarily concerned with the 'ideal child', where there is an emphasis on respect for parents, elders, and ancestors. It also governs the relationship of people outside of the family unit, to include persons who are in positions of authority.
Virtuous Ethics • Benevolence • Propriety • Righteousness	Each tenet mutually underpins one another, with the interplay supporting social stability. Benevolence (*ren*), propriety (*li*), and righteousness (*yi*) are concerned with the exercising virtuous ethics in one's conduct including respect, reciprocity, selflessness, and genuine care for oneself and others.
Doctrine of the Mean (*Zhongyong*)	This emphasises taking a moderate path to finding the best solution between two conflicting positions. The goal is to maintain balance and harmony in all undertakings.
Mandate of Heaven	In ancient texts, this refers to the legitimacy of the kings' right to rule over their subjects, where Heaven has blessed the king and given him absolute power to reign. Today, this manifests in an externalised locus of control where authority is obeyed.
Perfect Gentleman (*Junzi*)	The 'exemplary man' (and of course lady) is a status any man/woman can achieve by cultivating oneself, and following the paths described above. The *Junzi* rules by acting virtuously himself/herself, to inspire others by leading with example, and cultivating a lifelong passion for learning.
Continuous Learning (*Xue*)	A feature prominent to Confucianism is its commitment to study and learning. Historically, learning referred to the process beyond understanding and deliberating of academic study to include a pursuit of the 'Way of Heaven' through classics. Today, it is about transformation and betterment of the self through the continuous acquisition of knowledge.

Each says something about how individuals should conduct themselves, in its own right, but when taken together has implications for the mode of discipline that is prevalent within East Asian societies. All up, these Confucian tenets showcase the importance of education, which to this day remain obvious in East Asian societies, with their focus on education and performance. Because education and betterment are so important and central under Confucianism, a Confucian approach to pedagogy is somewhat unforgiving for underperformance, and this points in the direction of what we will explain next: Confucianism uses discipline as an integral part of pedagogy to guide students to strong (or at least improving) learning and academic performance.

Since originating in China, the essence of Confucianism has been reflected in all aspects of life, including arts, history, social life, and government. Over the course of history, Chinese civilisation has spread to almost all neighbouring states, at some point, and has brought with it the influence of Confucianism. These societies include Japan, South Korea (hereafter Korea), Taiwan, Hong Kong, Singapore, and Vietnam, which have adapted and interpreted Confucian thought in different ways, to serve its political, social, and economic transitions. In this book, and for the purpose of our analyses, we include these societies in a cluster labelled the 'Confucian Orbit'.

Contemporary Relevance

As with all '-isms', Confucianism has undergone a number of transformations, reinterpretations, and adaptations over time. Given its longstanding history, and the fact that the essence of his meaning was selected and edited by his disciples over time, it should come as no surprise that there are many teachings, even competing versions, and schools of thought of Confucius. Hall and Ames (1987) express that Confucianism is not a static, unified, or unchanging belief system, but is complex and constantly evolving and adapted to the contemporary milieu (Tan, 2016). Despite these apparent 'inconsistencies', the essence of Confucianism remains evident in East Asia societies today, in terms of how people view themselves, their relationship with others, and their obligations and duties, and not least, in how they educate their children and youth.

Popular and academic interest in Confucianism emerged when countries/societies like Japan, Korea, Taiwan, and Singapore started to make real economic strides, despite having a number of disadvantages levelled against them (i.e. lack of natural resources, economically disadvantaged, affected by war). The rapid rate of industrialisation and exceptionally high growth rates was characterised as 'The East Asian Miracle' in a World Bank (Preston, 1993) report, which credited a number of policies, state intervention, taxation, and the welfare state for the boom. Around the same time, Western scholars had begun to explore these links between culture, i.e. Confucianism, and economic development (e.g. Vogel, 1979; Hofheinz and Calder, 1982), in what Herman Kahn (1979) coined the 'post-Confucian hypothesis'. This line of reasoning argued that certain values associated with the tradition, when exercised together by a society, allowed them to make tremendous improvements to their economy in a short period of time:

> Observing their high performance at the national and industry levels, scholars were quick to point to Confucianism as being the common denominator within East Asia. Thus, from a theoretical perspective, many believed that the values propagated by Confucian teachings equipped these societies with a *modus operandi* to excel in industrialisation (Berger, 1988). Values such as future orientation, hard work, fervour for education, and frugality were considered the hallmark of Asia's success story and served as a basis from which other societies could follow.
>
> (Viengkham, Baumann and Winzar, 2018, p. 338)

This perspective was in contrast to Max Weber's view that Confucianism, with its emphasis on tradition and a need to maintain harmony, would be a hindrance to capitalism and growth. Since then, the meaning and significance of Confucianism to economic issues has grown tremendously, and we showcase some of these in Table 1.1. We only focus specifically on how the concept of Confucianism has evolved as it is related to business, economics, and management; and though we acknowledge that there has been a long tradition in sinology, theology, and anthropology subject areas focussing on Confucianism, we would not be able to do them justice by including them here.

A more concrete link between the ancient philosophy and contemporary education in East Asia can be drawn from the 'Six Arts' which formed the basis of education in Chinese culture. These six arts, which were thoroughly practiced by Confucius's faithful disciples, included: (1) rites, (2) music, (3) archery, (4) charioteering, (5) calligraphy, and (6) mathematics. Those who practiced these arts and were devoted to continuous learning were on the path to becoming a *junzi*, or perfect gentleman.

Culture as a Competitive Resource

Culture, by its simplest terms, is a system of meaning *shared* by a group of people, as a way to make sense of our reality, or as Hofstede (1991) put it: "the collective programming of the mind". Culture impacts how we think, how we speak, how we act, and how we experience the world around us. Generally, societies transmit and pursue aspects of culture that are considered important or useful, or that can be adapted to benefit their society (Kuczynski, Marshall and Schell, 1997; Youniss, 1994). Despite

Table 1.1 Evolution of Definition and Measurement of Confucianism

Ostensive Definition	Description	Operational Definition	Key Reference
Post-Confucian Hypothesis	Factors believed to attribute to the rapid economic success of East Asian societies were hypothesised as "the creation of dedicated, motivated, responsible, and educated individuals" and "the enhanced sense of commitment, organizational identity, and loyalty to various institutions".	Hypothesis	Kahn (1979) Berger (1988)
Confucian Dynamism	An emphasis on long-term orientation: characterisation of individuals who place importance on values associated with Confucian teachings that are future oriented (persistence, status-ordered relationships, thrift, sense of shame), and present/past oriented (steadiness and stability, protection of face, respect for tradition, reciprocity).	Likert scale	Hofstede and Bond (1988)
Confucian Ethics	Individuals are endowed with the mission of applying the 'Way of Humanity'—a central Confucian doctrine. Because of the innate desires of humans as biological organisms, humans should be regulated by an ethical system of: • Benevolence (*Ren*) • Righteousness (*Yi*) • Propriety (*Li*) "The Confucians set up appropriate ethical principles for a given role relationship according to superior/ inferior positions and the intimacy/distance of the relationship. . . . All major interpersonal relationships in one's lifetime should be arranged with reference to the deep structure of this ethical system". • Moral cultivation • Self-regulation • Harmony	Essay (conceptual)	Hwang (2001)

(Continued)

Table 1.1 (Continued)

Ostensive Definition	Description	Operational Definition	Key Reference
Confucian Work Ethic (CWE)	Evolving from Confucian Dynamism, and Max Weber's notion of the 'Protestant Work Ethic', CWE emphasises the values of thrift and hard work, harmony, and co-operation. CWE focusses on the accumulation of wealth in knowledge.	Likert scale	Lim (2003)
Confucian Values	"[A]n important factor influencing East Asians . . . such cultural values is considered to be instrumental for better understanding people's motivational tendencies in this region". • Face saving • Humility • Group orientation • Hierarchy • Reciprocity	Likert scale	Monkhouse, Barnes and Pham (2013)
Confucian Aspects	"Confucian teachings are essentially humanistic, in that they emphasize the importance of human relationships with any notion of the 'self' as being inextricably linked to the 'group'. . . . Confucianism is multifaceted . . . [it] has been instrumental to the architecture of each society's institutional development in different ways". • Relational aspect • Pedagogical aspect • Transformative aspect	Choice-based Best-Worst scaling	Viengkham et al. (2018)
Confucian Orbit	"The term 'Confucian orbit' is adopted because the cultures of these countries are all heavily influenced by Confucian values, albeit in different ways". Similar to the term 'Confucian Heritage Culture (CHC)'.	Cluster, segmentation	Baumann, Hamin, Tung and Hoadley (2016)

Confucianism shaping culture among East Asian societies in different ways, and having to compete with different philosophies, ideologies, and religions over time (e.g. the Communist revolution in China; Capitalism; Buddhism), the Confucian tradition has always emerged again as a pervasive force. That is not to say that Confucianism competes or dominates other ideologies that flourish within a society, but that given the syncretic characteristic of the region, operates alongside others to create unique blends of cultures.

Despite all the transformations and influences over the centuries, East Asia still clearly places a premium on certain values attributed to the Confucian culture; namely, the importance of education, of instilling hard work (a 'work ethic'), having strong family bonds, and maintaining harmonious relationships. Though these might be more contemporary interpretations of the Confucian classics, their survival and reinforcement over millennia have been deeply woven into the fabrics of East Asian society, so much so that they are a form of social capital (Fukuyama, 1999). Confucianism inspires co-operation between individuals within its societies, but also fosters a sense of cohesion across institutions and networks that manifest in how the household, school, and even business is run (e.g. Yeung and Tung, 1996; Kang, Matusik and Barclay, 2017; Fang, 1999; Warner, 2014; Wang, Wang, Ruona and Rojewski, 2005; Redding, 2013).

Confucianism's elaborate doctrines are in itself a form of what Bourdieu (1997) refers to as 'cultural capital'. Developed initially to explain why school children's academic performance differed between educational systems, the concept evolved to reflect the accumulation of knowledge, behaviours, and skills that promote social mobility within a society. Thus with its longstanding history, the Confucian doctrine, with its emphasis on education and respect for authority, have rendered it into a unique cultural asset. Clearly not all cultures are the same, nor are they easily replicable or replaceable, and this is arguably what makes culture under Confucianism a competitive resource in domains such as academic performance, not least driven by the aforementioned utilisation of strict discipline.

To be competitive means utilising all the resources to outperform the competition, but to maintain and sustain that competitiveness requires having a resource base (i.e. capabilities and assets) that is relatively unique. In our narrative we do not measure Confucianism directly, *per se*, but we analyse how the tradition, as deeply rooted in the psyche of East Asians, 'manifests' in certain ways of being and behaving. With this, and in a similar spirit to the post-Confucian hypothesis, we view Confucian culture as a competitive resource for success in the region. It would be naïve to assume that Confucianism is solely responsible for the successes we see in academic achievement, business performance, and overall economic growth of the East, but there is certainly some merit that Confucian culture forms the basis for important human resource competition for a number of reasons, as expressed by Cummings (1995):

- Adherence to Confucian values within these societies brings an element of social stability, transmitted from the home environment to the community at large. For example, in the classroom setting, teachers take an explicit approach to the instruction of students, which produces a focussed learning environment that optimises the transmission of knowledge and values.
- It fosters a level of competitiveness by virtue of always seeking improvement relative to oneself, and others. This can be seen in the student at the individual level, to corporations in the marketplace, competing to achieve higher levels of productivity.
- The state places cultural and educational policies at the centre of plans for national development, minimising involvement in the everyday management of schools, entrusting principals and teachers with the duty of care to manage schools and students.

The competitive advantage of Confucianism can be found, in essence, in the way it produces a mindset or worldview. This view is consistent with the belief that one is always capable of improving their situation, if they are willing to put the effort in. Second to this—a missing link in discussions on Confucianism and growth—is that there are certain ways this pursuit of improvement can be, should be, and has been done. This missing link is the role of discipline. While discipline is present in almost all cultures and societies, to some extent or another, how it is valued or applied as a tool is what we argue makes *the* difference in performance and competitiveness.

Spotlight

Confucianism and Discipline

Confucianism assigns substantial power to teachers where students have to obey rules and teachers demand respect (Chan and Young, 2012; Yuhan and Chen, 2013). Learning under Confucianism has a strong element of character building and an inherent element of school discipline with "forms of punishment which [are] related to learning, so as to raise . . . students' intrinsic ability to learn" (Hue, 2007, p. 26). Discipline and punishment under Confucianism are designed to be an integrative part of learning, i.e. to make the student a better learner and person through a 'no pain, no transformation' approach. After all, the Chinese believe that "Jade will never become a work of art without being carved" (Baumann, Tung and

Hamin, 2012, p. 1), suggesting that discipline indeed is not a necessary evil, but instead a very effective and useful tool to enhance learning, personal development and overall human betterment. This may be different in western discipline with detentions, time outs and suspensions that may not relate to learning and may not be effective to actually discipline the student since they—unlike under Confucianism—do not feel the pain of any consequences. In fact, students under the western paradigm sometimes later regret that their teachers and parents did not insist on more disciplined learning (Park and Abelmann, 2004), while in East Asia such regrets are uncommon since parents, teachers and the system never lose focus on a disciplined learning approach.

Source: Baumann and Krskova (2016) in *School Discipline, School Uniforms and Academic Performance*

Introducing Discipline

The Missing Link

With previous research on drivers of academic performance centring around the amount of funding provided for education (Jensen, Reichl and Kemp, 2011; Keller, 2006), classroom size (Finn, Gerber and Boyd-Zaharias, 2005; Hoxby, 2000; Jepsen and Rivkin, 2009), hours of schooling (Wiley and Harnischfeger, 1974), teacher qualifications (Croninger, Rice, Rathbun and Nishio, 2007), and teacher quality (Hanushek, 2011), we now turn the focus to an underexplored potential driver of performance and competitiveness: school discipline, or simply put, discipline (henceforth our referred term). Discipline is centre stage in education under Confucianism, and therefore a unique feature in education systems in East Asia.

It is not necessarily easy to 'capture' (or measure) discipline, not least because there is a lack of a generally accepted understanding, definition, and operationalisation of discipline. Perhaps the most general, if not generic, understanding centres around Romi and Freund (1999, p. 54): "discipline is a system of sanctions that addresses the breakdown when the code of conduct is broken"; or "all activities that are implemented to control learner behaviour, to enforce compliance and maintain order" (Bechuke and Debeila, 2012, p. 243). We align the understanding of discipline in our study with these definitions, notwithstanding that we will offer an extension to better incorporate the facets of school discipline that also allows a cross-cultural comparison later in Chapter 3.

There is some recent research aligned with our narrative suggesting that indeed higher levels of school discipline are associated with higher levels of academic performance (Baumann and Krskova, 2016), and that indeed there are substantial differences among discipline levels for different societies, nations, and cultures. It was further found that discipline is more effective in driving performance than educational investment (Krskova and Baumann, 2017):

> We found in our study that East Asia peak performs academically, and we have established that this directly relates to high levels of discipline in the classrooms. Homework is carefully checked by teachers in countries/places like Korea, Japan and Taiwan and students know that they can expect negative consequences if they do not complete their work. Respect for teachers in that part of the world is high and students are effectively disciplined for poor performance, disrespect and non-compliance with school policy and dress codes.
>
> (Baumann and Krskova, 2016)

Ultimately, discipline may be a matter of one's, or a society's, *Weltanschauung* (roughly translates into worldview). It would be reasonable to assume that all societies have some level of discipline in their education systems, functionally speaking, but how it is 'viewed', how it is practiced, how strict or laissez-faire it is, differs markedly. For example, it is not unusual for teachers in the Confucian Orbit to check students' homework with consequences for not having completed such, whereas in the West, generally that is seen as less important, subsequently with no or little consequences for poor performance. A similar pattern is found for punctuality, rudeness, talking out of turn, etc.—East Asia is much stricter on practically all discipline dimensions than the rest of the world, both in terms of enforcing it (i.e. standards are complied with), and in terms of the repercussions for non-compliance (i.e. consequences). Though there is a lack of a clear-cut measure of discipline, and all that it entails, the concept has been evolved over time to reflect a number of aspects from punitive dimensions, to motivational and self-directional. There are also distinctions between the roles on the enforcer and recipient of discipline, and we have outlined some of these definitions in Table 1.2.

Naturally, school discipline is not detached from the environment a student experiences at home, and non-surprisingly, the literature also 'links' parental and school discipline, and ultimately both are not least driven by societal values in a culture, which are in turn evident in certain institutions, such as schools. There are issues of fundamental differences in mindsets regarding values and socialisation between cultures/societies driving discipline at home and in schools, coupled with the changing nature of parental input; societal shifts see more working parents in the

Table 1.2 Evolution of Definition and Measurement of Discipline

Ostensive Definition	Description	Operational Definition	Key Reference
Discipline (noun)	"[A] system of sanctions that addresses the breakdown when the code of conduct is broken". Attitudes towards disruptive behaviour in the classroom.	Perception of various in-school discipline problems from the perspective of teachers, students, and parents. Likert scale.	Romi and Freund (1999)
Discipline (verb)	Approaches to parenting and classroom management, involving the enforcement of measures to correct behaviour. Attempts at moderating or correcting behaviours through 'external control'. "[A]ll activities that are implemented to control learner behaviour, to enforce compliance and maintain order".		Pellerin (2005b) Bechuke and Debeila (2012)
Parental Discipline	The behaviour utilised by parents in response to, and intended to correct, perceived misbehaviour by a child, with the aim of socialising children into the dominant culture. A typology of child-rearing strategies include: • Authoritative approach • Authoritarian approach • Permissive approach • Indifferent approach	Typology.	Baumrind (1967, 1971)

(Continued)

Table 1.2 (Continued)

Ostensive Definition	Description	Operational Definition	Key Reference
Self-Discipline (noun)	The possession of self-control and the ability to delay instant gratification, and making choices that require one to sacrifice short-term pleasure for long-term gain. "We suggest another reason for students falling short of their intellectual potential: their failure to exercise self-discipline".	A composite score produced with questionnaire data from students, teachers, and parents assessing each individual.	Duckworth and Seligman (2005)
Indiscipline	A lack of discipline, with a "view of pupils being either disruptive or disrupted" . . . "indiscipline is presented as a problem that emerges in the home and that is *carried* into school. Importantly, it is based on a deficit view of parents".	Multi-stakeholder perspective (students and teachers), using observations, interviews, and school documents.	Araújo (2005)
Punitive Discipline/ Corporal Punishment	Physical punitive discipline is the "use of tactics such as spanking, slapping, or hitting with an object in response to child transgression . . . consistent with the term corporal punishment". Verbally mediated punitive discipline is "psychological aggression defined as 'communication intended to cause the child to experience psychological pain' . . . yelling, name calling, and threats of abandonment".	Likert scale, frequency.	Fung and Lau (2009)

| Classroom Discipline/ Management | The policies and practices that are designed within school systems to ensure the well-being and safety students. Effective classroom management maintains appropriate student behaviour and reduces classroom disruption; whereas ineffective classroom management may concede to disruptive behaviour. "[A]ims to support students with behavioural problems and deals with disciplinary issues such as bullying and violence. It intends to promote students' social competence, such as self-discipline and self-management, and to prepare them to be civilised and responsible citizens". | An interactionist perspective is taken to examine how teachers defined their own and others' roles in the classroom context. | Hue (2007) Lewis (2001) |
| Disciplinary Climate | An aspect of the school climate, in which an orderly classroom environment is regarded as a way of improving academic performance . . . where "students' perceptions of classroom disciplinary climate may be associated with their confidence in and respect for the teacher" and may be adversely affected in the absence of disciplinary policies. | Programme for International Student Assessment (PISA) index summarises students' reports on the frequency of five dimensions. | Organisation for Economic Co-operation and Development (OECD) |

West as well as in East Asia, resulting in less time spent at home 'child-rearing'. There is a complex hybrid of the role of schools as the disciplinary force for students, yet this role is not always accepted by parents (typically in the West). That is, schools and their teachers do not have the 'authority' to discipline children and instil them with the 'right' values for a good society. This is in contrast to the Confucian Orbit where generally, parents and the education system work in the same direction—one towards a disciplined learning environment, with a focus on academic performance as preparation for life in the workforce. It has been reported that parents visit a school and request teachers be stricter with their children, or pay an after-school tutor to assume that strict educator role; this contrasts the West where parents often report to schools/teachers and 'cry' on their children's behalf. This shows a very different *Weltanschauung*—both by parents, the school, and society on discipline issues.

Authoritative parenting has been demonstrated to lead to high levels of performance for children and adolescents (Aunola, Stattin and Nurmi, 2000). Pellerin (2005a) was novel in bridging parental styles with types of school discipline and found 'authoritative schools' associate with highest levels of constructive student engagement. Her research applied Baumrind's prominent parenting typology (indifferent, permissive, authoritarian, and authoritative) to schools at the elementary, middle, and high school level. Theoretically, we align our study on Pellerin's notion of authoritative socialisation, a combination of responsiveness and demanding high performance simultaneously ultimately drives the highest level of performance. Pellerin's classification of discipline is as follows (Pellerin, 2005a):

- *Authoritative:* high demandingness and high responsiveness;
- *Authoritarian:* high demandingness and low responsiveness;
- *Permissive:* low demandingness and high responsiveness;
- *Indifferent:* low demandingness and low responsiveness.

At the risk of oversimplification, the education system under Confucianism follows an authoritative approach as opposed to the generally popular permissive approach in the 'West'. Naturally, students are exposed to a large number of influencing factors when forming their values and work ethic, beyond parents/relatives and schools also including (social) media, and cultural values being manifest through government policy in shaping and promoting educational agendas and resources.

There have also been seismic shifts over time in terms of education pedagogy ('how we teach') to curriculum design ('what we teach'), with this evolution depicted in Figure 1.5. While generally Western curriculum has been dominant globally, with other parts of the world adapting American, British, and European teaching material, the Confucian Orbit remained steadfast with a stricter approach to pedagogy and discipline in contrast to the 'West' that has generally moved towards a more permissive approach.

However, in 2017, for the first time in history, the UK adopted teaching material on math from China, a change that made media headlines at the

	Past	Present	Future
Pedagogy "How we teach"	East Asia and West are separate	East Asia and West are separate	East Asia → West
Curriculum "What we teach"	West → East Asia	East Asia → West	East Asia → West

Figure 1.5 Evolution of Pedagogy and Curriculum Design in East Vis-à-Vis the West

Source: Adapted from *Korea Times*: www.koreatimes.co.kr/www/nation/2017/08/181_234867.html

time. Prior to this, there had been attempts to investigate what methods had been working for Chinese teachers in their classrooms, and whether any such approaches could be adopted to British education. The controversial reports at the time, naturally met with scepticism by Western educators, concluded that a great deal can be learned from an East Asian approach, detailed in the 'Chalk and Talk' spotlight.

Spotlight

'Chalk and Talk' Teaching Might Be the Best Way After All

Seventy teachers from the UK were sent to Shanghai to study classroom methods to investigate why Chinese students perform so well. Upon their return, the teachers reported that much of China's success came from teaching methods the UK has been moving away from for the past 40 years.

The Chinese favour a 'chalk and talk' approach, whereas countries such as the UK, US, Australia, and New Zealand have been moving away from this direct form of teaching to a more collaborative form of learning where students take greater control.

Given China's success in international tests such as PISA, TIMSS, and PIRLS, it seems we have been misguided in abandoning the traditional, teacher-directed method of learning where the teacher spends more time standing at the front of the class, directing learning and controlling classroom activities. . . .

Based on this recent study of classrooms in the UK and China and a recent UK report titled What makes great teaching?, there is increasing evidence that these new-age education techniques, where teachers facilitate instead of teach and praise students on the basis that all must be winners, in open classrooms where what children learn is based on their immediate interests, lead to under-performance.

The UK report concludes that many of the approaches adopted in Australian education are counterproductive.

Often derided as 'drill and kill' or making children 'parrot' what is being taught, the UK report and other research suggests that memorisation and rote learning are important classroom strategies, which all teachers should be familiar with. . . .

One of the prevailing education orthodoxies for many years is that students must be continually praised and that there is no room for failure. The times when '4 out of 10' or an 'E' meant fail are long gone. Supposedly, telling children they are not good enough hurts their self-esteem.

The UK report says that, while praising students might appear affirming and positive, *the wrong kinds of praise can be very harmful to learning.* Overly praising students, especially those who under-perform, is especially counterproductive. It conveys the message that teachers have low expectations and reinforces the belief that near enough is good enough, instead of aiming high and expecting strong results.

Source: Kevin Donnelly (2014) in *The Conversation* https://theconversation.com/chalk-and-talk-teaching-might-be-the-best-way-after-all-34478

Our research will contribute to the debate on which approach to pedagogy results in better learning, with our overarching proposition being that the more disciplined Confucian approach would result in stronger academic performance. We include here as a disclaimer that our narrative is not focussed on which pedagogical learning styles are most effective (e.g. teacher-directed or student-directed, direct instruction, or inquiry learning, etc.), but rather that a more disciplined environment, with more disciplined students results in better performance. In other words, it is not all about the way one is taught, but also the environment in which it is taught.

If our overarching hypothesis is supported, then this could have major implications for other parts in the world that aspire to improve their academic performance, and ultimately their competitiveness. Who should follow whom with changes to their curriculum and pedagogy, who should be become stricter or not?

The shift in pedagogy is nicely reflected in the PISA survey instrument itself. The West has departed from an authoritative approach to a permissive approach over the past four decades or so, while East Asia has largely remained its authoritative approach. We can see an 'evolution' of PISA measures from when testing first started in 2000 (Table 1.3). There was a change in the question battery on disciplinary climate and classroom management, the changing questions demonstrating the different mindsets relating to disciplinary issues and educational policies. The most notable change is that the initial PISA questions on Achievement Pressure posted in 2000 (e.g. 'The Teacher wants students to work hard'; see Table 1.3 for

Table 1.3 Evolution of PISA Measurement Focus 2000 to 2015

Year	Dimension	Code	Question Statements	Scale
2000 Reading	2000 PISA DISCLIM Disciplinary Climate	ST26Q01	The teacher has to wait a long time for students to <quieten down>.	Four-point scale: *never, some lessons, most lessons,* and *every lesson.*
		ST26Q12	Students cannot work well.	
		ST26Q13	Students don't listen to what the teacher says.	
		ST26Q14	Students don't start working for a long time after lesson begins.	
		ST26Q16	There is noise and disorder.	
		ST26Q17	At the start of class, more than five minutes are spent doing nothing.	
	2000 PISA ACHPRESS Achievement Pressure	ST26Q02	The teacher wants students to work hard.	Four-point scale: *never, some lessons, most lessons,* and *every lesson.*
		ST26Q03	The teacher tells students that they can do better.	
		ST26Q04	The teacher does not like it when students deliver <careless> work.	
		ST26Q15	Students have to learn a lot.	
	2000 PISA TEACBEHA Teacher Related Factors on School Climate (Principal's Perception)*	SC19Q01	Teachers' low expectations of students.	Four-point scale: *not at all, very little, to some extent, and a lot.*
		SC19Q03	Poor student-teacher relations.	
		SC19Q07	Teachers not meeting individual students' needs.	
		SC19Q08	Teacher absenteeism.	
		SC19Q11	Staff resisting change.	
		SC19Q14	Teachers being too strict with students.	
		SC19Q16	Students not being encouraged to achieve their full potential.	

(Continued)

Table 1.3 (Continued)

Year	Dimension	Code	Question Statements	Scale
	2000 PISA STUDBEHA Student Related Factors on School Climate (Principal's Perception)*	SC19Q02	Student absenteeism.	Four-point scale: *not at all, very little, to some extent, and a lot.*
		SC19Q06	Disruption of classes by students.	
		SC19Q09	Students skipping classes.	
		SC19Q10	Students lacking respect for teachers.	
		SC19Q13	Student use of alcohol or illegal drugs.	
		SC19Q15	Students intimidating or bullying other students.	
2003 Math	2003 PISA DISCLIM Disciplinary Climate	ST38Q02	Students don't listen to what the teacher says.	Four-point scale: *every lesson, most lessons, some lessons, and never or hardly ever.*
		ST38Q06	There is noise and disorder.	
		ST38Q08	The teacher has to wait a long time for students to <quieten down>.	
		ST38Q09	Students cannot work well.	
		ST38Q11	Students don't start working for a long time after lesson begins.	
	2003 PISA TEACBEH Teachers' Behaviour	ST25Q11	Teachers being too strict with students.	Four-point scale: *not at all, very little, to some extent, and a lot.*
		ST25Q01	Teachers' low expectations of students.	
	2003 PISA STUREL Student–Teacher Relations	ST26Q01	Students get along well with most teachers.	Four-point scale: *strongly agree, agree, disagree, and strongly disagree.*
		ST26Q02	Most teachers are interested in students' well-being.	
		ST26Q03	Most of my teachers really listen to what I have to say.	
		ST26Q04	If I need extra help, I will receive it from my teachers.	
		ST26Q05	Most of my teachers treat me fairly.	

2006 Science	2006 PISA PQSCHOOL Parent Perception of School Climate	PA03Q04	I am satisfied with the disciplinary atmosphere in my child's school.	Four-point scale: *strongly agree, agree, disagree,* and *strongly disagree.*
2009 Reading	2009 PISA DISCLIMA Disciplinary Climate	ST36Q01	Students don't listen to what the teacher says.	Four-point scale: *every lesson, most lessons, some lessons,* to *never or hardly ever.*
		ST36Q02	There is noise and disorder.	
		ST36Q03	The teacher has to wait a long time for students to <quiet down>.	
		ST36Q04	Students cannot work well.	
		ST36Q05	Students don't start working for a long time after lesson begins.	
	PISA 2009 STUDREL Student-Teacher Relations	ST34Q01	I get along with most of my teachers.	
		ST34Q02	Most of my teachers are interested in my well-being.	
		ST34Q03	Most of my teachers really listen to what I have to say.	
		ST34Q04	If I need extra help, I will receive it from my teachers.	
		ST34Q05	Most of my teachers treat me fairly.	

(Continued)

Table 1.3 (Continued)

Year	Dimension	Code	Question Statements	Scale
2012 Math	PISA 2012 DISCLIMA Disciplinary Climate	ST81Q01	Students don't listen to what the teacher says.	Four-point scale: *every lesson, most lessons, some lessons,* to *never or hardly ever.*
		ST81Q02	There is noise and disorder.	
		ST81Q03	The teacher has to wait a long time for students to <quiet down>.	
		ST81Q04	Students cannot work well.	
		ST81Q05	Students don't start working for a long time after the lesson begins.	
	PISA 2012 CLSMAN Classroom Management	ST85Q01	My teacher gets students to listen to him or her.	Four-point scale: *every lesson, most lessons, some lessons, or never or hardly ever.*
		ST85Q02	My teacher keeps the class orderly.	
		ST85Q03	My teacher starts lessons on time.	
		ST85Q04	The teacher has to wait a long time for students to <quiet down>.	
	PISA 2012 STUDREL Student-Teacher Relation	ST86Q01	Students get along well with most teachers.	Four-point scale: *strongly agree, agree, disagree,* to *strongly disagree.*
		ST86Q02	Most teachers are interested in students' well-being.	
		ST86Q03	Most of my teachers really listen to what I have to say.	
		ST86Q04	If I need extra help, I will receive it from my teachers.	
		ST86Q05	Most of my teachers treat me fairly.	

2015 Science			Four-point scale: *in all lessons, in some lessons,* and *never or hardly ever.*
	PISA 2015 DISCLISCI Disciplinary Climate	ST097Q01TA	Students don't listen to what the teacher says.
		ST097Q02TA	There is noise and disorder.
		ST097Q03TA	The teacher has to wait a long time for students to quiet down.
		ST097Q04TA	Students cannot work well.
		ST097Q05TA	Students don't start working for a long time after the lesson begins.
	PISA 2015 Teacher Fairness *** Not included in data set.**	ST039Q01NA	Teachers called on me less often than they called on other students.
		ST039Q02NA	Teachers graded me harder than they graded other students.
		ST039Q03NA	Teachers gave me the impression that they think I am less smart than I really am.
		ST039Q04NA	Teachers disciplined me more harshly than other students.
		ST039Q05NA	Teachers ridiculed me in front of others.
		ST039Q06NA	Teachers said something insulting to me in front of others.

---

* Measures of School Climate relating to Teacher Behaviour (TEACBEHA) and Student Behaviour (STUDBEHA) from the principal's perspective were included in all waves of PISA data collection (2000–2015). We focus specifically on students' evaluation of school discipline because students would be the most honest in their assessment of how a classroom is managed; whereas teachers and principals may have conflicting interests.

the complete overview of questions over time) were dropped as of the 2003 testing. There has been a shift from discipline dimensions reflecting classroom atmosphere and behaviour to a focus on student welfare and bullying in the PISA survey instrument as outlined below. The zenith of a reflection of a permissive pedagogic mindset in the PISA questionnaire is evidenced by the new addition for 2015 on Teacher Fairness, implying that *de facto* a teacher would be 'bullying' a student rather than disciplining them. The distribution of that data was skewed and the OECD decided not to publish such results.

Introducing Competitiveness

Competitiveness: The Phenomenon CDC Explains

The dependent variable of CDC is competitiveness. The World Economic Forum in Davos (WEF) defines competitiveness as "the set of institutions, policies, and factors that determine the level of productivity of a country" (Schwab and Sala-i-Martin, 2013). While Confucianism (culture) as well as discipline in the education system of a nation remains relatively stable, the largest variation over time might be found in competitiveness. The WEF publishes annually a global ranking—a list of 'winners and losers'. The spotlight, taken directly from the World Economic Forum's web page, summarises the relevance and necessity of competitiveness for nations.

Spotlight

Why Competitiveness Matters

It matters how competitive your country is. Here are three reasons why:

It happens every year: as the World Economic Forum publishes its annual Global Competitiveness Report, national media around the world headline their reports with their own country's ranking, congratulating or criticising the government accordingly.

But this isn't a football league table, where one team's win is another's loss: it is possible for a country to go down in the ranking even if it improves its competitiveness. If that seems counter-intuitive, it's because the word 'competitiveness' can be misleading. It implies competition in the sporting sense, with countries pitted against each other in a zero-sum game—and that's not how to interpret the index.

Instead, think of a country's competitiveness as its level of productivity: its ability to produce more outputs with the same amount of inputs. Clearly, it is possible for all countries to improve at once. Competitiveness, in this sense, matters for three reasons.

1. The first, and ultimately most important, is that more productive countries can create greater wealth, higher living standards and more happiness for their citizens.
2. Secondly, more productive countries offer greater returns on investment. This matters to companies choosing whether to invest in physical

capital. But it also means that national investments in areas such as infrastructure, education and skills development have greater potential to translate into economic growth.

3. Finally, competitiveness implies economic stability and resilience. Data analysed in last year's Global Competitiveness Report found that the more competitive an economy was in 2007, the less severely it was affected by the recession that followed.

Source: World Economic Forum (www.weforum.org/agenda/2016/09/it-matters-how-competitive-your-country-is-here-are-three-reasons-why/)

Some critics would pose a rather valid question relating to why competitiveness even matters at all, and query why nations are so fixated on outranking and outperforming one another (see Krugman, 1994). While the World Economic Forum has provided an answer (see World Economic Forum spotlight) that nicely summarises the benefits of living in a competitive society, we add to this with a simple reasoning: *because competitiveness is not a matter of choice—we live in a competitive world.* While not the focus of our book, there is a long historical debate about the 'Survival of the Fittest', the catchphrase summarising Darwinian evolutionary theory's mechanism of natural selection (Darwin, 1869), and in nature (flora, fauna) we observe that everyday survival unobstructed. Of course, for our project on human subjects, our view is guided by our predominant training in business schools, but even the fact that national growth is contingent upon enterprise and innovation, places competitiveness at the forefront of concern for a number of stakeholders.

Our point is that competitiveness will always be at the forefront of concern not only for policy makers and government, but also ordinary citizens whose livelihoods are directly affected by the infrastructure, education, investments, etc. that are adopted within that nation. A goal of competitiveness is economic progress, where better income generates more wealth and lifestyle improvement, and better opportunities for all. If the infrastructure is not in place to allow people to perform, or achieve their potential, then the burden falls to the state in welfare allocations. All of these issues are a result of (or lack of) national competitiveness.

If competitiveness is going to occur regardless, then we may as well be preparing our students—the next generation—for this. This has usually translated into more funding and investment allocated toward schools across some nations, but with limited effect (Krskova and Baumann, 2017). Instead, and in line with our concept of CDC, we argue that one way of preparing students for the future is through a culture that promotes discipline. From a grassroots perspective, more discipline during the formative years of a child's education (i.e. home and school environment) would have longer lasting effects in their preparedness for outside of formal education, beyond technical knowledge. To some degree it can be assumed that discipline experienced at school would, in one way or another, result in some form of (self-)discipline—a useful trait later in life (for university and the workforce, for example).

Education and the Economy

It has long been clear that there must be 'some' association between a nation's education system and their economic strength, but the detailed mechanisms about how that works remain largely unclear. It is unclear because at both ends (for education and the economy) questions remain about measurement: which aspects should be included and excluded, and is there a time (lag) effect? The overarching argument is that if we teach the next generation well, we will gain economic benefits longer term.

Prominent work on the association between education and the economy has been conducted at America's elite universities, Harvard and Stanford. At Harvard, Barro and his colleagues (namely Barro and Lee, 1993a, 1993b; Barro, 1997; Barro and McCleary, 2003) explored education as a driver for developing economies to catch up with emerging and developed economies. In another study, Barro probed the association between years of schooling with economic performance (Barro and Lee, 1996). At Stanford, Hanushek and his colleagues studied gross domestic product (GDP) growth impacting the quality of schooling (Vessman and Hanushek, 2007a, 2007b). In a subsequent study, Hanushek and Woessmann (2010), like our study, also used Organisation for Economic Co-operation and Development (OECD) Programme for International Student Assessment (PISA) data to correlate education with economic metrics. Others have looked at the association between public expenditure per student and economic growth at the secondary school level (Keller, 2006), or contrasted the relative importance of school discipline (88 percent) to education investment (12 percent) on the effect on academic performance, both also directly driving competitiveness (Krskova and Baumann, 2017). The same study also demonstrated effects of discipline (students listen well in 2003 and students work well in 2009) on competitiveness in 2012.

In conclusion, there is supporting evidence for the generally accepted notion that education is paramount for a country's economic success and welfare, pointing toward the crucial role of the education system in the formation of human capital for a nation.

The most accepted conceptualisation and measurement of competitiveness is the national level index put forward by the World Economic Forum (WEF) in Davos, Switzerland (Schwab and Sala-i-Martin, 2014, p. 4). The WEF Global Competitiveness Index (GCI) contains the following 12 pillars (Figure 1.6) (Schwab and Sala-i-Martin, 2014):

In recent rankings, we typically saw Western countries rank high, with East Asian nations somewhere in the middle. This is despite Asian markets such as China, Korea, and India experiencing phenomenal economic growth over the past few decades beyond that of Western economies, with their saturated

Pillar Dimensions	Details
1. Institutions	Legal and administrative frameworks
2. Infrastructure	Critical for an effective economy
3. Macroeconomic Environment	Stability is important for businesses and the country overall
4. Health and Primary Education	Healthy workforce is vital for competitiveness
5. Higher Education and Training	Crucial for economies wishing to move up the value chain
6. Goods Market Efficiency	By producing the right mix of products and services
7. Labour Market Efficiency	Workers allocated effectively
8. Financial Market Development	Financial resources allocated to most productive uses
9. Technological Readiness	Agility of technology adoption
10. Market Size	Exploit economies of scale
11. Business Sophistication	Quality of a country's business network's operations, strategies, and firms
12. Innovation Technological	Emerging for technological and non-knowledge

Figure 1.6 World Economic Forum 12 Pillars of Competitiveness

markets. As previously alluded to, students from East Asian economies also consistently outperformed their peers from the rest of the world (Baumann and Winzar, 2016), yet despite this, are still ranked behind Western economies on a number of indices. To probe this anomaly, a study by Baumann and colleagues (2016) compared the competitiveness of individuals at the micro level across three country clusters (i.e. emerging economies in Asia, highly developed Western countries, and Confucian Orbit), and found that three factors (competitive attitude, willingness to serve, and speed) accounted for 81 to 93 percent in explaining workforce performance for the Confucian Orbit, alone. The study highlighted that a nation's competitiveness should be considered as an incorporation of various types of factors, from micro to macro data. In this instance, the underlying motivational mechanisms of individuals in the East Asian sample proved to be the driving force of their performance, beyond that of the West, suggesting that a nation's level of competitiveness is ultimately also impacted by the 'work ethic' of its citizens.

Table 1.4 Evolution of Definition and Measurement of Competitiveness

Ostensive Definition	Description	Operational Definition	Key Reference
Absolute Advantage	Trade is viewed as positive-sum: the outcome of a policy, decision, or negotiation, where no single one entity wins at the other's expense. In other words, the outcome is a win-win solution for all.	Empirical observation, e.g. in describing the division of labour or behaviour of rent-seeking groups	Smith (1776)
Comparative Advantage	In principle, describes the work gains in trade for nations, organisations, and/or individuals, as a result of differences in factor endowments, labour, and capital. In particular, the theory establishes the differences in labour productivity between free markets.	Opportunity cost ratios Production possibility frontier (PPF)	Ricardo (1817)
Competitive Advantage	Competitiveness through acts of *innovation*: the actions and strategies that allow one organisation to outperform its competitors. In effect, the ability to leverage skills, resources, and assets to differentiate oneself from rivals in the marketplace.	Five forces analysis Sustained profit Market share Return on investment	Porter (1985)

Model	Description	Reference
The Diamond Model	A two-pronged perspective of strategic analysis of firms: the industry-view and resourced-based view (RBV). Together, the model requires the consideration of the firm's endowments *and* the nation's institutional factors.	Four country-specific 'determinants', and two external variables, chance and government	Porter (1990)
Double Diamond Model	An extension of Porter's Diamond Model and incorporates multinational activities and the role of government. Organisations build upon both domestic and foreign diamonds to become globally competitive (i.e. survival, growth, and profitability). Previous models deemed applicable only for triad-markets (USA, EU, and Japan), but not small, open, trading economies (e.g. Canada).	Framework applied developed to assess the success of Canada's resource-based multinationals and foreign subsidiaries	Rugman and D'Cruz (1993)
The Nine-Factor Model	An extension to the Diamond Model; includes four groups of human factors in addition to four physical factors to explain national competitiveness, with chance events included as an external factor.	Explaining the role of, for example, Japanese foreign direct investment (FDI) in Korea, in *relation to* the performance of Japanese FDI in Korea	Cho (1994)

(Continued)

Table 1.4 (Continued)

Ostensive Definition	Description	Operational Definition	Key Reference
Global Competitiveness Index	An annual report that surveys a majority of the world's nations, reporting on aspects of development, wages, labour productivity, infrastructure, health, and education. Data are organised into 12 pillars of competitiveness, and countries are ranked accordingly. The index separates countries into three stages: factor-driven, efficiency-driven, and innovation-driven.	110 variables organised into 12 pillars of competitiveness	World Economic Forum (WEF)
Hypercompetitiveness	The indiscriminate need by individuals to compete and win (and to avoid losing), at any cost as a means of maintaining or enhancing feelings of one's self-worth. This is associated with a strong orientation towards manipulative, aggressive, exploitative, and denigrating behaviours of others.	Likert scale	Horney (1937) Ryckman, Libby, van den Borne, Gold and Lindner (1997)
Trait Competitiveness	"The enjoyment of interpersonal competition and the desire to win and be better than others".	Likert scale	King, MicInerney and Watkins (2012)

Personal Development Competition Orientation	The psychometric properties of individuals "in which the primary focus is not on the outcome (i.e. on winning), but rather more on enjoyment and mastery of the task. Individuals with such competitive attitudes are concerned more with self-discovery, self-improvement, and task-mastery than with comparisons with others". "Personal development competitors want to win and be successful, but not at the expense of other people".	Likert scale	Ryckman, Hammer and Gold (1996)
Competitive Productivity (CP)	At the micro level, "Individual Competitive Productivity (ICP) is both an attitude and behaviour directed at outperforming the competing individuals, and past performance through pragmatism".	Conceptual	Baumann and Pintado (2013) Baumann, Cherry and Chu (2019)

What Does This Mean for the Future of Work?

Our research on the association between education and competitiveness has not least to be viewed in the context of rapid economic changes. Historically, there have always been times of massive changes, more recently labelled disruptive innovation (Christensen, Raynor and McDonald, 2015).

Changes can be so substantial that they affect workers' everyday lives; often they are rapid, and often they had not been predicted. If so, this may also explain why education can only partially prepare the next generation for such massive changes. Education would always pass on a hybrid of facts and figures, skills, values, and inspiration, and some generic 'coping mechanisms' for times of change. At the time of this research, the developed world has entered the Fourth Industrial Revolution. Figure 1.7 provides a brief, but helpful, overview of the progression of industrial revolutions.

A recent *Forbes* article on the Fourth Industrial Revolution (Marr, 2016) puts the challenges of the workforce in a historical perspective:

> Many experts suggest that the fourth industrial revolution will benefit the rich much more than the poor, especially as low-skill, low-wage jobs disappear in favour of automation.
>
> But this isn't new. Historically, industrial revolutions have always begun with greater inequality followed by periods of political and institutional change. The industrial revolution that began at the beginning of the 19th century originally led to a huge polarization of wealth and power, before being followed by nearly 100 years of change including the spread of democracy, trade unions, progressive taxation and the development of social safety nets.
>
> It seems a safe bet to say, then, that our current political, business, and social structures may not be ready or capable of absorbing all the changes a fourth industrial revolution would bring, and that major changes to the very structure of our society may be inevitable.

We kept the technological advancements as a framework for our study in mind, asking ourselves to what extent education and discipline would be an important factor in the formation of competitiveness and economic growth. For example, students mastering math and science skills would appear to be likely success factors for workers wanting to be competitive in technology and innovation. We had previously alluded to East Asian societies being at the forefront of academic performance with strong economic performance during the Asian Miracle of the 1980s and 1990s.

China's data-sharing programmes promote collaboration and progress, for example in medicine and security, compared to the West

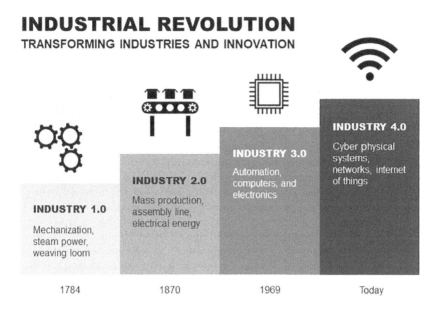

Figure 1.7 The Four Industrial Revolutions

Source: www.iffresearch.com/research-futures-seminar-summary-future-closer-think-technology-means-research/

where progression is often slower due to legal complexities, or a relative decrease in intensive investment strategies in research and development (Fu, 2015; Ma et al., 2015). In other words, while it has sometimes been argued that the stricter East Asian upbringing may hinder creativity and economic innovation, economic development and progression during the Asian Miracle and recent advancements in artificial intelligence, green technology (wind, water, and solar), and dramatic growth in services industries in East Asia tell us another picture—the generation that grew up under strict Confucian educational principals appears to be the one that ultimately forms a cutting-edge East Asian economic landscape driving the Fourth Industrial Revolution.

While it may be impossible to accurately predict the future landscape for the workforce of today's youth, and again, it is mere speculation of what *exact* skills they will need in the decades to come, it appears useful to summarise the transformative trends and likely drivers of future growth to at least attempt to prepare the youth and society at large for the future nature of work. Based on a recent Japanese broadcaster's outlook (NHK Documentary, 25 March 2018), the following economic trends and general considerations have been identified, providing a future outlook on what type of work environment students might have to be prepared for:

- **Artificial intelligence** (AI): examples of AI include stock trading systems such as automated buying and selling of stocks, engineering, medicine, law, education. With accurate algorithms and accurate predictions, future economic growth can be generated. Some new jobs will be generated, but many also made redundant.
- **Sharing economy** (sharing of resources) vis-à-vis conventional capitalist economy (consumption of services and goods): examples are UBER and Airbnb. These 'jobs' are often executed as a side business besides one's normal job, e.g. sharing a car, sharing a home, hosting, etc.
- **Creative destruction** (Joseph Schumpter 1883–1950): as the reference suggests, this is not a new phenomenon! New businesses destroying old ones would be as old as economic activity in itself, and this is often coupled with imitators emerging and offering similar services to the newly emerging ones. Creative destruction is *de facto* a call for continuing innovation as a key to survival, and healthy competition. In essence, in a competitive landscape, a (service) provider can never settle, but instead is constantly looking beyond the horizon to seek new opportunities. Entrepreneurs put pressure on established providers who have no choice but to embrace change, look ahead, and in turn predict (and drive) future developments. In effect, a never ending destruction is essential for economic growth, but this can also mean a complete 'shake out' for established businesses (e.g. hotels are losing customers because of Airbnb, jobs are destroyed). Given such pressures, the educational dimensions investigated in our research appear to make sense—especially with our focus on PISA 2015 science scores.
- **Humans continue their relentless pursuit of growth:** an example is Facebook that focusses on customers who do not yet have internet access. New technology might offer internet from the sky in the future, or even hotels in the sky. The sky is the limit, in the eyes of many entrepreneurs.
- **Invisible hand of the market** (manipulation . . .): "as we became more desperate, we lost the ability to think in a rational and calm way to manage our risk". Recent crises such as the burst of the IT bubble in the USA, the housing crises, the Asian crisis, the Global Financial crises (GFC) also warn us that humans' pursuit of growth assists economic progression, but can also 'collapse' systems when greed takes over. This warning may also remind us to educate the next generation to combine a hybrid of 'talent', one to dream and aspire, but also coupled with analytical skills to allow for realistic assessment of risks.

- *The Wealth of Nations* (**Adam Smith**): Smith wrote two seminal books. In 1759 he published his first book, *The Theory of Moral Sentiments*; in 1776, he published his most influential work, *An Inquiry into the Nature and Causes of the Wealth of Nations*. Nowadays the latter is more popular, more often discussed in schools and universities, even in the public domain, but the former is often forgotten, overlooked, and neglected (that piece was about moral sentiment, i.e. sympathy in society). Too much pursuit of growth through capitalism may lead to an 'obese society', i.e. there are (or should be) limits to our own material aspirations (e.g. more food and more material 'things' do not necessarily lead to [more] happiness). One is encouraged to look beyond a growth-based economy, when there are two approaches to growth: (1) more material output, but with limited sustainability, and (2) understanding the capacity of the economy, environmental protection, capacity to make choices, health, education with working towards a sustainable economy.

Source: NHK Documentary, 25 March 2018 1.10pm—*As Economic inequalities widen and growth slows, capitalism may be at a crossroads. We ask leading economists why, and document how governments and businesses are racing to adapt.* NHK Money World program

The Gig Economy

Traditionally, the education system in most developed markets aims to prepare workers for stable employment relationships; in East Asia there is further a long tradition of lifelong employment (e.g. in Japan, albeit that is also changing). Graduates often aspire to get a job with job security, pension plans, stable income streams and employment rights. More recent, however, there has been a drastic reduction of stable employment with a move towards the 'gig economy', defined as:

> an environment in which temporary positions are common and organizations contract with independent workers for short-term engagements. The trend toward a gig economy has begun. A study by Intuit predicted that by 2020, 40 percent of American workers would be independent contractors.
> (https://whatis.techtarget.com/definition/gig-economy)

In other words, the education system of today—knowingly or not—should be preparing students for 'non-stable' work situations they may soon face: temporary work or contracts, self-employment and rolling fixed-term contracts. Often workers get these gigs via online platforms, such as UBER and Fiverr, which provide opportunities for freelance work. More than half of workers in their twenties and thirties in developed economies rely on gigs and no longer rely on full-time employment.

Interestingly, in a recent article in the *Harvard Business Review* (HBR) on the gig economy (Petriglieri, Ashford and Wrzesniewski, 2018), and perhaps contrary to what would be expected at first sight, discipline issues were discussed in relation to workers in the gig economy. Indeed, the article refers to discipline three times:

> Interestingly, however, the people we talked with aren't just focusing on getting things done and sold. They care about both being at work—*having the discipline* to regularly generate products or services that find a market—and being into their work: having the courage to stay fully invested in the process and output of that labor.
>
> Sustaining productivity is a constant struggle. Distress and distractions can erode it, and both impediments abound in people's working lives. One executive coach gave a poignant description of an unproductive day: "It's when there is so much to do that I'm disorganized and can't get my act together. [In the evening,] the same e-mails I opened in the morning are still open. The documents I wanted to get done are not done. I got distracted and feel like I wasted time". A day like that, he said, leaves him full of self-doubt.
>
> (Petrieglieri et al., 2018, p. 3, emphasis added)

The HBR article points in the direction of the argument we are proposing in our work: discipline is a driver of performance. For workers in the gig economy—who would not report directly to a superior to 'enforce' some level of discipline as we might experience in a traditional work setting ('intervene' when employees are late, underperform, or lack presentation)—a higher degree of self-(discipline) would need to be evident in order to perform. Without it, their ability to obtain and maintain gigs would be compromised. This is evidenced by the following report in the same HBR article:

> "in the afternoon I schedule phone calls, more of the business or financial things that need to be done". This *discipline* even extends to his wardrobe: "I always get dressed for the office. Most days in summer I wear shorts when I'm not on the road, but still I shower and shave as if I were going to a workplace separate from home". That may sound rigid, but it helps Matthew pour himself into his work. He and other successful independent workers seem to follow the advice of the French novelist Gustave Flaubert: "Be regular and orderly in your life . . . so that you may be violent and original in your work".
>
> (Petriglieri et al., 2018, p. 5, emphasis added)

In sum, as an interviewed independent consultant, or gig worker, puts it: "the void she felt when between assignments; the exhilaration of landing the next engagement; the *discipline*, concentration, and grace that mastering her profession required" (Petriglieri et al., 2018, p. 1, emphasis added).

Such a dramatic shift in the nature of employment for the majority of future school graduates also calls for a review of which sets of skills students should learn while in a nation's education system. How can they be (better) prepared for a transitioning economy where they have to be—in many cases—on the constant lookout for new (and better) gigs? Do future mini-entrepreneurs need more discipline in order to obtain and maintain those gigs as the HBR article suggests? An argument could be made that discipline is even more important to form and maintain work ethic in the growing gig economy environment, in contrast to stable employment.

Tangible elements of competitiveness at the micro level—for each and every individual—are talent, discipline, grooming, etc., and they may play a more crucial role for gig seekers who are constantly on the 'hunt' for new jobs. For example, a courier at FedEx would require (self-)discipline for punctuality, respect, and politeness towards customers, or FedEx would not assign any more jobs, or gigs. The same would apply for gig workers in consulting, teaching, and tutoring, cleaning, design, pet sitting, to name a few.

In conclusion, discipline is—to some degree—detached from the complexity and seniority level of employment or job/function type. All workers—whether it is stable or gig employment—face negative consequences if they are not on time, do not perform well, are not friendly and polite, and do not have manners—values that start at home, and are shaped by the education system. A case could be made that for the gig economy, it is even more important to pass on discipline (no doubt coupled with creativity, passion, enthusiasm, and so on) to the next generation.

Data Sources and Methodology

Throughout the book, we utilise a number of secondary data sources and statistical approaches to answer the questions we posed earlier in this chapter. We briefly outline the nature of each, as they appear in this book:

Data Sources

- *Programme for International Student Assessment* (PISA) data as a measure of individual-level student academic performance and discipline, from the Organisation for Economic Co-operation and Development (OECD) database: 2000, 2003, 2006, 2009, 2012, and 2015 waves of collection. Data publicly available from: www.oecd.org/pisa/data/

- *Global Competitiveness Index* (GCI) data as a measure of macro-level national competitiveness scores, from the World Economic Forum (WEF) database: annual from 2000 to 2018. Data publicly available from: https://govdata360.worldbank.org/

Accompanying Technical Reports for both PISA and GCI, per wave of data collection, are also publicly available.

Statistical Methods

- Structural Equation Modelling (SEM): a form of causal modelling that combines factor analysis, regression, and path analysis, to determine the relationship between theoretical constructs (Hooper, Coughlan and Mullen, 2008).
- Inter-Ocular Testing (IOT): a method of 'eye-balling' the data, to avoid falling into a trap of simply accepting statistically significant differences as a reliable test, in isolation (Baumann, Winzar and Fang, 2018). Researchers are encouraged to also visually inspect the 'differences' and draw conclusions based on other assessments such as effect size (e.g. common-language effect size, Cohen's D, and η2).
- Two-stage Least Squares Regression (2SLS): a technique used in the analysis of structural equations.

Applications

- IBM SPSS Statistics AMOS;
- R (programming language);
- Tableau software;
- Microsoft Excel.

Notes

1. Previous work has justified classifying all countries into societal or geographic clusters on the basis of geography, language, ethnicity, work-related values, and religion (e.g. House, Hanges, Javidan, Dorfman and Gupta, 2004). We follow a similar approach, but also classify the countries on the basis that education systems within clusters would be, more or less, similar.
2. Though subject to debate on whether this cluster could be named 'Anglo-Saxon' or 'English-Speaking World', we decided on the former because the countries included in the cluster have a common British history, resulting in a shared language and common cultural heritage, and have similar patterns of economic development, for example rapid post-war growth (Baumann and Winzar, 2016).

3. We refer to Confucianism as a philosophy, ideology, tradition, doctrine, wisdom, and thought interchangeably throughout. While this is subject to much debate, for the purpose of our narrative, we view Confucianism as encompassing all of these qualities because it is multi-faceted, and interpretations of Confucianism are equally so.

4. The *Analects* is composed of a large collection of independent passages, the contents of which have been interpreted by reading scholars' commentaries on the book. One of the principal, and most well-known, interpreters of Confucianism was Mencius (Meng Ke), described as the 'second sage' after Confucius himself.

References

Araújo, Marta. "Disruptive or disrupt ed? A qualitative study on the construction of indiscipline." *International Journal of Inclusive Education* 9, no. 3 (2005): 241–268.

Aunola, Kaisa, Håkan Stattin, and Jari-Erik Nurmi. "Parenting styles and adolescents' achievement strategies." *Journal of Adolescence* 23, no. 2 (2000): 205–222.

Barro, Robert J. *Getting It Right: Markets and Choices in a Free Society.* Cambridge, MA: MIT Press, 1997.

Barro, Robert J., and Jong-Wha Lee. "International comparisons of educational attainment." *Journal of Monetary Economics* 32, no. 3 (1993a): 363–394.

Barro, Robert J., and Jong-Wha Lee. "Losers and winners in economic growth." *The World Bank Economic Review* 7, no. S1 (1993b): 267–298.

Barro, Robert J., and Rachel McCleary. *Religion and Economic Growth.* No. w9682. National Bureau of Economic Research, 2003.

Baumann, Chris, Michael Cherry, and Wujin Chu. "Competitive Productivity (CP) at Macro-Meso-Micro levels." *Cross Cultural & Strategic Management* (2019).

Baumann, Chris, Hamin, Rosalie L. Tung, and Susan Hoadley. "Competitiveness and workforce performance: Asia vis-à-vis the 'West'." *International Journal of Contemporary Hospitality Management* 28, no. 10 (2016): 2197–2217.

Baumann, Chris, and Marina Harvey. "Competitiveness vis-à-vis motivation and personality as drivers of academic performance: Introducing the MCP model." *International Journal of Educational Management* 32, no. 1 (2018): 185–202.

Baumann, Chris, and Hana Krskova. "School discipline, school uniforms and academic performance." *International Journal of Educational Management* 30, no. 6 (2016): 1003–1029.

Baumann, Chris, and Iggy Pintado. "Competitive productivity—A new perspective on effective output." *Journal of Institute of Management Services* 57, no. 1 (2013): 9–11.

Baumann, Chris, Rosalie L. Tung, and Hamin. "Jade will never become a work of art without being carved: Western versus Chinese attitudes toward discipline in education and society." *Virginia Review of Asian Studies* 10 (2012): 1–17.

Baumann, Chris, and Hume Winzar. "The role of secondary education in explaining competitiveness." *Asia Pacific Journal of Education* 36, no. 1 (2016): 13–30.

Baumann, Chris, Hume Winzar, and Tony Fang. "East Asian wisdom and relativity: Inter-ocular testing of Schwartz values from WVS with extension of the ReVaMB model." *Cross Cultural & Strategic Management* 25, no. 2 (2018): 210–230.

Baumrind, Diana. "Child care practices anteceding three patterns of preschool behavior." *Genetic Psychology Monographs* 75, no. 1 (1967): 43–88.

Baumrind, Diana. "Current patterns of parental authority." *Developmental Psychology* 4, no. 1p2 (1971): 1.

Baumrind, Diana. "Effective parenting during the early adolescent transition." *Family Transitions* 2, no. 1 (1991a): 1.

Baumrind, Diana. "The influence of parenting style on adolescent competence and substance use." *The Journal of Early Adolescence* 11, no. 1 (1991b): 56–95.

Bechuke, A. L., and J. R. Debeila. "Applying choice theory in fostering discipline: Managing and modifying challenging learners behaviours in South African schools." *International Journal of Humanities and Social Science* 2, no. 22 (2012): 240–255.

Berger, Peter L. "An East Asian development model?" In P. Berger and M. H. Hsiao (Eds.), *Search of an East Asian Development Model*. New Brunswick, NJ: Transaction Publications, 1988, pp. 3–11.

Bourdieu, Pierre "The forms of capital." In A. H. Halsey, H. Lauder, P. Brown and A. Stuart Wells (Eds.), *Education: Culture, Economy and Society*. Oxford: Oxford University Press, 1997, pp. 40–58.

Chan, Alex, and Angus Young. "Confucian principles of governance: Paternalistic order and relational obligations without legal rules." (January 17, 2012). Available at SSRN: https://ssrn.com/abstract=1986716 or http://dx.doi. org/10.2139/ssrn.1986716.

Cho, Dong-Sung. "A dynamic approach to international competitiveness: The case of Korea." *Asia Pacific Business Review* 1, no. 1 (1994): 17–36.

Christensen, Clayton M., Michael E. Raynor, and Rory McDonald. "What is disruptive innovation." *Harvard Business Review* 93, no. 12 (2015): 44–53.

Croninger, Robert G., Jennifer King Rice, Amy Rathbun, and Masako Nishio. "Teacher qualifications and early learning: Effects of certification, degree, and experience on first-grade student achievement." *Economics of Education Review* 26, no. 3 (2007): 312–324.

Cummings, William K. "The Asian human resource approach in global perspective." *Oxford Review of Education* 21, no. 1 (1995): 67–81.

Darwin, Charles. "Origin of species." *The Athenaeum* 2177 (1869): 82–82.

Donnelly, Kevin. *"Chalk and Talk" Teaching Might Be the Best Way After All*, 2014. Retrieved from the Conversation website: http://theconversation. com/chalk-and-talk-teaching-might-be-the-best-way-after-all-34478.

Dornbusch, Sanford M., Philip L. Ritter, P. Herbert Leiderman, Donald F. Roberts, and Michael J. Fraleigh. "The relation of parenting style to adolescent school performance." *Child Development* (1987): 1244–1257.

Duckworth, Angela L., and Martin E. P. Seligman. "Self-discipline outdoes IQ in predicting academic performance of adolescents." *Psychological Science* 16, no. 12 (2005): 939–944.

Ezra, Vogel. *Japan as Number One: Lessons for America*. Cambridge, MA: Harvard University Press, 1979.

Fang, Tony. *Chinese Business Negotiating Style*. Thousand Oaks, CA: Sage, 1999.

Finn, Jeremy D., Susan B. Gerber, and Jayne Boyd-Zaharias. "Small classes in the early grades, academic achievement, and graduating from high school." *Journal of Educational Psychology* 97, no. 2 (2005): 214.

Fu, Xiaolan. "Innovation in China since the reforms: An overview." In *China's Path to Innovation*. Cambridge: Cambridge University Press, 2015, pp. 15–44.

Fukuyama, Mr Francis. IMF Working Paper WP/00/74. JEL Classification Numbers: Z13, presented at IMF Institute conference on Second Generation Reforms, November 8-9, 1999.

Fung, Joey J., and Anna S. Lau. "Punitive discipline and child behavior problems in Chinese-American immigrant families: The moderating effects of indigenous child-rearing ideologies." *International Journal of Behavioral Development* 33, no. 6 (2009): 520–530.

Hall, David L., and Roger T. Ames. *Thinking Through Confucius*. New York: SUNY Press, 1987.

Hanushek, Eric A. "The economic value of higher teacher quality." *Economics of Education Review* 30, no. 3 (2011): 466–479.

Hanushek, Eric A., and Woessmann, Ludger. "Education and economic growth." *Economics of Education* (2010): 60–67.

Hofheinz, Roy, and Kent E. Calder. *The Eastasia Edge: Why an Entire Region Is Overtaking the West in Technology, Exports, and Management*. New York: Basic Books, 1982.

Hofstede, Geert. *Cultures and Organizations. Intercultural Cooperation and Its Importance for Survival. Software of the Mind*. London: McGraw-Hill, 1991.

Hofstede, Geert, and Michael Harris Bond. "The Confucius connection: From cultural roots to economic growth." *Organizational Dynamics* 16, no. 4 (1988): 5–21.

Hooper, Daire, Joseph Coughlan, and Michael Mullen. "Structural equation modelling: Guidelines for determining model fit." *Articles* (2008): 2.

Horney, K. (1937). *The Neurotic Personality of Our Time*. New York: Norton.

House, Robert J., Paul J. Hanges, Mansour Javidan, Peter W. Dorfman, and Vipin Gupta, eds. *Culture, Leadership, and Organizations: The GLOBE Study of 62 Societies*. Thousand Oaks, CA: Sage, 2004.

Hoxby, Caroline M. "The effects of class size on student achievement: New evidence from population variation." *The Quarterly Journal of Economics* 115, no. 4 (2000): 1239–1285.

Hue, Ming-Tak. "Emergence of Confucianism from teachers' definitions of guidance and discipline in Hong Kong secondary schools." *Research in Education* 78, no. 1 (2007): 21–33.

Hwang, Kwang-Kuo. "The deep structure of Confucianism: A social psychological approach." *Asian Philosophy* 11, no. 3 (2001): 179–204.

Jensen, Ben, Julian Reichl, and Andrew Kemp. "The real issue in school funding: An analysis of increasing government school expenditure and declining performance." *Australian Economic Review* 44, no. 3 (2011): 321–329.

Jepsen, Christopher, and Steven Rivkin. "Class size reduction and student achievement the potential tradeoff between teacher quality and class size." *Journal of Human Resources* 44, no. 1 (2009): 223–250.

Kahn, H. with the Hudson Institute. *World Economic Development: 1979 and Beyond*. Boulder, CO: Westview Press, 1979.

Kang, Jae Hyeung, James G. Matusik, and Lizabeth A. Barclay. "Affective and normative motives to work overtime in Asian organizations: Four cultural orientations from Confucian ethics." *Journal of Business Ethics* 140, no. 1 (2017): 115–130.

Keller, Katarina R. I. "Investment in primary, secondary, and higher education and the effects on economic growth." *Contemporary Economic Policy* 24, no. 1 (2006): 18–34.

King, Ronnel B., Dennis M. McInerney, and David A. Watkins. "Competitiveness is not that bad . . . at least in the East: Testing the hierarchical model of achievement motivation in the Asian setting." *International Journal of Intercultural Relations* 36, no. 3 (2012): 446–457.

Krskova, Hana, and Chris Baumann. "School discipline, investment, competitiveness and mediating educational performance." *International Journal of Educational Management* 31, no. 3 (2017): 293–319.

Krugman, Paul. "Competitiveness: A dangerous obsession." *Foreign Affairs* 73 (1994): 28.

Kuczynski, Leon, Sheila Marshall, and Kathleen Schell. "Value socialization in a bidirectional context." *Parenting and Children's Internalization of Values: A Handbook of Contemporary Theory* (1997): 23–50.

Legge, James. "The Four Books." In *The Chinese Classics*. Vols. 1–2. Oxford: Clarendon Press, reprinted by Culture Book Co., Taipei, 1992.

Lewis, Ramon. "Classroom discipline and student responsibility: The students' view." *Teaching and Teacher Education* 17, no. 3 (2001): 307–319.

Lim, Vivien K. G. "Money matters: An empirical investigation of money, face and Confucian work ethic." *Personality and Individual Differences* 35, no. 4 (2003): 953–970.

Ma, Zhenzhong, Mingyang Yu, Chongyan Gao, Jieru Zhou, and Zhenning Yang. "Institutional constraints of product innovation in China: Evidence from international joint ventures." *Journal of Business Research* 68, no. 5 (2015): 949–956.

Marr, Bernard. "Why everyone must get ready for the 4th industrial revolution." *The Forbes* (2016).

Monkhouse, Lien Le, Bradley R. Barnes, and Thi Song Hanh Pham. "Measuring Confucian values among East Asian consumers: A four country study." *Asia Pacific Business Review* 19, no. 3 (2013): 320–336.

Moon, Hwy-Chang. *From Adam Smith to Michael Porter: Evolution of Competitiveness Theory.* Vol. 2. River Edge, NJ: World Scientific, 2000.

Park, So Jin, and Nancy Abelmann. "Class and cosmopolitan striving: Mothers' management of English education in South Korea." *Anthropological Quarterly* (2004): 645–672.

Pellerin, Lisa A. "Applying Baumrind's parenting typology to high schools: Toward a middle-range theory of authoritative socialization." *Social Science Research* 34, no. 2 (2005a): 283–303.

Pellerin, Lisa A. "Student disengagement and the socialization styles of high schools." *Social Forces* 84, no. 2 (2005b): 1159–1179.

Petriglieri, Gianpiero, Susan J. Ashford, and Amy Wrzesniewski. "Agony and ecstasy in the gig economy: Cultivating holding environments for precarious and personalized work identities." *Administrative Science Quarterly* 64, no. 1 (2018): 124–170. doi:10.1177/0001839218759646.

Phillipson, Shane N. "Confucianism, learning self-concept and the development of exceptionality." *Exceptionality in East Asia: Explorations in the Actiotope Model of Giftedness* (2013): 40–64.

Porter, Michael E. *Competitive advantage: Creating and sustaining superior performance.* Vol. 43. New York: Free Press, 1985, p. 214.

Porter, Michael E. "The competitive advantage of nations." *Competitive Intelligence Review* 1, no. 1 (1990): 14.

Porter, Michael E. *Competitive Advantage of Nations: Creating and Sustaining Superior Performance.* Vol. 2. New York: Simon and Schuster, 2011.

Preston, Lewis T. *The East Asian Miracle: Economic Growth and Public Policy.* Vol. 1. Washington, DC: World Bank Publications, 1993.

Redding, Gordon. *The Spirit of Chinese Capitalism.* Vol. 22. Berlin: Walter de Gruyter, 2013.

Romi, Shlomo, and Mira Freund. "Teachers', students' and parents' attitudes towards disruptive behaviour problems in high school: A case study." *Educational Psychology* 19, no. 1 (1999): 53–70.

Rugman, Alan M., and Joseph R. D'cruz. "The 'double diamond' model of international competitiveness: The Canadian experience." *MIR: Management International Review* (1993): 17–39.

Ryckman, Richard M., Max Hammer, Linda M. Kaczor, and Joel A. Gold. "Construction of a personal development competitive attitude scale." *Journal of Personality Assessment* 66, no. 2 (1996): 374–385.

Ryckman, Richard M., Cary R. Libby, Bart van den Borne, Joel A. Gold, and Marc A. Lindner. "Values of hypercompetitive and personal development competitive individuals." *Journal of Personality Assessment* 69, no. 2 (1997): 271–283.

Schwab, Klaus, and Sala-i-Martin. "The global competitiveness report 2013–2014." *World Economic Forum.* Full Data Edition, 2013.

Smith, Adam. *The Wealth of Nations [1776].* New York: Modern Library, 1937.

Sun, Anna Xiao Dong. *Confusions Over Confucianism: Controversies Over the Religious Nature of Confucianism, 1870–2007.* Princeton: Princeton University Press, 2008.

Tan, Charlene. *Educational Policy Borrowing in China: Looking West or Looking East?* London: Routledge, 2016.

Tu, Wei-ming, ed. *Confucian Traditions in East Asian Modernity: Moral Education and Economic Culture in Japan and the Four Mini-Dragons.* Cambridge, MA: Harvard University Press, 1996.

Vessman, Ludger, and Eric Hanushek. "The role of education quality in economic growth (Part I)." *Educational Studies* 2 (2007a): 86–116.

Vessman, Ludger, and Eric Hanushek. "The role of education quality in economic growth (Part II)." *Educational Studies* 3 (2007b): 115–185.

Viengkham, Doris, Chris Baumann, and Hume Winzar. "Confucianism: Measurement and association with workforce performance." *Cross Cultural & Strategic Management* 25, no. 2 (2018): 337–374.

Wang, Jia, Greg G. Wang, Wendy E. A. Ruona, and Jay W. Rojewski. "Confucian values and the implications for international HRD." *Human Resource Development International* 8, no. 3 (2005): 311–326.

Warner, Malcolm. "In search of Confucian HRM: Theory and practice in Greater China and beyond." In *Confucian HRM in Greater China.* London: Routledge, 2014, pp. 9–34.

Wiley, David E., and Annegret Harnischfeger. "Explosion of a myth: Quantity of schooling and exposure to instruction, major educational vehicles." *Educational Researcher* 3, no. 4 (1974): 7–12.

Yao, Xinzhong. *An Introduction to Confucianism.* Cambridge: Cambridge University Press, 2000.

Yeung, Irene Y. M., and Rosalie L. Tung. "Achieving business success in Confucian societies: The importance of guanxi (connections)." *Organizational Dynamics* 25, no. 2 (1996): 54–65.

Youniss, James. "Rearing children for society." *New Directions for Child and Adolescent Development* 1994, no. 66 (1994): 37–50.

Yuhan, X. I. E., and G. E. Chen. "Confucius' thoughts on moral education in China." *Cross-Cultural Communication* 9, no. 4 (2013): 45–49.

2 The Confucianism-Discipline-Competitiveness (CDC) Model

In the previous chapter we introduced the overall narrative of this book, namely that Competitiveness-Discipline-Confucianism are interrelated, which we capture as the CDC model or framework. The literature reviewed for our research has provided us with good indication that these three dimensions are indeed interrelated, but there has not to date been empirical work done to support that argument. East Asian students themselves have often connected the dots about focus and discipline driving performance without scholarly evidence, for example at a Shanghainese school, where two girls concluded:

I already know the shame of failure.

(Wang Yu, age 19)[1]

Failure is not an option.

(Ma Li, age 18)

In this chapter, we provide precisely such, i.e. we have 'crunched' the numbers to explore to what degree the literature tells us is also supported when we look at actual student data. We focus this chapter on answering a fundamental question to our overall narrative: could school discipline be a driver—or at least contributing factor—to/of academic performance?

We next present the results of multivariate analyses, with a key focus on the association between discipline and academic performance. In essence, we want to establish whether there are principal (to a degree, universal/global) mechanisms as to how discipline drives academic performance. Will there be differences to our CDC model for the Confucian Orbit and the Anglo-Saxon clusters, as well as to other parts of the world?

Our overarching proposition is, as outlined in our introduction chapter, that the higher the discipline standards, the higher the academic performance. But would that mechanism in principal work simultaneously for the six geographic regions we test, albeit the actual standards (means and distribution) would presumably vary substantially (we will explore that question separately in Chapter 3)?

Our CDC Model at the Micro Level

Our model includes the following independent variable of family wealth as a 'starting point' to explaining academic performance (the dependent variable) across the six geographical clusters. Family wealth, as measured by PISA, is based on the reported availability of 16 household items including three 'country-specific household items' that are considered appropriate measures within that country's context. For instance, while students for all countries were asked to report on possessions such as books and the availability of a place to study, some possessions varied by country: Australian students were presented with 'Espresso Machine', whereas Korean students were presented with 'Clothing Dryer' as country-specific wealth items. We adopt the 'home possessions index' measured by PISA as a socioeconomic indicator for the purpose of our analysis—but some call for more national- or regional-specific item measures in future (Rutkowski and Rutkowski, 2010, 2013). Regardless of the actual 'wealth possessions' included in the measure across countries, we apply the composite indicator as the starting point to our model because it provides an objective baseline of students' socioeconomic status, from which we can determine in what way, if at all, student motivation and behaviour is affected by this.

Our inclusion of family wealth as the starting point in explaining academic performance is also aligned with the fact that wealth (which includes the availability of material resources) may operate differently between geographic clusters (Schulz, 2005). The link between the socioeconomic statuses of parents (i.e. family wealth) to their child's academic achievement is well established in the literature (Graetz, 1995; Coleman, 1968; Duncan, Morris and Rodrigues, 2011), but how this might impact the behavioural and motivational aspects of students' learning experience across 'cultures' is less known. We would suspect that, and in line with previous empirical studies, that more family wealth results in more available resources for learning as well as access to educational services (Considine and Zappalà, 2002) and higher academic performance; conversely, lower socioeconomic status households face a host of challenges including limited resources and stress that contribute to lower school performance (Willingham, 2012). But the relationship is not always clear cut. Other factors affect school performance, such as family size, where an increase in number of siblings results in 'resource dilution' (i.e. resources must be shared among siblings) thus reducing individual performance (Downey, 1995). Further, parents' socioeconomic status on student educational outcomes might also be neutralised or strengthened by contextual factors and individual characteristics; for example, if parents have a low income and/or low-status occupation, they may transmit, to make up for these 'deficiencies', a high educational aspiration in their children. In other words, academic achievement is not only contingent upon what parents *have*, but also what they *do* to encourage behavioural and motivational strategies for learning (Considine and Zappalà, 2002). We add that the balance between family wealth (availability of tangible resources) and social factors (availability of intangible resources, including support and encouragement) contributes to students' academic achievement in different ways between geographic clusters, simply as a matter of education being prioritised differently, or resources being allocated in a different way across cultures (Chao, 1996).

Though we do not measure culture directly, *per se*, we use the cultural clusters as a proxy to discern whether there are any differences in terms of how the models work across countries. In other words, does wealth or socioeconomic factors determine the types and degree of motivation and behaviour of students, and does this in turn explain academic achievement—and how might this differ around the world?

We argue that this factor would drive academic performance, not necessarily in a direct fashion, but indeed with the following intervening (or mediating) factors:

- **Student Truancy:** refers to any action taken by the student of staying away, or being late to, school for no good reason. These measures include frequency of classes skipped, school days skipped, and late arrival to school.
- **Student Motivation:** captures the underlying reason for students' actions, such as recognising the practical reasons to follow a path of action (i.e. instrumental motivation), and the need for success or attainment of excellence (i.e. achievement motivation).
- **Test Anxiety:** the subjective feeling of fear or dread related to the student's performance in an assessment or examination.
- **Interest in Subject:** the extent to which the student has a 'desire' for wanting to know or learn about something.
- **Disciplinary Climate:** the overall condition of students' level of discipline in the classroom/school, as perceived by students.

As part of our model (Figure 2.1), we conceive that these factors are driven by 'family wealth' (i.e. the independent variable), where behavioural and motivational approaches of students (i.e. mediating variables) may be a reflection of that wealth, i.e. rich, poor, or in-between, which in turn contribute to explaining students' academic performance (i.e. the dependent variable). Although previous literature demonstrates strong links between parents' socioeconomic status and their child's academic performance—higher socioeconomic status associated with stronger performance, and lower socioeconomic status with poorer performance (Fan, 2012)—we seek to determine whether wealth is 'used differently' between clusters, in terms of how they shape students' behaviours at school and motivations for learning.

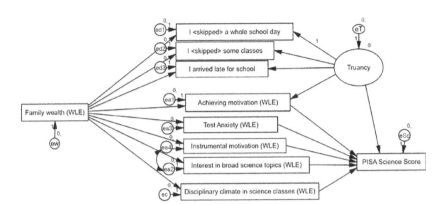

Figure 2.1 SEM Theoretical Model for CDC

Again, and in accordance with previous literature, we would expect that these would work differently among the clusters, both in the strength of the relationships and degree of intervention between factors. In other words, we expect to find that across the six geographic clusters, students' academic performance (i.e. PISA scores across math, science, and reading) will be explained by different relationships; in particular, and in line with our overarching hypothesis, we expect to find the higher the standards of discipline, the better the performance.

Unit of Analysis

Our unit of analysis is individual students who participated in the 2015 wave of PISA.[2] The PISA data are available for over half a million individual students (de-identified) from 72 countries. This data set allows us to evaluate our model at the individual (micro) level. Alongside assessing 15-year-old students on their math, science, and reading abilities, the PISA questionnaire gathers information from students relating to (1) various aspects of their home and family life, (2) school background, (3) educational resources, (4) classroom management, and (5) attitude and perceived abilities. Science was the major domain of focus for 2015 (subjects are rotated every three years that PISA is administered), which meant that students were asked to evaluate survey items, such as those that capture disciplinary climate, based on their experience during that particular subject class. While some may view this as problematic to generalise this to all class subjects, we contend that discipline in a science class would not be all that different to discipline in a math or reading (or even history or art!) class. In fact, if a school is well (or poorly) managed and enforces a high (or low) standard of discipline, then this will be reflected across all classes regardless. In other words, discipline in science classes would be highly correlated with discipline in math and reading classes.

We utilise PISA data, and effectiveness measures on student performance, because there exists a logical link between how students perform at school and how the country performs in the global arena (i.e. its competitiveness); this has been demonstrated empirically on numerous occasions (e.g. Baumann and Winzar, 2016; Hanushek and Woessmann, 2011a; Barro and Lee, 2001). But beyond capturing how students perform on test scores, PISA data allow us to explore the mechanisms that drive this, which is more important to our understanding of the dispositions that individuals carry with them into the workforce. After all, how students are educated and the values they cultivate during their formative years (i.e. childhood and school) ultimately make up how they engage with world, as adults, beyond formal education. This makes PISA data an appropriate proxy for the study of discipline and academic performance at the level of the individual.

To empirically test our model, and to make a comparison across the six cultural clusters, we apply the Structural Equation Modelling (SEM) technique. In our model, we specified that the factor of family wealth (independent variable)—through the available resources to service an education—influences students' cognitive and behavioural dispositions at school (mediating variables), which ultimately drive academic performance (dependent variable). Structural Equation Modelling allows us to simultaneously test the relationships between these measures. This procedure also involved generating overall fit indices (i.e. how well the model fits the data for each respective cluster), calculating path estimates between variables, and calculating squared multiple correlations (R-squared). We tested the same Structural Equation Model for each of the following geographic clusters:

Confucian Orbit	China, Hong Kong, Japan, Korea, Macao, Singapore, Taiwan, and Vietnam.
Anglo-Saxon	Australia, New Zealand, Canada, Ireland, United States of America (USA), United Kingdom (UK), and Puerto Rico.
Western Europe	Austria, Belgium, Denmark, Finland, France, Germany, Greece, Iceland, Italy, Luxembourg, Netherlands, Norway, Portugal, Spain, Sweden, Switzerland, Latvia, Malta, Lithuania, and Estonia.
Eastern Europe and Former Soviet Union	Albania, Bulgaria, Croatia, Georgia, Hungary, Poland, Romania, Russian Federation, Macedonia, Slovakia, Kosovo, Slovenia, Moldova, Montenegro, Czech Republic, and Turkey.
Latin America	Brazil, Chile, Argentina, Peru, Dominican Republic, Colombia, Trinidad and Tobago, Mexico, Costa Rica, and Uruguay.
North Africa and the Middle East	Algeria, Israel, Qatar, Jordan, Lebanon, United Arab Emirates (UAE), and Tunisia.

We approach the analysis for this chapter in two steps: firstly, we want to examine the association between school discipline and academic performance per geographic cluster and also for each country/society in the PISA 2015 data set. For this purpose, we only use the PISA variable 'Disciplinary Climate' and assess it for its link with academic performance (overall PISA science score). Secondly we are interested in additional PISA dimensions that drive performance with a broader view of discipline, including, for example, truancy. The second set of testing is in essence a statistical verification of our CDC model.

Association Between School Discipline and Academic Performance

Table 2.1 shows the correlations between school discipline and academic performance. Regional correlation coefficients are calculated by averaging the squared correlations and then finding the square root. This recognises that correlations are the square roots of the standardised variances, so the correct method of averaging is to square first and then average. We can see from our results that the highest correlation is found for the Anglo-Saxon cluster with a value of 0.205, lowest for Asia with 0.101 (that excludes the Confucian Orbit).

A possibly simplistic interpretation of the correlations is that, all else being equal, academic performance will go up by the number of R-squares for each standard deviation increase in school discipline. For example, the correlation for Anglo-Saxon is 0.205 and r^2 is 0.042, so a one standard deviation increase in school discipline will cause an increase of 0.042 standard deviations in academic performance. This also means that our

Table 2.1 Correlations Between School Discipline and Academic Performance per Geographic Cluster

Region	R-Squared	Correlation Between Disciplinary Climate and Science (r)
Anglo-Saxon	0.042	0.205
Asia	0.010	0.101
Confucian Orbit	0.028	0.166
Eastern Europe and Former Soviet Union	0.034	0.185
Latin America	0.025	0.158
North Africa and the Middle East	0.028	0.166
Western Europe	0.025	0.159

overarching proposition that the two constructs are related is statistically supported.

We further observe that all correlations are positive—i.e. the higher the discipline levels, the higher the performance. Naturally, discipline itself is not the strongest single factor determining performance, given that so many other factors determine human performance (e.g. IQ, EQ, talent for certain subjects, age and maturity, even mood, time of day of testing, physical and mental health, other circumstances). Nevertheless, the R-squared values range from 1 to 4 percent, indicating that indeed discipline determines—at least—this range of academic performance, and thus discipline is a valid area to further explore as a determinant of performance. Looking at the individual country/society level analysis (see the Appendix), we observe again solely positive associations, with relatively solid correlation overall. If we can increase discipline, we can increase performance. But how do these mechanisms work in more detail across geographic clusters?

CDC Under the SEM Probe

In our previous analysis we focussed solely on the association between discipline and academic performance. Next we extended our testing to include other factors that relate to discipline or performance determinants more broadly. Specifically, we included attitudes towards study, disciplinary climate, and behaviour towards study as drivers of academic performance. Family wealth, a student's financial background, was used as the independent variable based on the literature that such circumstances play a role in determining a student's academic performance (Duncan et al., 2011), and we included truancy, achieving motivation, test anxiety, interest and motivation, and also disciplinary climate as mediators to determine academic performance. Applying Structural Equation Modelling (SEM), we tested for appropriate goodness-of-fit measures and statistical significance in the parameter estimates. The model was run separately for each geographic cluster in our study, and given our focus on the Confucian Orbit (Figure 2.2, Panel A) in comparison to Anglo-Saxon (Figure 2.2, Panel B) and Western Europe (Figure 2.2, Panel C) regions, we present these models next (see Table 2.2); numbers show standardised coefficients with all associations significant at $p<0.05$. Note that we are dealing with very large sample sizes here, so we expect to see statistics that are 'statistically significant', without necessarily being very meaningful. In these cases, we should carefully consider less traditional measures of goodness of fit in Structural Equation Modelling (Bollen and Long, 1992; Byrne, 2016). The models for other geographic regions can be found in the Appendix.

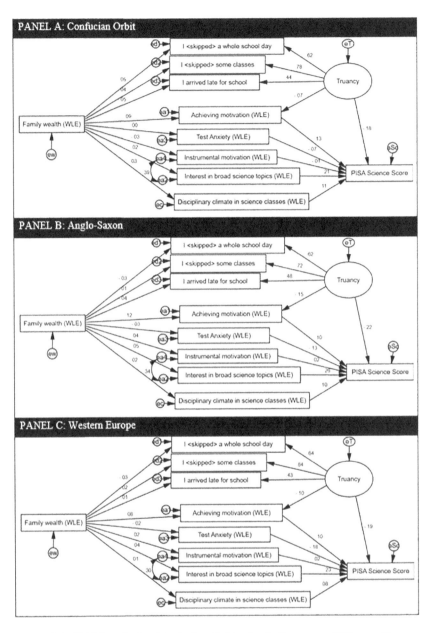

Figure 2.2 SEM Results for Confucian Orbit, Anglo-Saxon, and Western Europe Clusters

Table 2.2 Standardised Regression Coefficients for Cultural Groups

			Anglo-Saxon	Confucian Orbit	Western Europe	Eastern Europe and Former Soviet Union	Latin America	North Africa and the Middle East
WEALTH	→	MOTIVAT	0.121	0.092	0.085	-0.051	0.075	0.156
WEALTH	→	INTBRSCI	0.050	0.017	0.037	0.025	-0.009	0.027
WEALTH	→	INSTSCIE	0.039	-0.034	0.024	-0.085	-0.053	-0.022
WEALTH	→	DISCLISCI	0.018	0.026	0.010	-0.050	0.001	0.057
WEALTH	→	ANXTEST	-0.035	0.002	-0.024	-0.131	-0.041	0.030
WEALTH	→	ST062Q01TA	-0.031	0.054	-0.028	-0.012	0.013	0.069
WEALTH	→	ST062Q03TA	-0.040	-0.050	0.007	0.047	0.092	-0.022
WEALTH	→	ST062Q02TA	-0.012	0.035	-0.019	0.039	0.045	0.005
Truancy	→	MOTIVAT	-0.145	-0.068	-0.097	-0.053	-0.096	-0.134
Truancy	→	ST062Q01TA	0.623	0.624	0.642	0.674	0.634	0.583
Truancy	→	ST062Q02TA	0.721	0.779	0.839	0.859	0.759	0.755
Truancy	→	ST062Q03TA	0.476	0.445	0.432	0.504	0.345	0.524
Truancy	→	ScienceOverall	-0.218	-0.176	-0.188	-0.275	-0.197	-0.136
MOTIVAT	→	ScienceOverall	0.103	0.130	0.099	0.073	0.146	0.153
INTBRSCI	→	ScienceOverall	0.257	0.205	0.234	0.157	0.088	0.080
DISCLISCI	→	ScienceOverall	0.100	0.114	0.083	0.063	0.102	0.132
INSTSCIE	→	ScienceOverall	0.021	-0.015	0.022	-0.142	-0.080	0.052
ANXTEST	→	ScienceOverall	-0.128	-0.072	-0.185	-0.165	-0.148	-0.117

Table 2.3 brings together the regression coefficients for all six SEM models. The most notable outcome is that the estimates are very similar across all cultural groups. Focussing specifically on the effects of the PISA variables on academic performance, as measured by the PISA scores for science overall, we can see that all effects are remarkably comparable. For example, the association between truancy and performance is negative for all six geographic clusters; in other words, the more a student is late for school, skips classes, or skips an entire school day, the lower their academic performance. While there is a small—negligible—variation among the cultural groups, the nature of the link is *de facto* identical. A similar pattern of associations was found for disciplinary climate and performance, but naturally with a negative association: the better the disciplinary climate in classes, the higher the performance, and this was again the same for all geographic clusters. For the other four variables in the model, we again arrive at the same conclusion—there is no notable difference among the six geographic clusters: as we might expect, the higher the achieving motivation, the better the performance; the higher test anxiety, the lower performance; and of course interest in the subject taught has a positive effect on academic performance for all cultural groups. Instrumental motivation has practically no effect (close to zero) for all geographic clusters.

Our conclusion here is that it is not cultural differences within the model that actually make the difference in academic performance—the mechanisms are very similar for all geographic clusters. We only find very modest moderating influence of culture on the effects of discipline and

Table 2.3 Total Standardised Effects on Science Overall (Academic Achievement)

	Anglo-Saxon	Confucian Orbit	Western Europe	Eastern Europe and Former Soviet Union	Latin America	North Africa and the Middle East
Family Wealth	0.032	0.019	0.023	0.031	0.021	0.029
Truancy	−0.233	−0.184	−0.198	−0.278	−0.211	−0.157
Test Anxiety	−0.128	−0.072	−0.185	−0.165	−0.148	−0.117
Instrumental Motivation	0.021	−0.015	0.022	−0.142	−0.080	0.052
Disciplinary Climate	0.100	0.114	0.083	0.063	0.102	0.132
Interest in Science	0.257	0.205	0.234	0.157	0.088	0.080
Achieving Motivation	0.103	0.130	0.099	0.073	0.146	0.153

environmental influences on academic performance. This begs the question: why would there then be strong differences in academic performance nonetheless if the underlying mechanisms driving performance are so similar? We suspect it is not the associations then that are different, but indeed the actual spreads and means/medians that are different—i.e. it is not that discipline drives performance more in one region than another, but the fact that there are regions with higher discipline levels and that in turn results in higher academic performance—and as we have alluded to, the Confucian Orbit is a candidate where high levels of discipline have been suggested in anecdotal evidence in the literature. We next turn our attention to reasons why discipline and performance might be stronger in the Confucian Orbit.

Explaining the Difference: A Confucian Perspective

Previously, in Chapter 1, we provided an introduction to a historical overview of Confucianism to provide a foundation for its relevance to our narrative on discipline, performance, and competitiveness. In the proceeding section, we will discuss the role of Confucian culture in East Asia in the context of education and performance, by way of dissecting how certain aspects and understandings of the tradition have shaped the social, cognitive, and behavioural processes within their societies. In other words, we aim to paint a picture as to why culture, as stemming from—or at least being influenced by—Confucian traditions has propelled countries within the Confucian Orbit with a *modus operandi* to succeed.

The results from our Structural Equation Models (SEM) demonstrated that the drivers of academic performance work in similar ways across each geographic cluster, yet we continue to see that, generally, students in the Confucian Orbit outperform their peers on measures of math, science, and reading. An important reminder is that while we find that the six models work in a similar manner, one relationship consistently remains clear: the higher the discipline standards, the higher the academic performance, and the lower truancy (being late for school, skipping classes, or missing school), the better performance. Therefore, if in principle, these relationships operate in the same way regardless of which country a student is educated, then there is clearly 'something else' happening, or a number of factors 'tango together' in a different way, behind the scenes, which accounts for why students within the Confucian Orbit consistently outperform the rest. We simply put that under a long history of Confucian traditions, these societies have cultivated a pattern of activities and processes—normalised across contexts—which manifest as a unique form of discipline and work ethic.

While a great deal has been said (and debated) about the role of Confucian culture on performance, the conversation usually takes one of two paths: first, that any attempt to apply Confucianism as the key explanation for the rapid economic growth of East Asian countries is cultural essentialism (Morrison, 2006); and second, that it does play an important role in explaining performance, but the mechanisms through which this is understood is unclear. Our approach is one that agrees with the view that Confucianism *does* play an important role in shaping performance of individuals in the East, but with a critical addition: that performance is primarily achieved through the way culture has shaped views and practices of *discipline* among various stakeholders.

The home environment is an important starting point in 'setting kids up' in their attitude, approach, and capacity to perform at school from a young age, which continues to be nurtured in the school environment (Xu, 2017). Further, the logic is that the home environment and the underlying child socialisation priorities are shaped by a society's prevailing cultural system and offers a microcosmic snapshot of the values that are important in a society (Chen et al., 1998).

A question that emerges then is: what is it about the culture in the Confucian Orbit that cultivates a strong desire to succeed? We contend that it is a combination of systems (i.e. stakeholders, policies, institutions) that work together to 'produce' a cultural climate conducive to self-betterment, resilience, and, of most importance, discipline in its individuals. While our analyses at the individual level utilise data based on academic performance, we believe this represents an important departure for any understanding of the values a culture impresses on its persons, because it shapes their outlook on work, and ultimately how a nation performs. Thus Jacques (2009, p. 616, emphasis added) best summarises our approach:

> The success of East Asian countries, however, cannot solely be explained in terms of their educational systems: it is also a product of the way in which *those systems interact with the wider culture.* As mentioned earlier, Confucian societies place much greater emphasis on education than Western societies, as exemplified by the high performance levels that parents expect and demand of their children. The explanation for their present level of educational attainment is thus to be found in part in their cultural traditions.

In the following sections, we will discuss the role of Confucianism through four lenses, drawing from the literature to demonstrate how aspects of the traditional philosophy are imbibed by individuals to be utilised and experienced as drivers of performance. Figure 2.3 are impressions about Confucianism that originated in Confucius's hometown in China, Qufu. Confucianism is the dominant cultural foundation for Chinese culture, and has spread to the entire East Asian region over time (e.g. Japan, Korea).

Figure 2.3 Impressions of Confucianism

Photo description from top left to bottom right:

A. Birthplace of Confucius near Mountain Ni, 25 kilometres southeast of Qufu city, Shandong Province. Confucius was born in this cave.
B. Temple of Confucius in Qufu (Kong Miao), the Dacheng Hall (or main hall).
C. Statue of Confucius on the altar in the Dacheng Hall (the 'Hall of Great Perfection', the 'Hall of Great Achievement').
D. Tourist demonstrating traditional Confucian discipline at the Temple of Confucius/Kong Family Mansion (Kong Fu) in Qufu.
E. City view of modern Qufu with the Huai River. Qufu translates into 'crooked hill'.
F. Confucius Research Institute 'Kongzi Academe' in Qufu. The institute hosts a museum and conference centre about the life of Confucius and its global impact on today's world.

Photo credit: Dr Chris Baumann (2015)

Education as a Transformative Experience

A cornerstone of the Confucian worldview and tradition is that of education and the importance thereof, where it is perceived to have played an instrumental role in the rise of East Asian societies, including China, Japan, Korea, Hong Kong, Singapore, and Vietnam. Notably, the academic performance of these societies in international standardised examinations such as PISA—the foundation of our analyses in Chapters 2, 3, and 4—are what call for greater attention to understanding the underlying phenomena which explain their consistently high performance, despite diverging economic stages. In other words, while each society has developed and transitioned in relatively different ways, each can be seen to share a commonality towards its view of the importance of education in achieving growth (de Bary, 1996)— personally, economically, and nationally.

The overarching aim of education, as seen by Confucianism, is in developing one's innate ability and nature through moral (self-)cultivation. Self-cultivation refers to the process of educating oneself and following the path for continuous self-improvement. According to the ancient Confucian text, the *Analects*, this is achieved by following the *Way* (*dao*), which is modelled on the three sage-kings of ancient China's first three dynasties. The *Way*, explained by Tu (1985, p. 94), is "a process, a movement, and, indeed, a dynamic unfolding of the self as a vital force for personal, social, and cosmic transformation". Broadening the *Way* is achieved by making the conscious effort to seek betterment through learning, which is a task never complete, because there is always yet more to learn. If one can strive to follow the *Way*, then they are on the path to becoming a *junzi*—an exemplary and learned person (Hung, 2016). As Yao (2000, p. 47) explains:

> Confucianism does not emphasise transcendence as a delivery from without. It is concerned with human destiny, but this concern is based on, and in turn supported by, the belief in the possibility of sagehood or the perfectibility of every individual, visible in daily improvement in terms of moral quality and social progress. Confucianism does not hand out a blank cheque for those who are eager to embrace an eternal hope. It is fully aware of the imperfection of human individuals and the limitation of social reality. Therefore, it repeatedly warns that perfectibility will remain merely a possibility unless each individual engages in a life-long process of learning and practising, and is constantly under self-*discipline and education.*
>
> (emphasis added)

Some have argued that the transformation and reinterpretations of Confucianism over millennia means that there might be little resemblance between the original tenets and concepts of learning today, with potentially little relevance to East Asian education (Tu, 2000). However, Confucian education is an open tradition which has evolved over time (Tan, 2016), creating a unique pedagogic culture that emphasises a controlled learning environment and respect for education which still resonates in today's classrooms (Leung, 2002). The massive importance of education and betterment under Confucianism also points toward an obligation for parents and teachers to use discipline to have their students learn and become better humans. Discipline is an integral part of Confucian learning; there is no excuse under Confucianism to neglect learning and be 'lazy'.

To illustrate, in Mandarin Chinese, the word *xue* (学 learning) is both a noun and a verb—meaning a person who is undertaking study in a place (noun), or reflecting the action and process of learning (verb). In this sense, learning is an "action-dispositional property of the human person which enables a person to be more than what he is in a given state" (Cheng, 2016, p. 52). For modern education in Confucian heritage cultures, we see this concept applied in not only *what* students learn (i.e. curriculum), but also *how* students learn within a classroom (i.e. a Confucian approach to pedagogy with a strong focus on discipline). By 'how' we refer to a number of core Confucian tenets that are ingrained within the classroom experience that not only assist in its management, but also ultimately transmission of values and knowledge to the next generation. In other words, while education is viewed a vehicle for individual and social mobility, education under the Confucian tradition aims to inculcate students with the 'right' ethical values, virtues, morals, and attitudes considered necessary for a good society. We outline these briefly below:

Benevolence (ren): The expression of compassion and genuine concern, benevolence is the overarching quality which encompasses other virtues including generosity, diligence, respect, tolerance, empathy, and trustworthiness. In the context of learning, teachers relate to their students with genuine care and empathy, and through reciprocal trust, teachers expect students to be respectful and obedient (Hue and Wai-Shing, 2008).

Righteousness (yi): The pursuit of individual interest and goals should not be made at the expense of others, but instead guided by a moral code with the good of society in mind.

Propriety (li): *Li* provides the guidelines of social behaviour that mandates how individuals should behave in an ideal society. It is concerned primarily with the avoidance of inappropriate actions, and the maintenance of harmonious relationships. There are clear expectations laid before students on how they should behave, and carry themselves in the classroom, including punctuality, politeness, and tidiness of uniforms.

Doctrine of the Mean (zhong yong): The appreciation of central virtues that achieve a balance between extremes, where individuals adopt moderate forms of behaviours. In the classroom, students are expected to conform to a certain standard of behaviour, where if this expectation is broken, teachers are equipped with disciplinary methods to correct this to reinstate a 'balance of order'.

The centrality of education to the Confucian tradition has been largely understood in the context of historical texts, but its contemporary relevance and importance today is evident. A study by Viengkham, Baumann and Winzar (2018) demonstrated that individuals from Taiwan, Mainland China, and South Korea consistently prioritised the importance of value of knowledge (pedagogical) over relational and transformative aspects of Confucianism, and when taken together, could explain up to 25 percent of work-related performance measures. Hue (2007b) also explored how Confucianism is applied in practice by teachers by examining how certain tenets influence disciplinary measures. The Confucian tradition strongly influences educational institutions that are often seen as responsible for 'passing on' the instruments of values and traditions for a society, in which the classroom becomes an arena which reinforces and strengthens these cultural codes. Perhaps this is also why the Confucian Orbit societies have preserved their culture and its norms well in everyday life (e.g. students bow to teachers in Korea, and later on continue this custom when greeting elders or superiors).

Today, the belief that education can mobilise individuals and societies remains stronger than ever. For instance, many Korean families hold the dream of success through education for their children, where many are sent to private learning institutions called *hagwon*, often held after school, in the evenings, and on weekends (Kim and Lee, 2010). According to a survey conducted by the *Korea National Statistical Office*, parents spent approximately $17 billion USD on private tutoring in 2007, despite the cost being a relatively sizeable proportion of the household monthly expenditure. With this, the tangible goal is for the student to be admitted to a prestigious university because this would increase one's competitiveness in the job market and enhance financial mobility; going to an elite university even enhances the 'chances' on the 'marriage market'. The intangible outcomes of pursuing high academic achievement is rooted in a sense of indebtedness towards the parents who make sacrifices, and the teachers who help prepare them for their future (Kim and Park, 2006); students in Korea have to be respectful to teachers and professors, but in turn they feel obliged to teach and mentor them holistically and often throughout life. Thus, this outlook rests on a long-term perspective towards education. That is: my future lifestyle and the dividends I reap are dependent on the sacrifices I make and effort I put in, *now*. Since teachers feel obliged to help students learn and grow, they equally feel responsible, if not obliged, to discipline unruly and under-performing students. We find very similar attitudes and practices beyond Korea, throughout the Confucian Orbit.

Spotlight

The Value of Education: Results of
Japanese-American Interviews

In the Chicago study, we found that the differences in educational expectations between East Asian Americans and Euro-Americans could be traced to the East-Asian cultural tradition, which places a high value on education for self-improvement, self-esteem, and family honour, and the determination of some East Asian-American families to overcome occupational discrimination by investing in education (cf. Sue and Okazaki, 1990). . . . Unequivocally, the value of education was evident across all of the Japanese-American families, as demonstrated in the following quotations from several parents:

> I expect him to go to college because I want him to have the most options for later life. Hopefully, he will have the qualifications to do whatever he wants and then he can pick and choose. I want him to be prepared and have as many opportunities as possible and not be forced into a position because he is unprepared or unqualified.
>
> Education is important from an altruistic point of view. Education widens your perspective; it makes your life a lot richer. I think education is very, very, important, so that you can become more global. Not only in terms of what you know but how you think and how flexible you can become. From a pragmatic point of view, education is very important because it is the ticket to a better job, and especially for a nonmainstream person you are stalemated with it.

Source: Schneider, Hieshima, Lee and Plank (1994, pp. 324–325) in *Cross-cultural Roots of Minority Child Development*

Effort Over Ability

According to Confucian philosophy, every individual is born with the capacity to improve him- and herself, and it is only one's inhibiting attitude toward self-improvement that impedes this process. Confucianism rejects the categorisation of human beings as being born good or bad, instead emphasising that the potential for improvement— in individual performance, in social relations, in moral conduct—rests in *actively creating* favourable environments. In other words, people are malleable and can be moulded to achieve their goals, but only through effort, hard work, and persistence, as stated by the Chinese philosopher, Hsun Tzu:

> Achievement consists of never giving up. . . . If there is no dark and dogged will, there will be no shining accomplishment; if there is no dull and determined effort, there will be no brilliant achievement.
>
> (Quoted in Watson, 1967, p. 18)

The quote above depicts a common mindset with regards to East Asian students' approaches to learning and achievement. In most cases, if a student fails to perform according to their own expectations, or that of their parents and teachers, it is attributed to insufficient effort as opposed to a lack of ability (Stevenson, Lee and Stigler, 1986). With this, there is a belief that improvement only occurs by applying oneself to do better than the last performance, translating to more time invested, more practice, and more reflection. This also explains why Confucian educators discipline poor-performing students—ultimately, they want to send out a 'wake-up' call so that the student will do better next time, and for life.

While students' views on effort might be seen as being consistent with values of hard work, diligence, and persistence, they can also be seen to be an outcome of their cultural upbringing that fosters a positive attitude towards learning (Gan, 2009; Littlewood, 1999). Rather than believing that achievement comes from innate abilities, students in East Asia view persistent effort as the driving force to success—whether it is mastering a topic, winning a competition, or excelling in an examination; art/music/painting and sport achievements are often viewed the same way. Studies have demonstrated that students' pursuits of academic success were not only contingent upon their personal goals (i.e. getting a good job), but that success *and* failure were attributed to social goals such as a sense of indebtedness and wanting to please their parents and relatives (Chen, Wang, Wei, Fwu and Hwang, 2009; Kim and Park, 2006; Fwu, Wei, Chen and Wang, 2014). Clearly there is a different mindset at play in terms of East Asian students' attribution to success in contrast to many other parts of the world. When East Asians succeed, they nearly always acknowledge the help and support of their parents, teachers, and peers (often attributing most of their success to them and not themselves), whereas students from Western nations generally view their successes as the result of their own individual labours and effort. Each mindset is shaped by different cultural precepts, but ultimately, students from Asia see that their wins and losses are part of a network that extends beyond them.

Under the influence of Confucian culture, the motivation to excel is guided by both personal and social goals, in line with the doctrine of filial piety. Children are socialised to understand the importance of one's role within a hierarchy, and that one should fulfil the obligations associated with that role. For students, that means not only taking education seriously, but also making it their one and (nearly) only priority. This places on them an expectation to perform at a certain level, where parents set the bar to a very high standard—much more so than, say, American parents by comparison (Stevenson and Stigler, 1992). Therefore, while East Asian students can be seen to align their achievements with the amount of effort put in, this effort is also driven by the expectations (or demand) placed upon them by parents, relatives, and teachers (Fuligni, 1997). Heine and Hamamura (2007) found that individuals from Confucian heritage cultures view their 'successes' not in terms of their own beliefs, but by having significant others believe that they are meeting the consensual standards associated with their roles. This standard does not only apply to education, but also to extra-curricular activities such as learning an instrument. While many Asian parents have their children master the piano or violin, for example, to cultivate another skill set, it also prepares them for the pressures of a highly competitive environment external to formal schooling. Many parents also view the learning of a musical instrument as an additional formation of (self-)discipline, with music teachers often being instructed by parents to not let performance slip.

Naturally, a higher level of parental expectation would come with more severe consequences for non-performance, and it is these 'consequences' which compel students for self-improvement. In other words, without consequence—perceived or real—there might be little reason to put in the (extra) effort to do better, e.g. better than others in class, and/or better than one's own previous performance ('betterment'). In Confucian societies, parents and teachers help their children (students) realise these consequences through both strict and nurturing disciplinary methods. For example, Korean parents utilise *Ga-jung-kyo-yuk* (translated as 'home [or family] education') which involves physical disciplinary practices (e.g. hitting palms with a stick in the event of severe misbehaviour), but also exercise extensive non-verbal affection (Choi, Kim, Kim and Park, 2013).

We add that there is a time dimension to consequences, and that parents, in their role as moderators of their child's behaviour, utilise stringent measures whose benefits are most obvious in years to come, when they enter adulthood. For instance, in addition to completing all of their assigned school homework, the majority of students also attend private tutoring (e.g. *hagwon* in Korea, *juku* in Japan, and *buxiban* in Taiwan) during times that could be spent on activities for pleasure like playing video games. Though one important objective is to prepare students for the university entrance examination, a residual and arguably more important outcome is that it prepares students for a competitive work environment when they leave school (the job markets in China, Japan, and Korea are highly competitive with often hundreds if not thousands of applications for one position). Resilience, belief in effort, and the ability to cope under competitive and high-pressure conditions are qualities necessary for the changing economy (Korean High Schoolers often discuss the Industrial Revolution 4 in classes—so they are aware of future challenges). While technical skills and knowledge are important for being able to market yourself across job contexts, having self-discipline (including endurance, persistence, and good work ethic) is perhaps one of the most useful attributes in handling precarious work environments, such as those in the emerging gig economy.

Some would argue that the pressures placed on Asian students to peak perform are detrimental to their well-being or that it fosters negative self-concepts (Stankov, 2010), or that the over-glorification of academic excellence in Asia may lead to a reluctance to move away from rote memorisation learning (Ho and Hau, 2010; Tan, 2015). On the contrary, and in line with Confucian's view of malleability, students' tendencies for self-criticism enable them to identify areas of weakness for improvement; and students often are in favour of rather strict discipline in schools. In their study, Heine and colleagues (2001) found that Japanese subjects consistently worked harder after failure than they did after succeeding. In fact, during Japan's 'wonder' and economic boom from the 1960s, it was often speculated that part of their motivation and 'drive' was the notion that their (already high) performance levels were not seen as good enough. In a culture with a deep respect for education, a belief in effortful success and one that is socially motivated, students are able to foster resilience over time. Though controversial, we include a passage from Amy Chua's (2011) book, *Battle Hymn of the Tiger Mother*, which highlights the dynamic of this parent-child relationship in East Asia, and the notions of effort and resiliency:

> Western parents are extremely anxious about their children's self-esteem. They worry about how their children will feel if they fail at something, and they constantly try to reassure their children about how good they are notwithstanding a mediocre performance on a test or at a recital. In other words, Western parents are concerned about their children's psyches. Chinese parents aren't. They assume strength, not fragility, and as a result they behave very differently. . . . Chinese parents demand perfect grades because they believe that their child can get them. If their child doesn't get them, the Chinese parent assumes it's because the child didn't work hard enough.

In essence, there is a prevailing mindset within the Confucian Orbit that effort breeds success, where the old saying 'persistence pays off' is evident across a number of contexts. In viewing education as a vehicle for improvement (both for oneself and the family) under the Confucian tradition, those individuals are imbued with a form of self-discipline that helps them regulate their behaviour and focus their attention on achieving future goals, often by delaying immediate gratification.

When considering the academic success of East Asian students, peers can also be seen as a source of normative pressures (Phillipson, 2013). Students are motivated to perform under expectations by their parents and teachers, but they also feel the pressure to maintain their performance relative to the performance of their peer groups. In other words, when all students within a cohort strive to excel, some students might also feel compelled to perform better (relative to other students, as well as their own past performance). In a sense, students are determined to compete with their peers, but not at the detriment or expense of their peer networks. Instead, students strive to uplift one another to enhance their performances overall; Confucianism after all has a strong focus on the welfare of the immediate group of colleagues.

Spotlight

'Cram Schools' as a Social Practice: Highlight Examination Culture in the Region

[T]he element of competition in the education system . . . gives private tutoring its edge as families seek to gain a relative advantage for their children 'in the education race', whether it is at primary or secondary level. As long as there is a prize at the end of the race—whether it is entry to an elite secondary school or university—then competition becomes the dominating force that guides the behaviour of parents . . . the availability of tutoring in a meritocratic society where 'education was the major screening device for upward social mobility'. The real outcome of the 'race', therefore, is inter-generational social and economic gain. It is this for which parents are willing to pay and for which so many students suffer what the Koreans call, *'ipsi-jiok* . . . entrance examination hell' (Kim and Lee, 2002, p. 4). . . .
　　Gray (2001), in his review of Zeng (1999), makes the point that:

> the test [examination] is not viewed primarily as an aptitude or I.Q. test, as in the West; rather, what is being measured is how well trained a student is. In other words, what is valued is not the ability to acquire information, to efficiently learn new things, and make connections between them, but the personal qualities—discipline, obedience, 'spirit', a good memory, the ability to postpone gratification—of the individual who can successfully pass the test.

These are Confucian virtues both Gray (2001) and Zeng (1999) see as operating principles in modern Confucian heritage cultures.

Source: Kennedy and Lee (2007, pp. 75–76) in *The Changing Role of Schools in Asian Societies: Schools for the Knowledge Society*

Socialisation Under Filial Piety

Societies tend to socialise their children with the values that are important to them (Tam, Lee, Kim, Li and Chao, 2012). Therefore, it is no surprise that Confucian heritage cultures, which place a premium on education, excel when it comes to academic achievement. Socialisation refers to the process of learning to behave in a manner acceptable to society (Musgrave, 1965; Harris, 1995). Within Confucian societies, the guiding principles that govern methods of socialisation are embodied in the ethic of filial piety, which views one's elders as the authoritative figures presiding over all of a child's learning experiences. Children are 'stamped' with a fundamental distinction between what is right and wrong, which in the context of education, exerts a pervasive influence on the nature and dynamics of the teacher-student relationship, impulse control, and the child's attitude towards learning (Ho, 1994).

Filial piety refers to the virtue of respect for one's parents, elders, and ancestors. Though it finds it roots in the immediate family, it also extends beyond to relationships between teacher and student, master, and apprentice, or government and society at large. At its core is the ability to maintain a stable and harmonious relationship. Though filial piety is becoming less prominent as China modernises, it is being replaced with a version that stresses 'filial reciprocity'. Under reciprocity, there is a mutual benefit of sorts, or a 'return of favours'; reciprocity is also an important element of Confucianism in its own right. In the context of the parent-child relationship, this could be understood as the sense of duty and obligation of each side: to care and provide, and excel and improve, respectively. For the teacher-student relationship, this includes the previously alluded to respect and care obligations.

For parents, they are tasked with caring and providing for their child, and cognitively socialising them. Confucianism emphasises self-regulation and restraint, and parents spend the early formative years mastering impulse control in their children. The fundamental goal is to prepare children for the stringent school environment, or in other words, parents are responsible for acclimatising young children to the demands and conditions of formal education, which are highly regimented, and instilling in them a strong work ethic to succeed. This translates to having discipline, in the school context, where students are, for example, punctual, polite, orderly, and well-groomed, and if not, are indeed disciplined.

In a way, early socialisation practices of children within the Confucian Orbit are aligned with a 'training' ideology, where parents expose the child to explicit examples of proper behaviours which are acceptable and examples of undesirable behaviours (Ho, 1986). Asian parents' disciplinary approach tends to be characterised as strict and authoritative (i.e. high demandingness, and high responsiveness), which are based on their own sociocultural and historical traditions, different to the Western experience (Lau and Cheung, 1987). For instance, the Confucian approach to 'training' and authoritativeness is guided by the need for a set standard of conduct that enables parents to maintain harmony and run a smooth household. Conversely, in the Western historical tradition, authoritarian child-rearing approaches were often linked to evangelical religious fervour which stressed 'breaking the child's will' and 'domination', coherent with the concept of 'original sin' (Smuts and Hagen, 1986). Ultimately authoritarian approaches to child-rearing are rooted in different cultural experiences, with divergent implications for outcomes, including academic achievement (Chao, 1994).

For students, their responsibility while in school is to excel academically and continually strive to improve upon themselves—an onus placed upon them because their parents usually make a number of sacrifices to ensure that they receive the best education. There is strong documentation of the children of Asian migrants who excel in their academic and professional performance, relative to native individuals (Fuligni, 1997; Kao, 1995; Kao and Tienda, 1995); and even when all resources and curriculum are the same, East Asian students studying in Western secondary institutions still continue to outpace their peers by at least two years (Jerrim and Choi, 2014; Jerrim, 2015). Anecdotal evidence report of Korean students entering the Australian school system and within one or two years 'peaking' the class if not the entire school cohort—and often English is not their mother tongue. The peak performance of Asian students could be related to their view that school serves the role of teaching them to deal with complex challenges and helps them enter a high status college or career (Lau, Nicholls, Thorkildsen and Patashnick, 2000), or in other words, that school serves as both a springboard and practice for their future. When East Asian student prepare for important exams, it is not seldom that they combine careful revision of the to-be-examined material with prayers at a Confucian temple (this is very common in Taiwan but also in other parts of the Confucian Orbit).

Further, socialisation and enforcing discipline, under Confucianism, is also a 'whole family affair'. In the East, this duty does not only fall to the parents, but also to the grandparents and extended relatives such as aunts and uncles when it comes to child-rearing practices. The family unit acts as a sort of buffer between the individual and society, in which the family has a responsibility to 'prepare' the individual to act in accordance with, and contribute to society in a meaningful way. Above all else, this is a reflection of peoples' attitudes to power and authority, where higher acceptance of power inequality and the privileging of status differences, is generally stronger in East Asian cultures (Hofstede, 1991). 'Acceptance' of these power inequalities does not necessarily make it 'desirable', but it may simply imply that the scripts of behaviour are deeply ingrained in the lived experience or reality (i.e. an 'unavoidable fact of life'). Perhaps

Spotlight

Cultivating Morality Through Preschool Education: Prospective of Chinese Teachers and Parents

Teachers also put a great emphasis on morality at the preschool stage. Compared to learning knowledge, teachers thought it was more important to nurture a young child's heart and help the child to build appropriate moral standards and habit. Teacher Tang, who was also a mother of a five-year-old boy (he went to a public preschool), pointed out that her educational approaches and beliefs were consistent across classroom and home:

> Take my own son as an example. The school assigns a lot of homework in language, math, *et cetera*. My mother also urges him to do homework every day. But I never taught him on these subjects. I only taught him principles of how to "act human" (zuo ren). For instance, if he does bad things, like dirty talk against his grandma, I will point it out and scold him: "You don't respect elders, which violates moral bottom line. That's why you need to be punished. You can't watch cartoons or play video games. If you correct this mistake, I will forgive you". I won't punish him for not finishing some homework. That's how I educate my son.

Another teacher shared with me her educational ideal and goal:

> Human beings will be assimilated to the society as they grow up. Some good habits and moral characteristics will gradually lose or be abandoned. So you cannot get better, but only get worse and worse, eroded by the adult environment. That's why I want to build in young children a stronger moral foundation in the beginning. Then even if they get assimilated into society, the directions they are in will still be better than those who have no good moral foundation.

In addition to probing into the important of moral development in socialisers' eyes, I also examined how parents evaluated the forces that impacted moral development. . . .

A.   Families (Parents) . . . 49%
B.   Teachers . . . 10%
C.   Peer groups . . . 12%
D.   Broader social environment . . . 6%
E.   Equal (Same across all four categories) . . . 23%

Source: Xu (2017) in *The Good Child: Moral Development in a Chinese Preschool*

the difference is that in some parts of the world, disgruntled members of society engage in public protests, whereas East Asians view fate as in their own hands, work hard, and 'move up' without seeking State safety nets or generous State support programmes.

In sum, filial piety becomes the mechanism through which students are 'prepared' for formal education, and learn the discipline needed to succeed.

Role Clarity

Under the rubric of Confucianism, the 'rules of power' that exist between ruler and subject manifest through a number of relationships that include between parent and child, teacher/professor and student, and employer and employee. In particular, there is a clear understanding of the expectations and role between students, teachers/professors and parents in regards to the institution of education (Watkins and Biggs, 1996), which can be categorised as follows:

- **Student:** as the learner and receiver of knowledge.
- **Teacher:** as role models as learned scholars, who are respected in their role in disseminating knowledge.
- **Parent:** prepare their children for the school environment, and ease the transition from home to formal education. They ultimately entrust teachers to carry on, to an extent, the disciplinarian role that will mould their children for society.

Role clarity is high under Confucianism: a teacher behaves like a teacher, and a student behaves as a student. The utilisation of school uniforms also contributes to role clarity—students in the Confucian Orbit nearly always wear proper uniforms to send out a signal to all about their role as a student; and teachers and professors often also wear somewhat more formal or professional attire; for example, it is not impossible to find a professor at a Western educational institution in shorts, but this is unthinkable in the Confucian Orbit.

When there is a clear distinction in roles and duties of each party, it would make sense that this would contribute to overall less distraction to learning. Overall the model of East Asian academic success can be viewed as a process of interactions among parents, teachers, children, and their peer groups, as summarised by Schneider et al. (1994, p. 327):

> how families structure and monitor the learning activities of their children at home are dependent on family members' expectations. These expectations are formed in turn through family members' cultural and economic experiences, the expectations of the school and community, and family resources, such as the amount of time parents can devote to an activity.

With this, and outlined in previous sections, the expectations related to achievement of students within the Confucian Orbit result from a general consensus of the importance of education. Naturally, when there is agreement about a goal and how to achieve that goal, i.e. how to prepare students for the future and good of society, then we might expect to see a more smoothly run process. Conversely, if there is discord between teacher and student role clarity, as we sometimes see in the West (debates about discipline in American schools are sometimes around safety, or even about teachers being attacked by students), then the quality of learning would ultimately suffer because too much time and energy is being spent on getting the class 'back on track' when there are disruptions.

The difference in role clarity between cultures is simply a function of having mutual respect for one another, as well as recognising that the 'whole is greater than the sum of its parts'. In other words, teachers, students, and parents each contribute their own part while entrusting the others to do theirs. For teachers, this means they are not only educators and carers of their students, but also are expected to provide an appropriate model of behaviour and initiate harsh discipline when students are underperforming or stepping out of line (Ho, 1994). This is a role that parents must be comfortable with: whereas parents in Asia prepare their children for this, some parents in the West tend to feel uncomfortable with a stricter approach, or feel it is a criticism of their parenting abilities, or they are just simply disengaged (Steinberg, Brown and Dornbusch, 1996). Asian parents have been reported to approach teachers to be stricter, whereas in the West, parents are sometimes known as 'advocates' for their offspring's misdemeanour at school.

East Asian parents play a crucial role in equipping their children with the mode of behaviours suited for an intensive learning environment, or in other words, good habits start at home. This gives teachers the freedom to focus on providing meaningful feedback to students to improve their performance, including discipline if they find it is necessary. In any society, it is easy to simply not care or to criticise, out of fear for hurting someone's feelings, but in East Asian societies, this sort of toughness is a precursor for improvement (Stankov, 2010). In fact this is necessary in any society, but the only difference being that many children in East Asian societies are ingrained with this 'toughness' from an early age. Of course not all students are receptive to the same types of socialisation, and we would not expect that all students within the Confucian Orbit equally prescribe to the same type of method.

How the student views the teacher also has enormous impact on the overall learning experience. In East Asia, there is a general belief in the correlation between age and wisdom, which is ingrained in a tradition of hierarchy and status: the older you are, the wiser you are. This has implications for how the student views the teacher, which from an Eastern perspective is a respected and wise elder, and from a Western perspective, is often akin to a 'buddy'. Each has its own consequence on the power dynamics; teachers who are perceived as respected elders are likely to have more obedient students, whereas teachers who are perceived as a buddy may find it difficult to regain any sense of authority (Way, 2011), each of which affects how students behave in the classroom:

> The role of the teacher could only be played out successfully provided that students could do their part well, and vice versa. As the teachers described, the roles of teachers and students were 'mutually complementary and mutually interdependent' (*xiang fu xiang cheng*). From this relative point of view, teachers and students had their own roles to play and their jobs to do in the classroom. Furthermore, they had to avoid dominating one another.
>
> (Hue, 2007b, p. 41)

In some countries, the role of the teacher is viewed more as a babysitter than a respected role model. The popular saying of 'those who *can't do*, teach' in the West is an unfortunate reflection of the sentiment toward educators, with an insinuation that they lack the competency to do their job in the real world, and therefore have no choice but to teach. Such a statement says a lot about a culture's treatment of its educators, in fact one of the most important resources to building a good society. And yet it is a notion that is often forgotten. Teachers in East Asia, on the other hand, tend to be held in high esteem: 'those who *can*, teach'. Only the most ambitious, capable, and qualified are given the responsibilities of educating students, and this finds its roots in traditional Confucian culture, where the teacher is a moral and noble figure. In Taiwanese temples of worship, the teacher is always placed on the same level as 'heaven, earth, emperor, and parents' (*tien, di, jun, qin, shi*), a sentiment that is echoed in across the Confucian Orbit (Gao, 1999). This also means that students in East Asia don't 'talk back' to teachers or professors as they often do in the West; notwithstanding that East Asian educators often encourage healthy debates and do care about the students' opinions and voices, just in a polite manner and fashion.

Teachers in East Asian countries tend to enjoy relatively higher occupational prestige and satisfaction, compared to teachers around the world (Fwu and Wang, 2002), and also despite earning a relatively lower salary compared to other developed nations—notwithstanding that on the entire career life-span, Korean teachers earn a respectable salary comparable to a professional career with the same leadership responsibility. Higher level of enjoyment is likely attributed to favourable national policies under teacher education, but also based on how they are perceived and treated within inside the classroom setting. When teachers feel a lack of respect or too much mistreatment, it has a telling effect on attrition and turnover rates; it has been noted that a lack of discipline in Western classrooms has been so severe that teachers are often leaving their profession only after a short tenure (Hanushek, Kain and Rivkin, 2004). Teachers in East Asia are often given the power to discipline, which keeps them in the profession rather than having to 'run away' from constant disrespect from students as is noted in other parts of the world.

Given this alarming difference, one would question whether there is any hope to 'fixing this'. The good news is that even making the smallest changes to school discipline can have a telling effect on student performance. We argue that school uniforms are an integral part of school discipline, and the contribution of uniforms to smooth operations in everyday school life benefiting students and teachers has recently been researched. In a study on school uniform adoption in an urban southwest school in the USA, Gentile and Imberman (2012) found that uniform adoption not only improved attendance in secondary grades, but also generated an increase in teacher retention at the elementary level. In fact, the adoption of school uniforms affected outcomes across a number of issues beyond the previously mentioned improved visible role clarity: they improved attendance (Evans, Michael and Muthoni, 2008); they instilled in students a respect for authority which reduced classroom disruptions; and can be used as a safety measure to easily identify unauthorised visitors to a school (Stanley, 1996). From an economic perspective, they also reduce the pressure to dress well, especially for students of lower socioeconomic background. And from an efficiency perspective, the implementation of uniforms makes the process of dressing for school faster (Alspach, 2007).

Spotlight

Respect for Japanese Teachers Means Top Results

First thing in the morning, Japanese children bow to their teachers. It's a small gesture that says a lot. . . .

Here, respect is not a song title. It's the backbone of Japan's school system, which for decades has topped international rankings while spending the lowest amount on education among developed democracies: 3.3 percent of Japan's gross domestic product, or GDP, goes toward schooling compared to 5 percent in the United States.

How do they do so much with so little? By investing in top-notch teachers.

"Teachers are given a good deal of respect; they're expected to devote their life", said Catherine Lewis, distinguished research scholar at Mills

College. *"The whole system is set up to emphasize the development of teachers"*.

Retirement comes at 60 for Japanese educators with a salary of more than $62,000, compared to $53,000 in the United States.

But in return, teachers are tasked with transforming children into model citizens. If a student is caught shoplifting, for example, the child's teacher is usually alerted before a parent.

"If our students do something wrong outside the school, we tend to think, 'we should have taught them better'", said Japanese teacher Mitsuko Watanabe.

Inside the classroom, children learn responsibility. Changing into slippers at the school's entrance and cleaning the building themselves. At lunch, it's a similar story.

Children take turns dishing out food to their classmates and their teacher, and no one takes a bite until everyone is served.

Teaching everything from table manners to trigonometry takes time. But in Japan, teachers also have scheduled periods to compare notes. Their desks are even grouped together in one room.

"I spend 60 percent of my time with students and 40 percent with other teachers", said math teacher Kazunaga Yokota.

Classes are regularly videotaped, allowing senior teachers to mentor juniors—a technique that's gaining traction in the U.S. And ineffective teachers aren't fired or sidelined—they're given extensive retraining, explains the president of Japan's teachers' union.

"It's impossible for someone to get through the system who is incompetent", said Yuzuru Nakamura, president of Japan's Teachers' Union.

Despite all this, those all-important global test scores have slipped: Japan topped worldwide math rankings in 2000, but dropped to 6th in 2006: still far ahead the U.S. at number 25.

What hasn't changed in Japan is the value placed on education best summed up by a Japanese proverb: better than a thousand days of study is one day with a great teacher.

Source: Celia Hatton, CBS News (29 September 2010). www.cbsnews.com/news/respect-for-japanese-teachers-means-top-results/

Appendix

Details on Structural Equation Models discussed in Chapter 2.

Correlation Between Perceived Disciplinary Climate and Science Performance—All Clusters

In Chapter 2 we presented correlations between disciplinary climate and science performance for individual students summarised at the cluster level. The following tables show the same correlations for individual countries within those clusters.

Note that there is a wide range of values within each cluster. Anglo-Saxon students had an average correlation of discipline to performance of 0.21, but the correlation ranges from 0.09 (Ireland) to 0.26 (USA). Similarly, Western European students' correlation ranges from 0.08 (Iceland) to 0.26 (Malta), and in the Confucian Orbit the correlation ranges from 0.05 (Korea) to 0.22 (Japan).

Table A2.1 Correlation Between Perceived Disciplinary Climate and Science Performance

Cluster	Country	Correlation: Disciplinary Climate and Science
Anglo-Saxon	Australia	0.232
$\rho=0.21$	Canada	0.135
	Ireland	0.089
	New Zealand	0.172
	Puerto Rico (USA)	0.205
	United Kingdom	0.216
	United States	0.257
	USA (Massachusetts)	0.238
	USA (North Carolina)	0.241
Asia	Indonesia	0.117
$\rho=0.1$	Thailand	0.082

Cluster	Country	Correlation: Disciplinary Climate and Science
Confucian Orbit ρ=0.17	B-S-J-G (China)	0.193
	Chinese Taipei	0.095
	Hong Kong	0.148
	Japan	0.216
	Korea	0.048
	Macao	0.09
	Singapore	0.294
	Vietnam	0.09
Eastern Europe and Former Soviet Union	Bulgaria	0.191
ρ=0.19	Croatia	0.266
	Czech Republic	0.268
	FYROM	0.14
	Georgia	0.17
	Hungary	0.203
	Kosovo	0.138
	Moldova	0.047
	Montenegro	0.152
	Romania	0.221
	Russian Federation	0.112
	Slovak Republic	0.251
	Slovenia	0.161
	Turkey	0.127
Latin America ρ=0.16	Argentina	0.056
	Brazil	0.216
	Chile	0.157
	Colombia	0.124
	Costa Rica	0.083
	Dominican Republic	0.171
	Mexico	0.133
	Peru	0.074
	Trinidad and Tobago	0.286
	Uruguay	0.14
North Africa and Middle East	Algeria	0.062
ρ=0.17	Israel	0.161
	Jordan	0.147
	Lebanon	0.182
	Qatar	0.297
	Tunisia	0.031
	United Arab Emirates	0.141

(*Continued*)

Table A2.1 (Continued)

Cluster	Country	Correlation: Disciplinary Climate and Science
Western Europe ρ=0.16	Austria	0.16
	Belgium	0.136
	Denmark	0.108
	Estonia	0.114
	Finland	0.102
	France	0.19
	Germany	0.214
	Greece	0.22
	Iceland	0.077
	Italy	0.163
	Latvia	0.113
	Lithuania	0.175
	Luxembourg	0.244
	Malta	0.256
	Netherlands	0.141
	Norway	0.107
	Poland	0.093
	Portugal	0.168
	Spain	0.112
	Spain (regions)	0.115
	Sweden	0.124
	Switzerland	0.194

Structural Equation Modelling Results for Each Cluster

The notable result is that the coefficients in all clusters are very similar, suggesting that the relationships among exogenous variables and measures of discipline and academic performance are much the same across all cultures. That is, the structural relationships are the same, and it is only the strength of predictor variables (and moderators) that drive academic performance.

SEM Details

The total sample size for each cluster based on PISA 2015 data used in this study are presented below. A separate Structural Equation Model (SEM) was computed for each cluster separately. SEM is a set of statistical modelling techniques designed to test *a priori* conceptual or theoretical models. Due to its ability to estimate and test relationships among hypothesised latent constructs (i.e. multiple

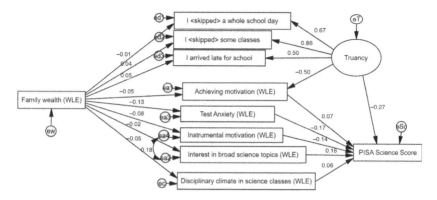

SEM: Eastern Europe and Former Soviet Union

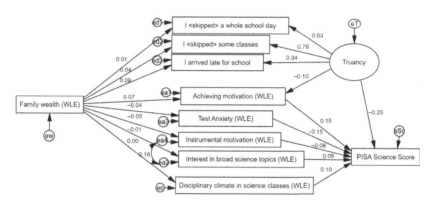

SEM: Latin America

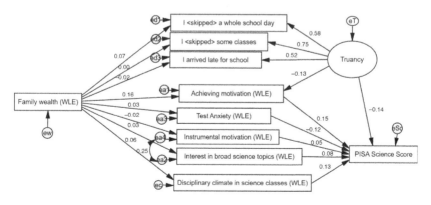

Figure A2.1 SEM: North Africa and the Middle East

Table A2.2 Total Standardised Effects on Science Overall (Academic Achievement)

	Anglo-Saxon	Confucian Orbit	Western Europe	Eastern Europe and Former Soviet Union	Latin America	North Africa and Middle
Family Wealth	0.032	0.019	0.023	0.031	0.021	0.029
Truancy	−0.233	−0.184	−0.198	−0.278	−0.211	−0.157
Test Anxiety	−0.128	−0.072	−0.185	−0.165	−0.148	−0.117
Instrumental Motivation	0.021	−0.015	0.022	−0.142	−0.080	0.052
Disciplinary Climate	0.100	0.114	0.083	0.063	0.102	0.132
Interest in Science	0.257	0.205	0.234	0.157	0.088	0.080
Achieving Motivation	0.103	0.130	0.099	0.073	0.146	0.153

independent, dependent, and mediating variables) simultaneously, it is considered the most suitable means of data analysis for this present study. Additionally, SEM is well regarded for its statistical efficiency because it does not designate a single statistical technique, but instead refers to a family of related procedures, providing the researcher with a versatile tool to understand causal effects via direct and indirect paths (we refer the interested reader to Hooper, Coughlan and Mullen, 2008 for a detailed technical description).

SEM PISA Measures of Attitude Towards Study, Disciplinary Climate, Behaviour, and Their Effects on Academic Performance

- Sample size = 69,655 (**Anglo-Saxon**);
- Sample size = 51,553 (**Confucian Orbit**);
- Sample size = 166,956 (**Western Europe**);
- Sample size = 80,308 (**Eastern Europe and Former Soviet Union**);
- Sample size = 80,545 (**Latin America**);
- Sample size = 55,555 (**North Africa and Middle East**);
- Chi-square = 80123.496;
- Degrees of freedom = 156;
- Probability level = .000.

Structural Equation Model Fit Summaries

Structural Equation Models requires that the data reflects the underlying theory, also known as model fit. As seen in the conceptual model, the use of directional lines indicates the relationship between variables: a line with one arrow head represents a hypothesised relationship, whereas a line with two arrow heads indicates a covariance with no implied directional effect between the exogenous variables.

In order to theoretically develop a unique estimate for each parameter, certain criteria within the model must first be identified, before proceeding with the assessment. We assess our model fit statistics, presented below, in line with recommendations made by Hooper et al. (2008). We generally found an adequate fit between our models and data.

CMIN

Model	NPAR	CMIN	DF	P	CMIN/DF
Default Model	234	80123.496	156	0.000	513.612
Saturated Model	390	0.000	0		
Independence Model	60	370567.544	330	0.000	1122.932

Baseline Comparisons

Model	NFI Delta1	RFI rho1	IFI Delta2	TLI rho2	CFI
Default Model	0.784	0.543	0.784	0.543	0.784
Saturated Model	1.000		1.000		1.000
Independence Model	0.000	0.000	0.000	0.000	0.000

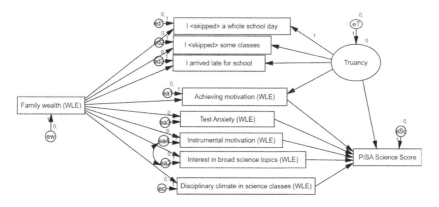

Figure A2.2 Conceptual Model

Parsimony-Adjusted Measures

Model	PRATIO	PNFI	PCFI
Default Model	0.473	0.371	0.371
Saturated Model	0.000	0.000	0.000
Independence Model	1.000	0.000	0.000

NCP

Model	NCP	LO 90	HI 90
Default Model	79967.496	79039.904	80901.367
Saturated Model	0.000	0.000	0.000
Independence Model	370237.544	368238.545	372242.820

FMIN

Model	FMIN	F0	LO 90	HI 90
Default Model	0.159	0.158	0.157	0.160
Saturated Model	0.000	0.000	0.000	0.000
Independence Model	0.734	0.734	0.730	0.738

RMSEA

Model	RMSEA	LO 90	HI 90	PCLOSE
Default Model	0.032	0.032	0.032	1.000
Independence Model	0.047	0.047	0.047	1.000

AIC

Model	AIC	BCC	BIC	CAIC
Default Model	80591.496	80591.568		
Saturated Model	780.000	780.120		
Independence Model	370687.544	370687.563		

ECVI

Model	ECVI	LO 90	HI 90	MECVI
Default Model	0.160	0.158	0.162	0.160
Saturated Model	0.002	0.002	0.002	0.002
Independence Model	0.735	0.731	0.739	0.735

HOELTER

Model	HOELTER 0.05	HOELTER 0.01
Default Model	1178	1265
Independence Model	514	540

Notes

1. Former student from Zhabei Number 8 High School, Shanghai, China, interviewed for the BBC: www.bbc.com/news/world-asia-china-18349873.
2. Data from the 2015 wave of PISA, used in our analyses, is available from: www.oecd.org/pisa/data/2015database/.

References

Alspach, Kyle. "Measured look at uniforms: Alternative to dress code." *The Boston Globe*, 2007.

Barro, Robert J., and Jong-Wha Lee. "International data on educational attainment: Updates and implications." *Oxford Economic Papers* 53, no. 3 (2001): 541–563.

Baumann, Chris, and Hume Winzar. "The role of secondary education in explaining competitiveness." *Asia Pacific Journal of Education* 36, no. 1 (2016): 13–30.

Bollen, Kenneth A., and J. Scott Long. "Tests for structural equation models: Introduction." *Sociological Methods & Research* 21, no. 2 (1992): 123–131.

Byrne, Barbara M. *Structural Equation Modeling With AMOS: Basic Concepts, Applications, and Programming*. New York: Routledge, 2016.

Chao, Ruth K. "Beyond parental control and authoritarian parenting style: Understanding Chinese parenting through the cultural notion of training." *Child development* 65, no. 4 (1994): 1111–1119.

Chao, Ruth K. "Chinese and European American mothers' beliefs about the role of parenting in children's school success." *Journal of Cross-Cultural Psychology* 27, no. 4 (1996): 403–423.

Chen, Shun-Wen, Hsiou-Huai Wang, Chih-Fen Wei, Bih-Jen Fwu, and Kwang-Kuo Hwang. "Taiwanese students' self-attributions for two types of achievement goals." *The Journal of Social psychology* 149, no. 2 (2009): 179–194.

Chen, Xinyin, Paul D. Hastings, Kenneth H. Rubin, Huichang Chen, Guozhen Cen, and Shannon L. Stewart. "Child-rearing attitudes and behavioral inhibition in Chinese and Canadian toddlers: A cross-cultural study." *Developmental Psychology* 34, no. 4 (1998): 677.

Cheng, Chung-ying. "A theory of learning (学) in Confucian perspective." *Educational Philosophy and Theory* 48, no. 1 (2016): 52–63.

Choi, Yoonsun, You Seung Kim, Su Yeong Kim, and Irene J. K. Park. "Is Asian American parenting controlling and harsh? Empirical testing of relationships between Korean American and Western parenting measures." *Asian American Journal of Psychology* 4, no. 1 (2013): 19.

Chua, Amy. *Battle Hymn of the Tiger Mother*. New York: Bloomsbury Publishing, 2011.

Coleman, James S. "Equality of educational opportunity." *Integrated Education* 6, no. 5 (1968): 19–28.

Considine, Gillian, and Gianni Zappalà. "The influence of social and economic disadvantage in the academic performance of school students in Australia." *Journal of Sociology* 38, no. 2 (2002): 129–148.

De Bary, William Theodore. "Confucian education in premodern East Asia." *Confucian Traditions in East Asian Modernity* 21 (1996): 37.

Downey, Douglas B. "When bigger is not better: Family size, parental resources, and children's educational performance." *American Sociological Review* (1995): 746–761.

Duncan, Greg J., Pamela A. Morris, and Chris Rodrigues. "Does money really matter? Estimating impacts of family income on young children's achievement with data from random-assignment experiments." *Developmental Psychology* 47, no. 5 (2011): 1263.

Evans, David, Michael Kremer, and Muthoni Ngatia. *The Impact of Distributing School Uniforms on Children's Education in Kenya*, 2008.

Fan, F. A. "The relationship between the socio-economic status of parents and students' academic achievements in social studies." *Research in Education* 87, no. 1 (2012): 99–103.

Fuligni, Andrew J. "The academic achievement of adolescents from immigrant families: The role of family background, attitudes, and behavior." *Child Development* 68, no. 2 (1997): 351–363.

Fwu, Bih-Jen, and Hsiou-Huai Wang. "The social status of teachers in Taiwan." *Comparative Education* 38, no. 2 (2002): 211–224.

Fwu, Bih-Jen, Chih-Fen Wei, Shun-Wen Chen, and Hsiou-huai Wang. "Effort counts: The moral significance of effort in the patterns of credit assignment on math learning in the Confucian cultural context." *International Journal of Educational Development* 39 (2014): 157–162.

Gan, Zhengdong. "'Asian learners' re-examined: An empirical study of language learning attitudes, strategies and motivation among mainland Chinese and Hong Kong students." *Journal of Multilingual and Multicultural Development* 30, no. 1 (2009): 41–58.

Gao, M. S. *The History of Chinese Educational System (Zhong Guo Jiao Yu Shi Lun)*. Taipei, Lian-jing Bookstore, 1999. [in Chinese].

Gentile, Elisabetta, and Scott A. Imberman. "Dressed for success? The effect of school uniforms on student achievement and behavior." *Journal of Urban Economics* 71, no. 1 (2012): 1–17.

Graetz, Brian. "Socioeconomic status in education research and policy." *Socioeconomic Status and School Education* (1995): 23–51.

Gray, B. "Review: Dragon gate: Competitive examinations and their consequences." *TESL-EJ* 5, no. 2 (2001).

Hanushek, Eric A., John F. Kain, and Steven G. Rivkin. "Why public schools lose teachers." *Journal of Human Resources* 39, no. 2 (2004): 326–354.

Hanushek, Eric A., and Ludger Woessmann. "The economics of international differences in educational achievement." In *Handbook of the Economics of Education*. Vol. 3. Elsevier, North Holland, 2011a, pp. 89–200.

Hanushek, Eric A., and Ludger Woessmann. "How much do educational outcomes matter in OECD countries?" *Economic Policy* 26, no. 67 (2011b): 427–491.

Harris, Judith Rich. "Where is the child's environment? A group socialization theory of development." *Psychological Review* 102, no. 3 (1995): 458.

Heine, Steven J., and Takeshi Hamamura. "In search of East Asian self-enhancement." *Personality and Social Psychology Review* 11, no. 1 (2007): 4–27.

Heine, Steven J., Shinobu Kitayama, Darrin R. Lehman, Toshitake Takata, Eugene Ide, Cecilia Leung, and Hisaya Matsumoto. "Divergent consequences of success and failure in Japan and North America: an investigation of self-improving motivations and malleable selves." *Journal of Personality and Social Psychology* 81, no. 4 (2001): 599.

Ho, David Yau-fai. "Chinese patterns of socialization: A critical review." In M. H. Bond (Ed.), *The Psychology of the Chinese People*. New York, NY: Oxford University Press, 1986, pp. 1–37.

Ho, David Yau-fai. "Cognitive socialization in Confucian heritage cultures." In *Cross-cultural Roots of Minority Child Development*, 1994, pp. 285–313.

Ho, Irene T., and Kit-Tai Hau. "Consequences of the Confucian culture: High achievement but negative psychological attributes?" *Learning and Individual Differences* 20, no. 6 (2010): 571–573.

Hofstede, Geert. *Cultures and Organizations: Intercultural Cooperation and Its Importance for Survival: Software of the Mind*. London: McGraw-Hill, 1991.

Hooper, Daire, Joseph Coughlan, and Michael Mullen. "Structural equation modelling: Guidelines for determining model fit." *Articles* (2008): 2.

Hue, Ming-Tak. "Emergence of Confucianism from teachers' definitions of guidance and discipline in Hong Kong secondary schools." *Research in Education* 78, no. 1 (2007a): 21–33.

Hue, Ming-Tak. "The influence of classic Chinese philosophy of Confucianism, Taoism and Legalism on classroom discipline in Hong Kong junior secondary schools." *Pastoral Care in Education* 25, no. 2 (2007b): 38–45.

Hue, Ming-Tak, and Wai-shing Li. *Classroom Management: Creating a Positive Learning Environment*. Vol. 1. Hong Kong: Hong Kong University Press, 2008.

Hung, Ruyu. "A critique of Confucian learning: On learners and knowledge." *Educational Philosophy and Theory* 48, no. 1 (2016): 85–96.

Jacques, Martin. *When China Rules the World: The Rise of the Middle Kingdom and the End of the Western World*. London: Allen Lane, 2009.

Jerrim, John. "Why do East Asian children perform so well in PISA? An investigation of Western-born children of East Asian descent." *Oxford Review of Education* 41, no. 3 (2015): 310–333.

Jerrim, John, and Álvaro Choi. "The mathematics skills of school children: How does England compare to the high-performing East Asian jurisdictions?" *Journal of Education Policy* 29, no. 3 (2014): 349–376.

Kao, Grace. "Asian Americans as model minorities? A look at their academic performance." *American Journal of Education* 103, no. 2 (1995): 121–159.

Kao, Grace, and Marta Tienda. "Optimism and achievement: The educational performance of immigrant youth." *Social Science Quarterly* (1995): 1–19.

Kennedy, Kerry J., and John Chi-Kin Lee. *The Changing Role of Schools in Asian Societies: Schools for the Knowledge Society*. London: Routledge, 2007.

Kim, Sunwoong, and Ju-Ho Lee. 2002. *Private Tutoring and Demand for Education in South Korea*, 2002. Retrieved December 29, 2006, from http://www.kdischool.ac.kr/faculty/resume/juholee/Tutor4.pdf

Kim, Sunwoong, and Ju-Ho Lee. "Private tutoring and demand for education in South Korea." *Economic Development and Cultural Change* 58, no. 2 (2010): 259–296.

Kim, Uichol, and Young-Shin Park. "Indigenous psychological analysis of academic achievement in Korea: The influence of self-efficacy, parents, and culture." *International Journal of Psychology* 41, no. 4 (2006): 287–292.

Lau, Sing, and Ping Chung Cheung. "Relations between Chinese adolescents' perception of parental control and organization and their perception of parental warmth." *Developmental Psychology* 23, no. 5 (1987): 726.

Lau, Sing, John G. Nicholls, Theresa A. Thorkildsen, and Michael Patashnick. "Chinese and American Adolescents' perceptions of the purposes of education and beliefs about the world of work." *Social Behavior and Personality: An International Journal* 28, no. 1 (2000): 73–89.

Leung, Frederick K. S. "Behind the high achievement of East Asian students." *Educational Research and Evaluation* 8, no. 1 (2002): 87–108.

Littlewood, William. "Defining and developing autonomy in East Asian contexts." *Applied Linguistics* 20, no. 1 (1999): 71–94.

Morrison, Keith. "Paradox lost: Toward a robust test of the Chinese learner." *Education Journal-Hong Kong-Chinese University of Hong Kong* 34, no. 1 (2006): 1.

Musgrave, P. W. "Sociology in the training of teachers." In *Aspects of Education: Three: The Professional Education of Teachers*, 1965.

Phillipson, Shane N. "Confucianism, learning self-concept and the development of exceptionality." In *Exceptionality in East Asia: Explorations in the Actiotope Model of Giftedness*. London: Routledge, 2013, pp. 40–64.

Rutkowski, Leslie, and David Rutkowski. "Getting it 'better': The importance of improving background questionnaires in international large-scale assessment." *Journal of Curriculum Studies* 42, no. 3 (2010): 411–430.

Rutkowski, David, and Leslie Rutkowski. "Measuring socioeconomic background in PISA: One size might not fit all." *Research in Comparative and International Education* 8, no. 3 (2013): 259–278.

Schneider, Barbara, Joyce A. Hieshima, Sehahn Lee, and Stephen Plank. "East-Asian academic success in the United States: Family, school, and community explanations." In *Cross-cultural Roots of Minority Child Development*. New York: Psychology Press, 1994, pp. 323–350.

Schulz, Wolfram. *Measuring the Socio-economic Background of Students and Its Effect on Achievement on PISA 2000 and PISA 2003*. Online Submission, Paper prepared for the Annual Meeting of the American Educational Research Association. San Francisco, CA, April 7–11, 2005.

Smuts, Alice Boardman, and John W. Hagen. *History and Research in Child Development*. No. 211. Chicago: University of Chicago Press, 1986.

Stankov, Lazar. "Unforgiving Confucian culture: A breeding ground for high academic achievement, test anxiety and self-doubt?" *Learning and Individual Differences* 20, no. 6 (2010): 555–563.

Stanley, M. Sue. "School uniforms and safety." *Education and Urban Society* 28, no. 4 (1996): 424–435.

Steinberg, Laurence, Benson Bradford Brown, and Sanford M. Dornbusch. *Beyond the Classroom: Why Schools Are Failing and What Parents Need to Do.* New York: Simon & Schuster, 1996.

Stevenson, Harold W., Shin-Ying Lee, and James W. Stigler. "Mathematics achievement of Chinese, Japanese, and American children." *Science* 231, no. 4739 (1986): 693–699.

Stevenson, Harold W., and James W. Stigler. *The Learning Gap.* New York: Simon and Schuster, 1992.

Stevenson, Harold W., and James W. Stigler. *Learning Gap: Why Our Schools Are Failing and What We Can Learn From Japanese and Chinese Educ.* New York: Simon & Schuster, 1992.

Sue, Stanley, and Sumie Okazaki. "Asian-American educational achievements: A phenomenon in search of an explanation." *American Psychologist* 45, no. 8 (1990): 913.

Sun, Qi. "To be Ren and Jun Zi: A Confucian perspective on the practice of contemporary education." *Journal of Thought* 39, no. 2 (2004): 77–90.

Tam, Kim-Pong, Sau-Lai Lee, Young-Hoon Kim, Yanmei Li, and Melody Manchi Chao. "Intersubjective model of value transmission: Parents using perceived norms as reference when socializing children." *Personality and Social Psychology Bulletin* 38, no. 8 (2012): 1041–1052.

Tan, Charlene. "Beyond rote-memorisation: Confucius' concept of thinking." *Educational Philosophy and Theory* 47, no.5 (2015): 428–439.

Tan, Charlene. *Educational Policy Borrowing in China: Looking West or Looking East?* London: Routledge, 2016.

Tu, Weiming. *Confucian Thought: Selfhood as Creative Transformation.* New York: SUNY Press, 1985.

Tu, Weiming. "Implications of the Rise of 'Confucian' East Asia." *Daedalus* 129, no. 1 (2000): 195–218.

Viengkham, Doris, Chris Baumann, and Hume Winzar. "Confucianism: Measurement and association with workforce performance." *Cross Cultural & Strategic Management* 25, no. 2 (2018): 337–374.

Watkins, David A., and John B. Biggs. *The Chinese Learner: Cultural, Psychological, and Contextual Influences.* Comparative Education Research Centre, Faculty of Education, University of Hong Kong, Pokfulam Road, Hong Kong; The Australian Council for Educational Research, Ltd., 19 Prospect Hill Road, Camberwell, Melbourne, Victoria 3124, Australia., 1996.

Watson, Burton. *Basic Writings of Mo Tzu, Hsün Tzu, and Han Fei Tzu.* New York: Columbia University Press, 1967.

Way, Sandra M. "School discipline and disruptive classroom behavior: The moderating effects of student perceptions." *The Sociological Quarterly* 52, no. 3 (2011): 346–375.

Willingham, Daniel T. "Ask the cognitive scientist: Why does family wealth affect learning?" *American Educator* 36, no. 1 (2012): 33–39.

Xu, Jing. *The Good Child: Moral Development in a Chinese Preschool*. Stanford, CA: Stanford University Press, 2017.

Yao, Xinzhong. *An Introduction to Confucianism*. Cambridge: Cambridge University Press, 2000.

Zeng, K. 1999. *Dragon Gate: Competitive Examinations and their Consequences*. London: Cassell.

3 Discipline and Academic Performance Under the Microscope

> Nurturing is always two-way—one has to be receptive to what is being conveyed.
>
> Rosalie L. Tung (2018, personal correspondence)

The previous chapter of this book provided the results of multivariate analyses, with a key focus on the association between discipline and academic performance. That analysis provided evidence that the principal mechanisms 'work' in similar ways for the Confucian Orbit and the Anglo-Saxon cluster as well as other parts of the world: the higher the discipline standards, the higher the academic performance. Afterall, a Chinese proverb reads "Jade will never become a work of art without being carved". But are there differences in discipline standards and academic performance among the geographic clusters?

Next, in Chapter 3, we want to explore such differences for each performance and discipline dimension for each geographic cluster, posing the question: could it be that under Confucianism, school discipline is stronger with also stronger academic performance? The following variables were tested in bivariate analyses for this purpose, and we structure this chapter along these topics:

1. Academic Performance;
2. Disciplinary Climate (please note: we use the term school discipline, whereas PISA uses disciplinary climate);
3. Student Truancy;
4. Student Learning Time;
5. Student Motivation;
6. Student Well-Being;
7. Student Outlook on Education;
8. Teacher Performance.

The units of analysis are all the individual students in each cluster, and we again use the PISA 2015 data set. Inter-Ocular Test (IOT) charts (an approach introduced by Baumann, Winzar and Fang, 2018) allow for an easy-to-comprehend visualisation of the:

1. Mean and median;
2. Spread; and
3. Differences among the six geographical clusters (for a list of countries/societies per cluster, refer to Figure 1.3 in Chapter 1):
   - Confucian Orbit;
   - Anglo-Saxon;
   - Eastern Europe and Former Soviet Union;
   - Western Europe;
   - Latin America;
   - North Africa and the Middle East.

A comparison of the six geographical clusters along each of the PISA dimensions included in our analysis resulted in statistically significant differences ($p \leq 0.001$), which was anticipated given the large sample size. Therefore, we refer to our Inter-Ocular Test (IOT), or in other words, 'looking at the data', to determine the extent to which geographic clusters actually differ on PISA dimensions. In order to analyse our Inter-Ocular Test (IOT) charts methodologically, we explore the following for each box plot. The box represents 50 percent of the sample; the vertical line represents the median (i.e. the 'middle value'), the diamond represents mean, or average:

1. What is the median, mean, box spread (50 percent of sample) and the overall range (range is from lowest to highest value)?
2. Are there differences between the six clusters on each dimension?
3. Is there a pattern? In other words: which dimension(s) 'stand out' in terms of geographic cluster differences?

Academic Performance

Academic performance in PISA is split into three areas of examination: science, math, and reading. Table 3.1 provides Inter-Ocular Tests (IOT) for each dimension with the six geographic clusters plotted separately. We wanted to see whether there are differences in the median, mean, and distribution of the three academic performance dimensions among the geographic clusters, and indeed we found there to be substantial differences for all three performance dimensions.

There is a clear pattern with the Confucian Orbit topping the ranking for science, math, and reading. The performance differences are very substantial as evidenced by, for example, the median for the Confucian Orbit science performance levelling with the top 50 percent for Eastern Europe and former Soviet Union, and indeed surpassing the top 50 percent

Table 3.1 Comparison of PISA Results: Academic Performance

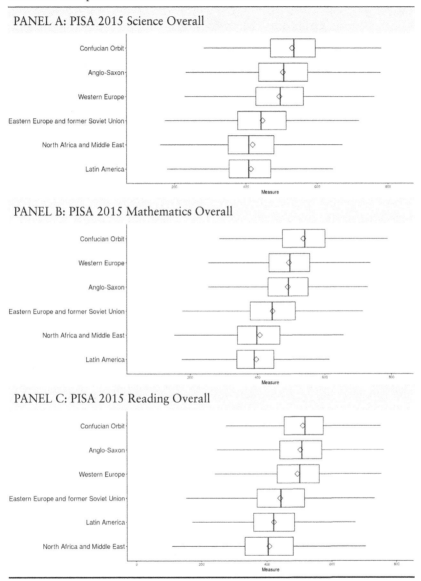

PANEL A: PISA 2015 Science Overall

PANEL B: PISA 2015 Mathematics Overall

PANEL C: PISA 2015 Reading Overall

for North Africa and the Middle East as well as Latin America. The pattern of the Confucian Orbit peak performing is similar for math and reading—albeit for math, the bottom of the 50 percent Confucian Orbit performers is higher than the median for Eastern Europe and the former Soviet Union, and remarkably, that is also higher than the highest 50 percent for North Africa and the Middle East as well as Latin America. In other words, the *bottom* of the Confucian Orbit performs stronger than the *top* of some other parts of the world—and that is very remarkable. The Confucian Orbit does clearly stand out with the strongest academic performance globally.

It should also be noted that while we analyse the PISA data 2015, Baumann and Krskova (2016) used 2012 PISA data for their study and found similarly strong academic performance for the East Asian cluster with equally high levels of discipline, as did Shin, Lee and Kim (2009) based on PISA 2003 data. In other words, the Confucian Orbit has consistently outperformed the rest of the world in terms of successfully applying school discipline to enhance—or at least maintain—high academic performance levels. Baumann and Krskova's (2016) work is a seminal study that specifically—and perhaps for the first time—linked school discipline with academic performance empirically, and our work presented in this book aligns with their work, notwithstanding that we now add Inter-Ocular Test (IOT) evidence, i.e. we plot the data, and we have more recent PISA data.

School Discipline

Discipline within the context of the classroom is defined as the misbehaviour of students, and the reactionary approaches teachers take to 'correct' this poor behaviour (Charles, 2002). It has been shown that discipline standards differ between countries, where a number of characteristics relating to the school environment factors, the teachers, the country's wealth levels, and gender could be major determinants of a school's level of discipline (Chiu and McBride-Chang, 2006). However, contrary to the belief that wealthier countries have better school discipline (because they have better resources to manage classrooms), the opposite was found by Chiu and Chow (2011) where poorer countries reported better classroom discipline; often poorer countries have big classes where teachers value discipline to manage those large classes effectively. In the same study, richer countries associated better discipline more strongly with positive teacher-student relations. These findings indicate that how students relate to teachers, or perhaps even attend more to their teacher's instruction, is a better indicator of how disciplined a classroom or school will be as opposed to degree of wealth, overall. Also in line with this is our finding from Chapter 2, where the six geographic cluster models resulted in very little difference between family wealth and discipline. We were both surprised and pleased with this result, because this means that how a classroom is managed, and how students are engaged, is not a function of more money or resources, or that greater (lower) wealth produces more qualified (unqualified) teachers. But instead that school discipline quite literally comes down to the ecosystem of management strategies between the school, teacher, student, and peers. To reiterate, we found a positive association between discipline and performance, and that was the same for all geographic clusters. If discipline can be increased, performance also improves.

A key reason for the varying levels of school discipline across countries is that the expectations and understanding of what constitutes 'good discipline' varies since discipline is not least culturally driven. Naturally, if there is discord between teachers and students as to what is considered good discipline, then there is larger room for error and miscommunication in meeting that standard. In contrast, if both 'sides' agree on the value and practice of discipline, then there should by default be some degree of harmony.

In their study on the 'dual perspective' of discipline between teachers and students, Haroun and O'Hanlon (1997) identified a number of points where both parties' views converged and diverged on matters of discipline. Generally, there was consensus on the students' part that discipline is an 'external power' used to control their behaviour, and that teachers are responsible for maintaining the discipline in the classroom. Notably, only three students (of 800) mentioned discipline as serving an important function in facilitating communication between teachers and students, helping achieve learning aims, and creating a positive environment. A critical issue this highlights is that a lack of discipline could be the result of a lack of agreement on what the 'purpose' of discipline is, either on the part of the teacher, student, parent, or even the school. Perhaps often forgotten is that the ultimate goal of schooling is to create a positive learning environment so students can learn and grow, and that discipline is only a means by which to achieve that, leaving open to interpretation which types of issues need to be addressed and which to let 'slide by'. Teachers, regardless of the country they are teaching, have to deal with misbehaving students, and teenagers wanting to 'push the limit', but where the line is drawn on an 'infraction' may vary greatly. For example, some schools may only prioritise disciplinary action if the student 'acts out' violently whereas others impose serious repercussions for being a minute late to class. These discrepancies are a matter of school policy and their societal contexts, but not necessarily how rich or poor anyone is.

The majority of focus on school discipline matters relates to the disruptive behaviours of students. But what is considered disruptive, and the severity of it also lacks a clear definition, let alone what type of consequences should be imposed. Romi and Freund (1999) conducted a 'triad perspective' study on the teacher, parent, and students' views of 'severe' disruptive behaviour in Israeli classrooms and found a large gap between the three groups. There was most agreement among the teachers, where over 80 percent regarded verbal and physical violence aimed at students and vandalism among the top issues; for students, there was consensus of around 50 percent regarding issues of theft from classmates, throwing items, and abuse; and for parents, the only agreement was on physical violence directed at students. The implications of this lack of agreement are that each party perceives the conduct of students differently, and most likely, in accordance to a different standard held than to that of the teachers or students. Worse yet is when parents and students share a perception of disruptive behaviours which differ substantially from teachers'; this may result in the escalation of behavioural issues because students feel they cannot 'meet the expectations' of their teachers, and simultaneously, teachers sometimes feel they do not have the support or understanding of their need to discipline students, from parents and/or the school system (principal, legal framework). Logically then, establishing disciplinary standards needs to be a 'joint venture' between teachers, parents, and students, where clear expectations and boundaries are set for students' behaviours.

Aptitude levels aside, when students are well behaved and less disruptive, they are likely to perform better in school (Blank and Shavit, 2016). This is because students are better able to engage with the material, but also because good discipline likely fosters positive learning skills which in turn affect academic performance (Yang, 2009). Discipline alone is not enough to help students achieve academic excellence—a number of other preconditions including personality, motivation, intelligence, and self-image (Wong, 1991) also contribute to this. However, discipline helps students to realise their capacity to achieving stronger performance through learning skills such as perseverance, an ability to meet schedules, set goals, and complete unpleasant tasks (Pasternak, 2013). These issues relate to having self-discipline, because each requires an internal process or *will* to undertake the task. They do not, however, occur in a vacuum, but instead are positively and significantly related to students' conduct within the classroom *and* their respect for the teacher (Pasternak, 2013). In other words, discipline is not an 'inherent or innate characteristic'; teachers and parents, regardless of their socioeconomic or cultural background, have the ability to influence a student's habits, attitudes, and performance. Therefore discipline is not only about good classroom management relating to noise control and disruption, but also about establishing management expectation of what students can achieve if they put their best foot forward; it is about improvement, however incremental. Good discipline may help weaker students to 'catch up', and stronger students to excel.

In the classroom setting, or even the home environment, the expectations relate to the minimum standard of behaviour considered 'acceptable' as enforced by teachers, parents, and school policy. The perceived severity of poor discipline (such as disruptive behaviours) has been demonstrated to vary greatly between parents, teachers, and students (Romi and Freund, 1999), which would suggest that the minimum standard of what is expected of students would also vary between teachers and parents as previously alluded to. Expected standards are important because they establish a benchmark that allows students to—either consciously or passively—evaluate their behaviour and performance, and determine where adjustments can be made. Setting a standard of expectation would foster a sense of accountability and responsibility of oneself (for the student) and toward the teacher or parent (Ingersoll, 2007). More importantly, setting a standard that is shared and understood between educators, students, and their parents is likely to produce the best outcome, because there is accountability on multiple sides.

For schools in East Asia, we see this type of 'planning' early in a child's academic career. Teachers often "emphasize [their] authority, reinforcing discipline and manners consistently. During the whole class activity in one classroom, a teacher called out the names of the disruptive and inattentive children and she did not ignore children's misbehaviour'" (Kwon, 2004, p. 307). 'Isolation techniques' are also common, for example unruly kindergarten students are made to stand in the corner to reflect on their behaviour and manners (Kwon, 2004), whereas in the West, conferences are used between teacher, student, and parents, often as a last resort, when teachers feel they are 'out of options'. This also raises the issue of immediacy and pragmatism—in East Asia, the signal that behaviour or performance is not acceptable is 'sent out' immediately without bureaucracy, whereas in the West, there is concern that due to lack of a teacher's right to discipline a student, they just let it slip in order to avoid paperwork and triggering a bureaucratic 'machinery'. Ultimately such a constellation benefits no one: the student misses a chance to reflect and improve behaviour and performance, teachers are dissatisfied because they know they should have disciplined the student, and ultimately this results in a vicious circle—the situation in terms of behaviour and performance gets worse and worse (and there are countries in PISA where this is occurring).

The link between disciplinary climate and academic performance has been demonstrated in the literature on numerous occasions. Shin et al. (2009), using PISA 2003 data, found that better disciplinary climate were associated with better mathematics performance in their comparison of Japan, Korea, and American students. Analysis of PISA 2009 data by Ma, Jong and Yuan (2013) also revealed a strong link between disciplinary climate and math, science, and reading performance for students in Hong Kong, Taiwan, and Japan. And more recently, Krskova and Baumann (2017) revealed the relative importance of school discipline compared to education investment as almost nine to one, respectively, suggesting that a country has much more leverage when improving school discipline rather than spending more on education (where often, the individual student benefits only little when funds are used to enhance bureaucratic purposes).

In our study, we analysed the most recent PISA 2015 data, and found similar results that provide further evidence of a strong link between disciplinary climate and academic performance.

There are a number of different terms used for—*de facto*—a very similar construct: school discipline (PISA labels it disciplinary climate, while others call it school climate, classroom management). What we consider school discipline, or just discipline, is captured by PISA's disciplinary climate based on five questions that students answer while doing the PISA testing:

- ST097Q01TA   Students don't listen to what the teacher says.
- ST097Q02TA   There is noise and disorder.
- ST097Q03TA   The teacher has to wait a long time for students to quiet down.
- ST097Q04TA   Students cannot work well.
- ST097Q05TA   Students don't start working for a long time after the lesson begins.

While PISA does capture an evaluation of school climate from the principal's and teachers' perspectives, we refer to the student's judgement of disciplinary climate because they are the ones who are both experiencing and being affected by it. Perhaps the student's lens here may well be most accurate since students have no or little incentive to 'paint' a rosy picture of their in-class situations—they can feel free to 'tell it as it is'. Looking at the distributions of the variables we see from the student-reported discipline dimensions, we also do not find evidence of abnormality or any type of bias—in sum, we conclude the data to be a realistic reflection of the actual classroom situation in terms of discipline.

It is those five PISA discipline variables that we next factor-scored (i.e. 'made just one variable') to represent school discipline holistically in our study. Our Inter-Ocular Test (IOT) for discipline in Table 3.2 shows a very clear pattern, which largely aligns with the previously explored academic performance pattern. For discipline, we observe that the Confucian Orbit is again top with the highest median and mean, and highest 50 percent box plot range, but this time—in contrast to the performance dimensions—the medians of the other five geographic clusters pretty much align (i.e. being more or less the same). In fact, the bottom of the 50 percent box plot of the Confucian Orbit are on par with the median and mean of the rest of the PISA world. What this means is that school discipline in the Confucian Orbit is *de facto* uniquely distinctive to the rest of the world, and this top ranking for school discipline also aligns with the Confucian Orbit's equally superior academic performance. In sum, the Confucian Orbit has the highest levels of academic performance that seems to be not least triggered by the highest levels of discipline.

In order to showcase the vast differences in school discipline among the geographic clusters, we further plotted the five PISA disciplinary dimensions with the percentages for each that students indicated 'never or hardly ever happens' (see Figure 3.1). For each discipline dimension, we can see strict discipline reflected in the Confucian Orbit where any of the five discipline issues hardly ever happen—i.e. only a mere 5–7 percent

Table 3.2 Disciplinary Climate

PANEL A: *Disciplinary Climate (DISCLISCI)*	
Code	*Statement(s)*
ST097Q01TA	Students don't listen to what the teacher says.
ST097Q02TA	There is noise and disorder.
ST097Q03TA	The teacher has to wait a long time for students to quiet down.
ST097Q04TA	Students cannot work well.
ST097Q05TA	Students don't start working for a long time after the lesson begins.

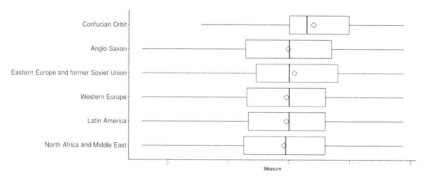

Higher points indicate better disciplinary climate; lower points indicate worse disciplinary climate.

Four-point scale: *Every lesson, most lessons, some lessons,* or *never or hardly ever.*

Disciplinary Climate Components
'Percent Never or Hardly Ever Happens'

Region

	Students Don't Listen	Teacher Must Wait	Start Work Late	Students Can't Work	Noise and Disorder
North Africa and Middle East	13	17	17	12	16
Eastern Europe and former ..	12	10	11	8	10
Anglo-Saxon	11	9	7	6	12
Latin America	10	11	11	7	12
Western Europe	9	10	10	6	10
Confucian Orbit	5	5	5	5	7

Figure 3.1 Disciplinary Climate Components ('Percent Never or Hardly Ever Happens')

of students reported problems in those areas. This is followed by Western Europe (6 to 10 percent), Latin America (7 to 12 percent) and the Anglo-Saxon cluster with 6 to 12 percent. The highest level of discipline problems is reported in Eastern Europe and former Soviet Union with 7–12 percent, or indeed markedly highest discipline problems in North Africa and the Middle East with 12 to 17 percent. In simple terms, the latter thus has roughly three times (yes, three times) as many discipline issues/problems than the Confucian Orbit, other areas have up to twice (that is still double the trouble) as many discipline problems reported as the Confucian Orbit. For a teacher who has to teach many hours each day, having twice or even triple the problems of a teacher in the better disciplined Confucian Orbit is not to be neglected. It perhaps comes as no surprise that teachers often leave the profession if they face such substantial discipline problems, with no legal support or tools to discipline students (e.g. in the West where the 'teacher waiting times' have been reported twice as problematic in comparison to the Confucian Orbit).

Which Discipline?

There are multiple understandings of discipline in the literature (in addition to the definitions we included in Chapter 1), for example:

- Discipline is concerned with "effective classroom management" (Haroun and O'Hanlon, 1997, p. 237), or indeed the "management of student behavior";
- Romi and Freund (1999, p. 54) argue that "discipline is a system of sanctions that addresses the breakdown when the code of conduct is broken";
- "Generally, school discipline is defined as school policies and actions taken by school personnel with students to prevent or intervene with unwanted behaviors" (Cameron, 2006, p. 219);
- Discipline also relates, or is used as a synonym for "classroom practices" (Cohen, McCabe, Michelli and Pickeral, 2009);
- School discipline was recently defined as "all activities that are implemented to control learner behaviour, to enforce compliance and maintain order" (Bechuke and Debeila, 2012, p. 243).

Alongside the numerous definitions of discipline are also the understanding of *when, how,* and *under which circumstances* it should be enforced. Discussions are often centred on the notion of student welfare in at least two ways: first, that discipline is a necessary tool to help students become better versions of themselves; and second, that use of discipline should not be in violation of students' rights and liberties. Additional to this is whether discipline should be purely punitive (i.e. punishing bad behaviour after it has occurred), or whether it should be preventative (i.e. using positive reinforcement to curtail bad behaviours before they can occur). Each is rather complex in its own right, let alone that there are hybrid versions to this.

Often times discipline is understood to be synonymous with 'punishment', but as Maag (2001, p. 178) points out, discipline (according to the *American Heritage Dictionary*) refers to "training that is expected to produce a specific character or pattern of behaviour, especially training that produces moral or mental *improvement*" (emphasis added). This definition reminds us of the origin of the term itself "via Old French from Latin *disciplina* 'instruction, knowledge', from *discipulus*", in other words, originally, while many now might assume that discipline is predominantly about punitive action, it is about instruction and knowledge.

Discipline that focusses purely on punishment, with a 'zero tolerance policy', risks breeding a hostile environment and creating more difficult-to-manage issues for educators (Skiba and Peterson, 2000); but while strict forms of punishment on bad behaviour may work in terms of removing the offending students, though temporarily, overly strict discipline may have little effectiveness in encouraging those students to behave in socially appropriate ways in the long run (Maag, 2001; Lewis, 2001). Alternatively, the use of positive reinforcement as a form of discipline is considered another approach, but it could be viewed as equally problematic to students' behaviours in the long term if misused. For example, if students are constantly praised for what would be considered mediocre performance, or simply even for participation, then how does that prepare them for competitive entry into tertiary education and/or the workforce?

Perhaps an issue is that the use of discipline operates in 'polar extremes'—where severely poor behaviour receives (negative) attention and really good behaviour receives (positive) attention—with very little in between. We similarly see this in the academic literature, and popular press, where approaches to discipline are often pitted again each other: it is either too harsh or lenient, too strict or laissez-faire, or too authoritative or permissive. Most notable in these comparisons is that they are often associated with Eastern vis-à-vis Western approaches, respectively. And there are many 'shades of grey' in between.

Concerns for the Asian students whose parents supposedly inflict disciplinary 'cruelty' upon them became apparent after Amy Chua's memoir *Battle Hymn of the Tiger Mother* was released, and many were quick to voice their opinions over which parenting style was better. Though controversial at the time, Chua's book inspired a series of academic research from education, child and family psychology, and cultural studies which gave insight to the dynamic of discipline and child-rearing strategies of Asian families; see Juang, Qin, and Park's (2013) special issue on aspects of parenting unique to Asian-heritage families. The key finding from this series of work is that 'tiger parenting', defined as the demanding, harsh, and emotionally unsupportive approach is present, but not exclusive. Asian-heritage parents are also warm, supporting, and loving towards their children. In other words, there is a balance between the two which is often overlooked in the literature. While some Asian parents view the 'tiger' approach to parenting as an 'outdated' view of Chinese parenting style (Way et al., 2013), others see the importance in blending approaches of strictness and nurturance in helping their children reach their developmental goals—both academic and psychosocial (Kim, Wang, Orozco-Lapray, Shen and Murtuza, 2013).

Spotlight

A 'Yin Yang' View on Discipline

We adopt the illusion that we can only adopt a *single* attitude to offenders; and then either (a) we yield totally to our feelings of indignation, perhaps even classifying them as 'evil', and are concerned only to punish them, or (b) as kind-hearted liberals we remember that they too are God's children and need love and understanding. . . .

The truth is that both attitudes have to be developed wholeheartedly in order to produce the required results. That is particularly important in the case of children, who learn to become responsible adults largely by coming to understand both (a) and (b) and being able to distinguish between them. They have to see the parent or teacher both as a (sometimes punitive) authority and as a friend or helper. Currently in many liberal societies, including the UK, it is difficult for them to see the teacher as an authority, simply because teachers are not granted the powers necessary to make their authority stick: they are not able to enforce obedience. The result is not only a lack of discipline which sometimes amounts to anarchy but—what may be even more important—a failure to communicate to children the whole idea and rationale that lies behind authority, prescriptive rules, and punishment. Even very well-ordered schools (of which of course there are many) may fail to communicate this idea, because they may rely on other kinds of motivation to keep good order, and hence not stress the particular notion of discipline which is connected to the concept of obedience to legitimate authority as such (see Wilson, 1977).

Source: Wilson (2002, pp. 412–413) in *Corporal Punishment Revisited*

A Confucian Approach to Discipline

Though we have previously expressed, in line with our findings from Chapter 2, that discipline (i.e. having it or lacking it) is not a cultural issue, *per se*, we view that culture under Confucianism has been successful in producing an 'approach' to discipline that has seen the academic success of its students, and competitiveness of its nations. In other words, culture associates with performance for all six geographic clusters, but the level of discipline—and associated academic performance—differ. Also drawing on our discussions from previous chapters, we consider three reasons for this:

1. A balanced approach to discipline is exercised;
2. A shared understanding in setting standards and expectations;
3. Consequences for non-compliance, on issues big *and* small.

The cornerstone of the Confucian tradition is that no one is unchangeable, and that everybody possesses the capacity to transform themselves, regardless how little. This is achieved through a balance of soft and hard approaches, each of which is adapted to the student and the situation at hand (Hue and Li, 2008). Confucianism's emphasis on humaneness means that all should be treated with compassion and understanding, and this view is echoed in the classrooms of Hong Kong (among other East Asian) teachers who believe that even if they had a student who was not performing as well as the others, or was behaving badly, that they were still capable of being a good learner in other domains and this just meant helping them find their 'way' (Hue, 2007a, p. 25), not least through the application of discipline. In this sense, educators believe that their role is to teach without distinction, and that by acknowledging students' inherent differences, apply appropriate methods to engaging if they fall behind—again, those methods including effective discipline.

The 'soft' and 'harsh' approaches to discipline are embedded in the Taoist[1] and Legalist[2] traditions, respectively (Hue, 2007b). The Taoist approach stresses taking 'action through inaction', which should not be confused with doing nothing at all, but could mean that teachers encourage students to use self-reflection as a tool for behavioural management. In Japanese classrooms, students perform *Hansei*—a self-reflection activity—often once or twice daily, either as a whole class or individually. *Hansei*—through that reflection—acknowledges human imperfection, identifying where one has gone wrong, but equally to find a way for improvement, and this in turn reflects the spirit of constant and lifelong zest for *betterment* under Confucianism. At Japanese schools, the aim is to have students purposefully thinking about their progress, what they have achieved, and identify goals for further self-improvement (Lewis, 1995a). On the other hand, the Legalist approach stresses a clear system of punishment and rewards aimed at discouraging bad behaviour through very explicit sanctions such as time-out, kneeling, or standing at the back of the room. Confucian teachers often feel that a physical 'wake-up call' is most effective to get a point across, e.g. that a student's behaviour was not correct, that her/his performance was not good enough, that one should be punctual, and if not, then consequences should be 'felt'.

Discipline in East Asia takes the form of Yin and Yang, which embraces opposites and paradox. The principle highlights to reconciliation of seemingly contrasting practices: Yin (black) represents female elements of passivity, where Yang (white) is a positive principle characterised by activity (Figure 3.2) (Fang, 2012). On their own, each approach to discipline can be an effective tool to dealing with a specific problem, and taken together, provides teachers and parents with a comprehensive toolset to help develop strong academic skills and nurture individuals to becoming good citizens, pass on values, and create work ethic.

In East Asia, discipline strategies are focussed on fostering self-reliance, rather than an over-dependence on authority, surveillance, or acting by a system of rewards and punishments (Lewis, 1984, 1989). In Japan, for example, students are encouraged to develop their leadership skills and be accountable for not only their own behaviours, but to also encourage their peers to act in accordance with what is expected. Teachers utilise the *toban* system, which "capitalizes on children's natural interests—for attention, prestige, and a chance to lead others—and gives children a chance to experience the pleasure, and headaches, of responsibility" (Lewis, 1997, p. 22). For example, students will take turns being tasked to stand at the front of the room to help quieten down the classroom; over the course

Figure 3.2 Yin Yang Symbol—Balance of Harsh and Soft Discipline

of the school year, students will help shape the rules and norms of the classroom, discuss class goals, and assess on their progress and areas for improvement. Responsibility also manifests in a physical manner, where students perform *o-soji*; a few days a week, students help 'take care' of their learning environment by cleaning in groups with brooms and cloths. In Korea, student 'helpers' often assist teachers at the school gate to greet students, check their uniforms and overall appearance, and alert teaching staff of late students; in one way or another, students are sometimes integrated in the discipline structure of Confucian schools.

Contrary to popular beliefs that East Asian schooling is characterised by harsh disciplinary practices, a study by Lewis, Romi, Qui, and Katz (2005) found that, in general, Chinese teachers were less punitive and aggressive than teachers from Israel and Australia. Additionally, those students from China also reported that their teachers were more inclusive and supportive of their voices, and less aggressive, when it came to discipline in the classroom. From another angle, in their survey of Chinese teachers, Ding, Li, Li, and Kulm (2008) found that the most 'problematic' classroom misbehaviour was that of students 'day dreaming' or being inattentive at times. This is in contrast to teachers from the West who identified disruptions such as speaking out of turn, and chit chat. These findings suggest that a less punitive—or perhaps more balanced approach, such as Confucian discipline—fosters a learning environment where less disruptions to other students occur (i.e. too much chatter and noise); this is supported by Mitchell and Bradshaw's (2013) conclusion that a *greater* use of exclusionary discipline strategies (such as confronting the student, or yelling) are associated with lower order and discipline in the classroom. Students who feel as though they are constantly under attack are less likely to want to co-operate in creating a positive learning environment, either for themselves or their peers. Following Confucianism, a 'stern talking to' may well be effective, ordering a student to stand in the corner to reflect may assist in betterment, but yelling appears out of place (and would also be non-Confucian, none-wise; teachers can't expect students to become gentlemen/ladies if they do not act that way as role models themselves in the first instance). In sum, perhaps, it is better to have harsh 'tools' used when really necessary (like in East Asia), but then not having to use them as often in contrast to having constant disruptions with endless discipline issues, but no power to effectively discipline students, if at all, as is the case under permissive contexts. See Figure 3.2 that symbolises the harmony of both, harsh and soft discipline.

The Confucian approach to discipline is not only exercised in the school environment, but also the home domain. Co-operation between teachers and parents exists not only relating to the perceived importance of education, but also that there is a mutual role to be played in instilling in students the values of hard work, diligence, and an understanding that the strict discipline is sometimes necessary to achieve these goals. Through

Structural Equation Modelling, a statistical technique we also apply in Chapter 2 of this book, Martin, Marsh, McInerney, Green, and Dowson (2007) demonstrated that teacher-student *and* parent-child relationships are both significantly associated with a student's academic motivation and engagement, including self-concept and self-esteem. Though those researchers found that teacher effects were stronger in relation to school, the findings reiterate that co-operative efforts between teachers and parents are the optimal approach to improving academic success. Beyond achievement at school, teachers and parents share a responsibility for preparing students to be civilised and responsible citizens; as such, discipline is used not only to address behavioural problems, but in promoting students' social competence, their self management, and adjustment into adult life (Hue, 2007b). While early socialisation in the home environment introduces students to core values of Confucianism, there is strong evidence that the school environment also acts as an arena where these cultural beliefs and practices are reiterated and reinforced (Hue, 2001, 2005). To summarise Hue's (2007a, p. 30) conclusions, five key themes are identified relating to Confucianism's influence on how teachers approach discipline in the classroom:

- Discipline can be used to reveal the natural tendencies of the students;
- There is an emphasis in individual effort, rather than belief in innate ability;
- Discipline is used with benevolence and kindness, not only harshness (i.e. discipline should be 'felt', but of course it should never be abusive);
- Discipline has an emphasis on politeness;
- The goal is students become *junzi*—the perfect gentlemen or ladies.

Perhaps the most important aspect of the Confucian approach to discipline is that there are consequences for non-compliance, not only for *major* infractions, but also for what many would consider the 'small things'. Basic principles such as how one takes care in their appearance and attire, being polite, or just simply being on time. While these are issues most people strive to meet, the lack of consequence in many societies means that there is very little incentive to improve upon them. Confucianism is concerned with *betterment*, and the development of sound self-regulation strategies (Woods and Lamond, 2011; McInerney, 2011): the systematic effort of regulating one's own thoughts, and feelings, and actions towards attaining personal goals (Bandura, 1991). Within the Confucian Orbit, this starts simply by being punctual, being well presented, being respectful, greeting teaching staff politely (and often with a bow), and putting effort into things—all things which are introduced at an early age, and passed on in school and society. When the fundamentals of good discipline are established, the rest will follow.

This approach to discipline also means that it need not be all about correcting big behavioural issues only, or reinforcing good behaviours overzealously. It is also about instilling in students a sense of responsibility by showing them that putting effort into the basic things can be a path to achieving greater things later on. Though this seems like common sense, these are the issues that schools often let 'slide' in the West: ensuring uniforms are worn properly (if there are uniforms at all), that students are punctual to every class, and that they are respectful to their teachers and peers. The consequences that result, when there is non-compliance, are sometimes non-existent, and that is a worrying message to be sending to students. Often publicised in the mainstream media is that the strict expectations placed upon students (in both demeanour and performance) in the classroom are cruel and rob them of their individuality; however, what may very well be the 'crueller' approach is being complacent with students, or giving them the impression that little effort is enough to get by in life (either because someone else will pick up the slack, or that there will be no consequences for underperformance).

In a study on the perceptions of strict discipline and obedience among Chinese in China, and Chinese in Canada and Australia, the findings indicated that the *overseas* Chinese (i.e. living in the West) favoured stricter schools than the Chinese in China (Baumann, Tung and Hamin, 2012). This is despite previous studies finding that students perceived teachers in the West, such as Australia, as more punitive and authoritarian than Chinese teachers (Lewis et al., 2005); again, this could be a result of Western teachers constantly having to apply non-effective discipline, whereas East Asian teachers apply effective discipline and in turn do not have to even use stricter punishment all that often. From a parent's perspective, they may feel that the emphasis is placed on the 'wrong kind' of strictness; whereas the literature gives us evidence that high- and low-level disturbances, such as too much noise or disengagement, are often addressed in Western classrooms, other disciplinary issues such as non-completion of homework or underperformance could take precedence.

In a study on the poor behaviour and disengagement of students in South Australian schools, findings indicated high frequency of unproductive student behaviour, but that teachers felt that they were lacking the resources and training to deal with the problems (Sullivan, Johnson, Conway, Owens and Taddeo, 2012); this contrasts to the Confucian Orbit where teachers—by and large—do have the power and 'tools' to discipline students. Further, teachers mostly attributed students' poor in-school behaviour with factors external to the classroom/school (i.e. problem behaviours stemmed from individual and/or home factors). This is a rather common theme that presents itself in the West, in contrast to schools in the Confucian Orbit. In the West, teachers often feel overwhelmed by the disruptive behaviour or lack of attention of their students, but also feel powerless to do anything about it—likely due to a lack of administrative support *and* respect from students (and parents). In the East, the onus is on the teacher to guide their students toward the correct behaviour, and again, are equipped with the support to do so.

The PISA discipline dimensions measure the 'outcome of discipline', i.e. the more disciplined students are, the higher the PISA score since there would be (a perception of) good discipline in the classroom. However, this measure does not include the tools used by teachers, the school policy applied, to discipline students for various forms of 'misbehaviour' or poor performance attempts. In simple terms, there is a difference between 'to discipline' (the teacher's action for misbehaviour) and 'to be disciplined'; the latter can take two forms:

1. A student *being disciplined* by a teacher for their misbehaviour (i.e. the punitive notion); and
2. A student that *is (self-)disciplined* (i.e. demonstrates good behaviour).

We contribute to this rather complex mechanism by adding our categorisation of discipline as a 'taxonomy of discipline dimensions', i.e. areas of everyday school life that inflict *consequences* for non-compliance. Much like Newton's Third Law, discipline functions under a paradigm of (in)action and reaction. For example, if a student does something wrong such as behave inappropriately (e.g. talking too loud, causing a distraction, being rude to the teacher or other students), then they are met with the consequence of punishment. Similarly, if a student is underperforming, this could be regarded as inaction on their behalf due to a 'lack of trying', which would also be met with punishment under a Confucian classroom approach (sometimes consequences directly correlate with mistakes made, for example in a class test; i.e. the more mistakes, the more consequences). Discipline under Confucianism is about 'concerted cultivation' (Lareau, 2003), a strategy which entails high levels of parental (and teacher) intervention in children's school lives to prepare them for the future; this is a necessary effort to boost the education potentialities of children, who cannot yet realise it on their own. Interviews with Chinese (and other ethnic) parents who moved their families to Australia paint a clear picture of their expectation of the education system in 'handling this':

> When children are small you have to control them like tree, small tree. When they are young we have to hold them up straight. When they are bigger, grow up, they understand what is right and what is wrong, and what they can do and what they can't do.
>
> (Mary, a parent of Chinese background—quoted from
> Cardona, Watkins and Noble, 2009, p. 23)

The literature has helpful and impressive work on discipline (which we showcase in Chapter 1, Table 1.2). Through our work on the topic for this book, we feel that we have developed a refined comprehension of issues and dimension that 'make up' discipline. We thus aspire to advance the understanding and definition of discipline where we incorporate a focus on the consequences for non-compliance students experience for the following dimensions of education, not least based on the notion that on the following dimensions of discipline, there are marked differences among geographic clusters how discipline manifests. Our new *taxonomy of discipline dimensions* is as follows:

- Behaviour, conduct, and deportment;
- Manners;
- Respect for teachers, education, and other students;
- Punctuality;
- Uniform/dress standard;
- Academic performance;
- Homework (e.g. checks by teachers for completion).

Traditionally, in one way or another, understanding of discipline in theory and practice would have centred on these dimensions; however, there appear to be a number of crucial differences in terms of discipline among geographic regions in how it is actually practiced in the classroom, justifying our split of discipline into these dimensions to better allow for a geographic comparison. In addition, this categorisation will also be of use to practitioners and policy makers wishing to better discipline standards in classrooms, and subsequently better academic performance. We add that imposing a tangible consequence for non-compliance on these 'everyday issues', when done with consistency, helps build good habits, which are conducive to a positive and co-operative learning environment. Better yet still, is that monitoring these issues requires little to no additional funding, resources, or training—only a willingness to more consequently have better discipline in classrooms. We illustrate this concept in Figure 3.3, which we introduce as the *taxonomy of discipline*

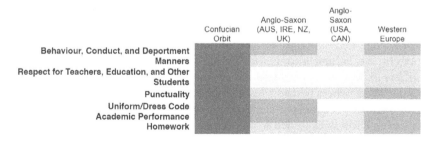

Figure 3.3 Taxonomy of Discipline Dimensions: Consequences for Non-compliance

Legend: The more intense the shading, the greater the extent to which that particular trait is manifested in that country/region. It should be noted that for the uniform and dress code dimension, the Anglo-Saxon cluster typically has school uniforms in Australia, Ireland, the UK, and New Zealand, but not so in Canada and the USA, where school uniforms are sometimes used in the private school sector only.

dimensions: consequences for non-compliance, showing that societies within the Confucian Orbit have more 'serious' consequences for non-compliance on a number of issues, compared to Western societies that may have a tendency to let these things slide if they fall below a certain standard.

Comparing discipline and academic performance among the geographic clusters as we have done for this study, it can be concluded that the stricter East Asian approach does indeed directly result in better performance. At the risk of oversimplification, we categorise our novel understanding of discipline as follows, with a comparison of the Confucian Orbit to the 'West' as an illustration.

Firstly, the level of enforcement ('strictness') differs with the Confucian Orbit generally expressing the highest level of discipline. This contrasts to the more permissive approach to education in the 'West' where discipline standards have generally become more relaxed. While darker shades indicate that there is greater consequence for non-compliance, in general, it would be reasonable to assume that over time, students will become inculcated with the expectations to conform to these behaviours, and result in a form of self-discipline to regulate these actions without reminding. In contrast, a more permissive environment with lower level consequences, if at all, may not solve the problem, and result in continuous interruptions, problems, and lower-level learning/performance. As we have previously suggested—if there are harsher consequences for non-compliance at school, they have to be used less often.

Behaviour, Conduct, Deportment, and Manners

It would be reasonable to assume that—more or less—schools around the world aspire to have students on good behaviour in the classroom without walking around, chit chatting, talking out of turn, or interrupting class otherwise. Good manners, however, are paramount in the Confucian Orbit where values of general betterment beyond academic performance are passed on in the classroom ('become a better person' under Confucianism, which is not the explicit goal of Western education where typically simply knowledge and skills are passed on with no/little attention to personal betterment, values, morals, or obvious character building). Parents and society expect teachers in East Asia to pass on good manners—in contrast to the 'West' where teachers have limited options to discipline students for poor behaviour or bad manners; in many Western countries, this dimension has been entirely excluded from performance evaluation. Teachers in the Confucian Orbit command a high level of respect on how they have to be addressed, often combined with respectful bowing to teaching staff—a Confucian custom that would be unthinkable in the English speaking world or Western Europe where students are often treated—more or less—as equal to teaching staff. Confucian education includes conduct, deportment, respect, communication, and overall behavioural standards. Confucian values are passed on in East Asian classrooms.

Respect for Teachers, Education, and Other Students

Respect for education is deeply ingrained within Confucian societies, and this high regard often translates to a deeply founded respect for the teachers and the whole institution of learning, indeed for knowledge itself. Although respect is a fundamental component in any society, regardless of cultural differences, the way in which it manifests or is displayed towards certain professions varies substantially. In China, the teaching profession is considered one of the noblest and similar in status to doctors; teachers are often revered on the same standing as 'gods' (Fwu and Wang, 2002). Similar levels of respect for teaching staff can be found throughout the Confucian Orbit. Conversely, in the UK, teachers are considered to be more on par with nurses and social workers—with only a fifth of adults believing that students demonstrate any respect for their teachers or school (Coughlan, 2013).

Students' respect for their teachers is not only the result of the importance of education, but also shaped by the hierarchical nature of their value systems. As elders, and thus wiser individuals, teachers are viewed as an important mediator between students' performance at school and their ability to succeed in the outside world. If there is little to no respect for the individual (from both students and parents) who is tasked with shaping a quality future for the students, then society ultimately suffers as a whole; a lack of respect encourages a cycle where students underperform, and quality educators are being deterred from entering or staying in the profession (Riggs, 2013). Further, respect for teachers and peers within the Confucian Orbit are also a matter of 'saving face'—where the actions taken are often in consideration of the public self-image and dignity of oneself and others (Kim and Nam, 1998; Ho, 1976). In Korea, for example, unruly students are sometimes requested to stand in front of the class for a short period of time—this 'loss of face' is the punishment, and sends out the clear signal: this was not right—so don't do it again. In turn, in maintaining harmony, students in the East are less likely to 'challenge' their teacher's authority in a direct or public manner.

Spotlight

Who Are the World's Most Valued Teachers?

All over the world, proud parents drop their children at the gates of schools, dreaming about what they might accomplish after years of study and homework. They entrust teachers with the duty of nurturing their development and opening their eyes to a world of possibilities. It's a huge responsibility—but is that responsibility reflected in their social status and pay?

October 5 is World Teachers' Day, so here's a look at how the world values teachers.

A 2013 study by the Varkey Foundation looked at the social status of teachers and found that there was great respect for teachers in many Asian societies—especially in China, South Korea and Singapore. For much of the Western parts of the world, levels of respect were lower.

The Global Teacher Status Index found that of the 21 countries surveyed, on average, teachers ranked 7th in a poll on 14 respected professions, just above social workers and librarians. China was the only country where teachers were considered as highly skilled as doctors.

Professor Peter Dolton, author of the Global Teacher Status Index which compared attitudes to teachers in 21 countries, said that teacher status measures differently 'based on the history and values and mores of a particular culture'.

For example, he cites New York City, where society is focussed on financial earnings, status correlates to how much a teacher is earning. Whereas in China, where cultural norms are to respect your elders, teachers are given higher status despite the lack of a high salary.

Source: Katie Pisa (5 October 2017) in *CNN International Edition* https://edition. cnn.com/2017/10/04/health/teacher-pay-and-status/index.html

Punctuality

Punctuality is strictly enforced in the Confucian Orbit with negative consequences for lateness, sending out a clear signal that lateness is not acceptable; it is viewed as disrespectful to the teacher and to education in principal, not least also to fellow students since the class is interrupted by 'latecomers'. This contrasts to the Anglo-Saxon part and Western Europe where punctuality is less of a 'big deal'—students of course are encouraged to be on time, but there are much less severe consequences for lateness in contrast to East Asia, if at all (often a 'late slip' from the school office will be the only action triggered, but students are indifferent to such 'consequences'). As an example of the importance of punctuality, Japan's Central Railway Company website promotes the timeliness of its *Shinkansen* (i.e. bullet trains), highlighting an annual average delay of 0.9 minutes per operational train—a statistic that also includes both human error and delays due to uncontrollable factors such as natural disasters! As the spotlight demonstrates, punctuality is so deeply ingrained in the Japanese culture starting from the home, to school, and spilling into the workforce and society at large.

Spotlight

Why Is Japan so Obsessed With Punctuality?

There was an 'incident' this week on a Japanese train. It was described by a rail company spokesperson as 'truly inexcusable', prompted a flurry of high-level apologies and staff are now being trained to prevent it from happening again.

The misdemeanor in question? The train departed from a station 25 seconds ahead of schedule.

The very notion of an 'early' train—as opposed to an eternally delayed one (never mind the fact it is worthy of an apology)—is no doubt an alien concept for UK's long-suffering National Rail season ticket holders.

Yet the incident casts a sharp light on one of the most famed preoccupations of Japanese society—its longstanding obsession with punctuality, right down to the second.

Japan is renowned as a nation steeped in its own unique rituals, quirks and customs—from the two-handed-bowing-head manouevre while exchanging business cards and the strict rules that govern where you can wear shoes or how to have a bath, to passengers not being allowed to open or close taxi doors (because that's the driver's job).

But one particularly baffling element of Japanese life is society's meticulous and painstaking attention to punctuality—as embodied by the nation's entire transport system, which is so punctual you can normally tell the time by its arrivals and departures.

Late trains are so unusual in Japan that when schedules are on rare occasions delayed, there is normally an immediate assumption that there has either been an earthquake or a suicide on the tracks.

Not to forget the fact that rail officials then diligently hand out apologetic 'late notes' to delayed commuters, so they can give them to their bosses to explain their tardiness. . . .

But it seems that early trains are equally worthy of an apology. The recent 'early' train scandal unfolded when a 7.12am train at Notogawa Station in central Japan departed at 7.11am and 35 seconds.

A very serious sounding internal investigation by West Japan Railway Company concluded that the train conductor had misunderstood the departure time and closed the doors prematurely. While the incident had no impact on other travel schedules, one passenger complained after missing the train.

Perhaps even more surprising is the fact that this was not an isolated incident: last autumn, another rail company in Japan publicly apologised after a train left a station 20 seconds early.

It is difficult to overestimate the importance of punctuality in Japanese society—a quality that perfectly complements a raft of other national characteristics such as 'hard-working', 'disciplined' and 'respectfully orderly'.

Japanese children are drilled in the utmost importance of punctuality from a young age at school, while many office workers will arrive at work extra early on a daily basis in order to avoid potential tardiness.

Punctuality is perhaps also one key reason why Tokyo—despite its megalopolis dimensions and status as one of the most densely packed cities on the planet—somehow manages to maintain an impressive sense of order and functions so smoothly.

Punctuality is certainly something that I had hoped would rub off on me when I relocated from London to Tokyo over ten years ago—yet I confess my ability to consistently arrive on time remains a work in progress (although, just like a train, I do now find myself emailing an instant apology if I'm running even seconds behind schedule).

But I do, however, live in hope—as does my patient (and punctual) Japanese husband who not only bought me a watch for my birthday, but set it four minutes fast, in an unsubtle attempt to bring my relaxed Western relationship with time in line with fellow Tokyoites.

Source: Danielle Demetriou, Telegraph UK (16 May 2018) www.telegraph.co.uk/travel/destinations/asia/japan/articles/why-japan-so-obsessed-with-punctuality/

Uniform and Dress Code

The Confucian Orbit as well as large parts of the Anglo-Saxon world (namely Australia, Ireland, UK, and New Zealand) have formal uniforms for students to wear at school, including the journey to/from where students are encouraged to uphold standards since they represent their school in public. Uniforms are often a sense of pride and contribute to a sense of belonging to the school community. Not least do uniforms contribute to equality, and make life easier for students and parents, plus they are inexpensive in comparison to fashion clothes. Research has also shown that school uniforms contribute to better school discipline (Murray, 1997). However, the level of enforcement of uniform and dress standards varies around the globe quite markedly. In Hong Kong, Japan, Korea, Singapore, and Taiwan, correct wearing of the uniform is strictly enforced with consequences for sloppy appearance (i.e. uniform, hair style), whereas in other parts of the world, such as North America, dress standards are more relaxed ('jeans and t-shirt OK'), or in Western Europe, there is no uniform at all, with little or no dress standards enforced (Figure 3.4).

Uniforms in East Asia and also in Australia, UK, Ireland, and New Zealand are often neat and proper, sending out a positive signal to students about the value of education, and often students wear them with pride. We do not argue that the adoption of school uniforms improves academic performance directly, but instead by improving the behaviour of students and their overall conduct. This is because the adoption of school uniform has three clear benefits from a disciplinary perspective:

1. Uniforms establish a clear standard and expectation for students in terms of their presentation;
2. Uniforms signal that the student represents a school, which would entail more responsibility in maintaining its image or reputation; and
3. Uniforms eliminate a great deal of time wasted for administration (and students) regarding what is considered appropriate attire. In fact, we hear far too often news stories from the USA where students are being pulled out of class, handed detentions, or being sent home for 'inappropriate clothing' (ripped jeans, shorts considered too short, etc.), all of time and effort which could be better spent on more pressing issues, such as how to improve students' academic performance.

The adoption of school uniforms has been found to improve student attendance (Evans, Michael and Muthoni, 2008), as well as increase teacher retention (Gentile and Imberman, 2012). From an economic perspective, they also reduce the pressure to dress well, especially for students of lower socioeconomic background. And from an efficiency perspective, the implementation of uniforms makes the process of dressing for school faster (Alspach, 2007). Therefore school uniforms have clear advantages, which also include establishing a sense of 'equality' among student peers, where no one can be judged on their attire, or conclusions drawn on their socioeconomic background because of what they do or do not have. Uniforms remove the competitive nature of appearances. The adoption of school uniform has also been found to have a positive effect on the school's climate and discipline (Murray, 1997), and be positively correlated with academic achievement (Bodine, 2003).

School uniforms not only establish equality at school, but they also serve to differentiate students on factors including seniority (i.e. different types of uniforms for juniors and seniors), distinction of merit (i.e. sport captain or club president), and leadership (i.e. school captaincy, student representative councils). Therefore, how students present themselves wearing uniforms allows them to signal both pride and achievement in what they represent, but also what they have achieved. An objective of schooling is to prepare students for the workforce, and to become good citizens in society, where the notion of 'dressing for success' is firmly ingrained through uniforms, establishing good habits for their future selves (Gentile and Imberman, 2012). In Figure 3.4 we compare some of the uniforms from East Asian countries with those in the West—where

Figure 3.4 School Uniforms in Confucian Orbit Vis-à-Vis Western Schools

Photo description from top to bottom:

1. Korean pupils waiting for class to begin.
2. Japanese high school students between classes.
3. North America: this student got into disciplinary trouble for wearing these jeans. In the Australian school system, for example, she would be wearing a school uniform tunic or skirt and shirt/blouse, avoiding all trouble and discussion whether jeans of this nature would be acceptable or not for school.

Photo credits (top to bottom): Michael Prewett, Jacob Plumb, Rogério Martins.

uniforms in the latter are often non-existent (with the exception of some private and religious schools).

Academic Performance and Homework

Perhaps the largest divergence on the understanding of discipline is how academic performance is viewed and treated—is it treated as part of discipline as in the Confucian Orbit, or not (as in the West and most other parts of the world). Based on the Confucian philosophy of human betterment and self-cultivation (Tan, 2017), the education approach in East Asia is that students generally should be able to achieve/learn what is expected of them, at least during school years where the material is not yet at the tertiary level that could be out of reach to some. Failure to perform is therefore viewed as a discipline issue, i.e. a poor test result is viewed as the outcome of a lack of trying, or not trying hard enough; insufficient study time has been allocated to sufficiently prepare for an exam or an assignment. This triggers educators to discipline students for poor performance in the Confucian Orbit, with often better results subsequently since students did 'get' the signal that their performance was disappointing and they need to try and study harder.

One controversial method (in the West, anyway) is the public display of students' results on assessments, examinations, and behaviour evaluation, and the 'jury' may well still be out on this issue—there are, of course, encouraging and discouraging effects of public display of this nature. It could have motivating effects for students with potential of betterment that just need a 'wake-up call' that they have to aspire more; it could motivate students in the mid-performance segment to reach for higher goals; and of course it could encourage simply lazy students since they have on display that their efforts are non-sufficient. It would also be helpful for students to see what actually is possible—e.g. if a student obtained 75 percent for their paper and 'thinks' that's already very good, they can then see the *relativity* of their performance if many other students received a score of 85 percent or above. Good, or bad, is always relative. On the flip side, public display could also discourage simply weak students with little/no potential for growth, e.g. students with limited academic talent in general, or for a specific subject (i.e. even if they tried harder/spent more time studying, they simply can't improve their performance). In this particular case, constant reminders of one's limitations could be demotivating. Singapore, for example, decided to abolish rankings for primary and secondary students as of 2019 in school reports:

> Whether a child finishes first or last will no longer be indicated in primary and secondary school report books from next year—a move

which Education Minister Ong Ye Kung hopes will show students that "learning is not a competition".

Report books will not just stop showing a student's position in relation to class or cohort. The information to be dropped includes:

- Class and level mean
- Minimum and maximum marks
- Underlining and/or colouring of failing marks
- Pass/fail for end-of-year result
- Mean subject grades
- Overall total marks
- L1R5 (English plus five relevant subjects), L1R4, EMB3 (English, maths, best three subjects) and EMB1 for lower secondary levels

The Ministry of Education (MOE) said on Friday (Sept 28) that the change is to allow each student to focus on his or her learning progress and discourage them from being overly concerned about comparisons.

(www.straitstimes.com/singapore/education/learning-is-not-a-competition-no-more-1st–2nd-or-last-in-class-for-primary-and)

Singapore is a peak PISA performer and also ranks high in terms of global competitiveness according to the WEF. What effects these changes will have remains to be seen. Looking to Japan, reflecting on the—now abolished—Japanese *Yutori* education approach, a softening of the approach to education, does not always result in favourable outcomes. In Japan, the *Yutori* education policy reduced hours at school, reduced curriculum content at the primary school level, but also resulted in a decline of scholastic ability and reduced work ethic. Subsequently, Japan has now abolished the *Yutori* approach (see Chapter 5 for a more detailed discussion), and it remains to be seen how Singapore's changing approach will impact PISA results and—longer term—WEF competitiveness.

Regardless, this important view of performance being a discipline issue is not least a contributing factor in the strong performance of the Confucian Orbit. This is in stark contrast to the West where performance is not viewed as a discipline issue, namely in the Anglo-Saxon part of the world nor in Europe. Failure is much more acceptable and there are few negative consequences. In fact, failure is even 'celebrated' in some Western schools, sending out a questionable signal to students. In fact, the relationship is reverse to the Confucian Orbit. While in the latter poor performance is not rewarded (but instead disciplined), in the West, often poor performing students get more attention from teaching staff, with generously funded support programmes that are often poorly attended (there are cases were students have to be 'lured' to school with free food). This sends out the signal to students that it is OK to fail, and there would not be negative, but rather positive outcomes (i.e. more attention, more support, more 'pampering'). This divergence does not least demonstrate the equally diverging value and standing of education—in East Asia, there is a view that education is a helpful tool to later succeed in life, whereas in the West, where additional support is free and plenty, the offer is not 'picked up' (again, there are sometimes incentive programmes for students to attend these programs—an approach unthinkable under Confucianism: the reward for education is betterment and a bright future).

PISA Dimensions Under the Microscope

Having established the link that higher discipline in the classroom is associated with higher academic performance, and considering the mechanisms under which this occurs, we next turn our attention to comparing the six geographic clusters on a number of other PISA dimensions. We seek to examine whether any other major differences emerge, which could in turn provide a more holistic picture for the Confucian Orbit's high performance.

Student Truancy

There is good evidence in the literature that absenteeism non-surprisingly associates with lower performance (Oluremi, 2013; Miller and Plant, 1999; Finn, 1989). If a student is not in class, or missed part of the lesson, then how can they learn? Our analysis in the previous chapter also provided clear support of this notion since we too found—in our multivariate analyses presented in Chapter 2—that higher absenteeism links with poor academic performance.

For the purpose of this chapter (our bivariate analysis) we analysed PISA data on:

1. Skipping class;
2. Arriving late for school.

For both tests (Table 3.3) we found the Confucian Orbit to have the lowest levels of absenteeism. In fact, for skipping some classes, the Confucian Orbit was the only geographic cluster with low levels of absenteeism (i.e. nearly none), contrasting the other five clusters with one or two times absent during the last two full weeks of school on average. Keeping in mind that the Confucian Orbit is also the peak performing cluster on all three PISA academic performance dimensions (math, reading, and science), it appears reasonable and logical to assume there to be at least some kind of link between truancy and performance. For punctuality, we see an even bigger difference between the Confucian

Table 3.3 Student Truancy

PANEL A: *Skipped Some Classes*

Code	Statement(s)
ST062Q02TA	In the last two full weeks of school, how often: I <skipped> some classes.

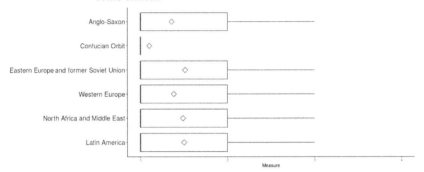

Higher points indicate more classes skipped; lower points indicate fewer classes skipped.

Four-point scale: *None, one or two times, three or four times,* or *five or more times.*

PANEL B: *Arrived Late for School*

Code	Statement(s)
ST062Q03TA	In the last two full weeks of school, how often: I arrived late for school.

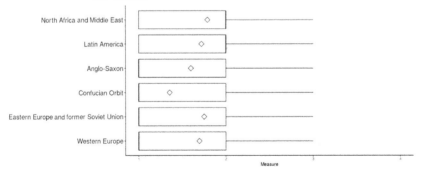

Higher points indicate being late for school on more occasions; lower points indicate fewer occasions being late for school.

Four-point scale: *None, one or two times, three or four times,* or *five or more times.*

Orbit with close to no lateness when arriving for school, to one or two times being late for school on average in the other geographic clusters. The highest level of arriving late for school is reported in North Africa and the Middle East, followed by Latin America and Eastern Europe and the former Soviet Union, followed by Western Europe and then the Anglo-Saxon world.

In East Asia, there are quite severe consequences for arriving late for school or class, let alone for skipping class. Punctuality is important under Confucianism and students being late for class not seldom face some form of punishment, a message sent out that students ought to be on time. While this is a prerequisite for solid learning, and also polite not to disturb the class by arriving late, this is also good preparation for future tertiary education and a professional career, and, as we found in our analysis in Chapter 2, also contributes to better academic performance.

Student Learning Time

Research indicates that the amount of time students spent on learning, both inside and outside of school instructional hours, can have a direct effect on levels of academic achievement (Jez and Wassmer, 2015). This is perhaps not a surprise, but the question we want to explore in our research is again what the differences would be around the globe—do some students really study more (in terms of study hours) in and out of the classroom?

The media has picked up on this topic with reports of students in Asia often studying long hours, far beyond what is common in the West (see, e.g. Weale, 2014). Academic research does indeed reveal longer study time in East Asia in contrast to Western nations (see Baumann, Hamin and Yang, 2016). But the correlation between study time and 'success' may not necessarily be of a linear nature (i.e. the more one studies, the more one succeeds). Other issues come into play, such as of course individual learning differences (some students are simply fast, others not), passion and talent for a topic (some students love math, others less so), what else is 'going on in life' (family and personal situation of a student), and of course also health (including mental health) and happiness. One issue perhaps overlooked both in public discussion and also in the scholarly literature may well be the key topic of our study: discipline. Could it be that better discipline leads to more effective use of class time and thus contribute to better learning?

Our analysis points exactly in the direction outlined above since the total learning time (Table 3.4, Panel A) varies to some degree globally, but it's not necessarily the case that the academic peak performers also study the longest hours—it does seem to depend on how *disciplined* those study hours are spent. The Confucian Orbit has long study hours, but so does North Africa, the Middle East, and Latin America. However,

Table 3.4 Student Learning Time

PANEL A: Total Learning Time (TMINS)	
Code	Statement(s)
ST060, ST061	Learning time in total (TMINS) was computed using information about the average minutes in a <class period> (ST061) in relation to information about the number of class periods per week attended in total (ST060).

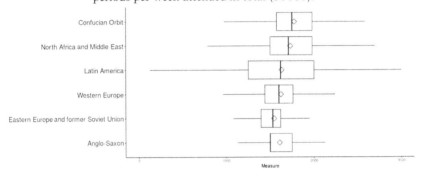

Learning time (minutes per week)—in total.

PANEL B: Out-of-School Study Time (OUTHOURS)	
Code	Statement(s)
ST071	Students were asked in a slider-format question how much time they spent studying in addition to their required school schedule. The index OUTHOURS was computed by summing the time spent studying for different school subjects.

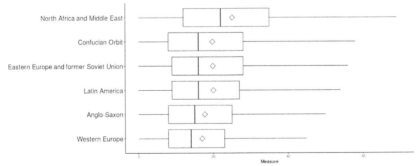

Out-of-school study time (hours per week)—in total.

while the former two have the longest study hours, that did not result in equally high academic performance as we have found for the Confucian Orbit with the highest output (or performance). This finding is further supported by the median, globally being more or less fairly similar (so also for Western Europe and Anglo-Saxon countries), but again with varying academic performance.

Students in PISA testing also indicated how much time they spend studying out of the classroom (Table 3.4, Panel B), and that analysis revealed a perhaps surprising finding: on average, students around the globe study about the same amount of time out of the classroom, and that amount appears detached from academic performance. Surprisingly, students in North Africa and the Middle East indicate the highest out-of-school study time, yet their performance was previously found to be in the bottom category (Table 3.1).

What appears to make the difference in terms of how out-of-school study time is spent and academic performance is the guidance, i.e. whether this study time is spent in a disciplined environment. Students in East Asia often attend classes at tutoring services (*hagwon* in Korea, *juku* in Japan, and *buxiban* in Taiwan). Parents personally fund these tutoring services, and often select such based on the ones that are strictest, i.e. check that students did complete their homework, participate in class and engage with the material. In fact, often parents in the Confucian Orbit instruct their tutoring services instructors not to be lenient with their children to optimise learning. This appears to contribute to the peak academic performance in the East Asian cluster since, as demonstrated here, the study time is not substantially higher than in other parts of the world, but that time is spent in a more structured, more guided, and more disciplined environment. These efforts by parents to support their children with their learning is not detached from the Confucian culture that inspires parents to have their children grow and become better human beings.

Student Self-Efficacy

Students' level of perceived self-efficacy in a particular subject matter has been demonstrated to affect a student's academic grades (Jung, Zhou and Lee, 2017). If a student believes they have efficacy, they believe they have the capability of producing a desired or intended result (Bandura, 1997), which in the context of schooling, translates to the student's personal judgement of "I am capable of doing/ understanding this".

This is related to how much emphasis students place on the belief that *effort* or innate *ability* drives performance and their overall ability to succeed academically (Zimmerman, 2000). As we have discussed in the previous chapter, students within the Confucian Orbit tend to emphasise effort as largely contributing to their success at school (or a lack of effort to their failures), whereas students from the West (Anglo-Saxon and Western Europe) tend to view this as linked to innate ability or luck (Kim and Park, 2006). With divergent views related to beliefs about 'modes of input' and outcomes between Eastern and Western students, we might expect to find that degrees of self-efficacy might also be different.

The PISA data presents a negligible difference between students from the six geographical clusters (Table 3.5). In other words, all students view themselves as equally capable of performing the (science-related) tasks at hand. Yet students from the Confucian Orbit substantially outperform

Table 3.5 Student Self-Efficacy

PANEL A: Perceived Self-Efficacy in Science (SCIEEFF)	
Code	Statement(s)

How easy do you think it would be for you to perform the following tasks on your own?

ST129Q01TA	Recognise the science question that underlies a newspaper report on a health issue.
ST129Q02TA	Explain why earthquakes occur more frequently in some areas than others.
ST129Q03TA	Describe the role of antibiotics in the treatment of disease.
ST129Q04TA	Identify the science question associated with the disposal of garbage.
ST129Q05TA	Predict how changes to an environment will affect the survival of certain species.
ST129Q06TA	Interpret the scientific information provided on the labelling of food items.
ST129Q07TA	Discuss how new evidence can lead you to change your understanding about the possibility of life on Mars.
ST129Q08TA	Identify the better of two explanations for the formation of acid rain.

Higher points indicate stronger perceived ability to complete the task; lower points indicate weaker perceived ability.

Four-point scale: *Strongly disagree, disagree, agree,* or *strongly agree.*

their peers in science (as well as math and reading), which leads to two possible conclusions.

These results highlight that having a belief that one can complete a task successfully or competently is very different to the level of work and commitment required to succeed at it. In other words, just because 'I think I can do it' does not mean it goes without effort. Fundamentally, this could reflect the difference between students in East Asia with the rest of the world where the latter place prominence on continuous learning (or a view that 'one is never done learning' or more can be done), vis-à-vis a Western perspective where one just needs to apply themselves enough to 'get the job done'. This has implications for the approach to learning that underlies students' educational experience: when students feel they 'know it all', they would perhaps be more complacent and self-assured in their ability, thus not feeling the need to improve their performance. On the contrary, when students hold the view that there is always more to learn, always more improvements to be made, we should not be surprised when their performance are leaps and bounds ahead of the rest—as we see with the Confucian Orbit.

The levelling of self-efficacy scores between clusters might also be a reflection of cultural effects on modesty. In East Asia, students tend to downplay their achievements or appraisal of performance whereas students in the West have been known to display more confidence (Farh, Dobbins and Cheng, 1991).

Student Motivation

Without any form of motivation, i.e. having *reasons* for acting or behaving in a certain manner, it would be almost impossible for individuals to meaningfully work towards a goal, or even care about their performance (Steinmayr and Spinath, 2009). In the context of education, these 'reasons' for learning can be intrinsic (i.e. interest in the subject) or extrinsic (i.e. reward and punishment) and influenced by many different factors (Deci, Koestner and Ryan, 2001). Academic performance is in itself an outcome of students' learning objectives, and given the substantial differences between clusters on performance measures, we might expect to see that students' levels of motivations—both intrinsic and extrinsic—might be different across geographic clusters.

PISA tested students on their level of instrumental (extrinsic) motivation, which represents the extent to which they are 'driven' by the utilitarian value of their education, such as assisting in their future career. Or in other words, "I work hard at this subject because it will be useful for some tangible outcome later". In comparing the data in Table 3.6, we find that the difference between clusters is in fact minimal.

Testing of students' achievement (intrinsic) motivation was also used as a gauge of competitive spirit at the individual level, focussing on 'intangible'

Table 3.6 Student Motivation

Code	Statement(s)
ST113Q01TA	Making an effort in my <school science> subject(s) is worth it because this will help me in the work I want to do later on. (R)
ST113Q02TA	What I learn in my <school science> subject(s) is important for me because I need this for what I want to do later on. (R)
ST113Q03TA	Studying my <school science> subject(s) is worthwhile for me because what I learn will improve my career prospects. (R)
ST113Q04TA	Many things that I learn in my <school science> subject(s) will help me to get a job. (R)

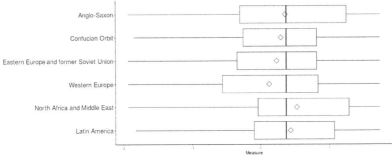

Higher points indicate stronger instrumental motivation; lower points indicate weaker instrumental motivation.

Four-point scale: *Strongly agree, agree, disagree,* or *strongly disagree.*

(R) = reverse coded

PANEL B: *Achievement Motivation (MOTIVAT)*

Code	Statement(s)
ST119Q01NA	I want top <grades> in most or all of my courses.
ST119Q02NA	I want to be able to select from among the best opportunities available when I graduate.
ST119Q03NA	I want to be the best, whatever I do.
ST119Q04NA	I see myself as an ambitious person.
ST119Q05NA	I want to be one of the best students in my class.

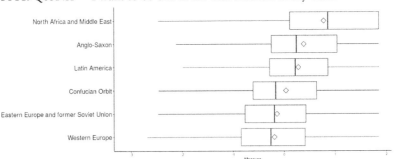

Higher points indicate stronger achievement motivation; lower points indicate weaker achievement motivation.

Four-point scale: *Strongly disagree, disagree, agree,* or *strongly agree.*

rewards most aligned with self-actualisation and -esteem (e.g. 'I want to be one of the best students in my class'). When comparing the six clusters on this dimension, we can arrange them at three levels: North Africa and the Middle East as showing the highest level of achievement motivation; Anglo-Saxon and Latin America as second; followed by Confucian Orbit, Eastern Europe, and the former Soviet Union, and Western Europe last.

Students' motivational goals, as well as their intensity, are often the product of their cultural upbringing and socialisation (King and McInerney, 2014; McInerney, Roche, McInerney and Marsh, 1997), and have been found to be comprised of behavioural, affective, and cognitive components (Dowson and McInerney, 2003). As we discussed in Chapter 2, students within the Confucian Orbit are highly motivated to excel academically as a result of the encouragement they receive from their parents, teachers, peers, as well as the expectations they place upon themselves. Keeping in mind that this cluster also outperforms the rest on all performance dimensions, there is evidently something else at play in supporting and transforming this motivation into high performance.

We argue that it is the structured environment of a strong classroom discipline that allows students within the Confucian Orbit to effectively act on their motivation to succeed. Baumann and Harvey (2018) found that *both* intrinsic and extrinsic motivations are significantly associated with academic performance, and we build on this by arguing that both internal (i.e. motivation) and external (i.e. discipline) factors, combined, drive performance. To illustrate, imagine academic performance as a 'vehicle' travelling on a journey from point A to point B; students' level of motivation to perform and succeed is internalised and acts as a driving force (i.e. the 'fuel'), but the way the classroom is organised and run (i.e. the 'engine') is ultimately what keeps everything running at optimal performance. Without a fine-tuned engine, the entire system underperforms.

Therefore, motivation is only one part of the equation to succeed, and students also require the guidance and discipline from teachers to realise and act on this potential (Doménech-Betoret, Abellán-Roselló and Gómez-Artiga, 2017; Ning and Downing, 2010). In fact we would not be surprised if the Confucian Orbit were to score highly on a measure of achievement pressure, another form of external motivation, which was initially included in the 2000 PISA wave, but subsequently—regrettably—removed. This dimension measured:

- The teacher wants students to work hard;
- The teacher tells students they can do better;
- The teacher does not like it when the students deliver careless work; and
- Students have a lot to learn.

In our argument, discipline is something enforced as an 'external pressure' as well as being internally driven. Thus the teachers' expectations for a student to achieve (and of course, how seriously students take those expectations) might be an important force in pushing students' performance that one step higher. While we do not have the evidence in this wave of PISA data, its (re)inclusion in future studies should be considered.

We also see a somewhat inverse pattern on student motivation and disciplinary climates, most evident for North Africa and the Middle East, and Confucian Orbit. Where students from North Africa and the Middle East reported to be highly motivated, they were less disciplined and performed worst academically on all three PISA dimensions (science, reading, math). For the Confucian Orbit, who were moderate in their motivational scores, they demonstrated strong discipline and consistently stronger performance overall. This offers some evidence toward our thinking about the additive effect (if not multiplying) of motivation *and* discipline as drivers of performance at the individual level, or as Baumann and Harvey (2018) put it: effective learning requires the 'carrot and the stick'.

Student Well-Being

For a long time, the mainstream Western media has been critical of the East Asian approach to education. They often describe the 'detrimental consequences' that strict disciplinary approaches and performance pressure places on the students' well-being (Yang, 2015), with little attention that in fact mental health issues have become quite severe in Western education (Harvey et al., 2017). The PISA dimensions we have included for student well-being include students' (1) sense of belonging at school and (2) test anxiety. Both measures capture the impact of the school environment and activities on the student's level of 'emotional welfare'; and we also suggest that, when taken together, these dimensions are indicative of how students feel about their experience in formal schooling overall. In other words, we can get a sense for how students perceive their learning environment by how integrated they feel at school (i.e. belonging) and the pressures they endure (i.e. anxiety).

In fact, much of the conversation surrounding the East Asian approach to education has lamented that although students outperform the rest, it *must be* because they are miserable at school and constantly feel the pressure to perform (Stankov, 2010), with some research findings pointing to higher scores on anxiety and lower scores on self-concept of Asian students (Lee, 2009; Wilkins, 2004). On the contrary, and as the PISA testing highlights, students within the Confucian Orbit are no different than students from any cluster in either their sense of belonging at school or test anxiety (Table 3.7).

Table 3.7 Student Well-Being

PANEL A: Sense of Belonging to School (BELONG)	

Code	Statement(s)
ST034Q01TA	I feel like an outsider (or left out of things) at school.
ST034Q02TA	I make friends easily at school. (R)
ST034Q03TA	I feel like I belong at school. (R)
ST034Q04TA	I feel awkward and out of place in my school.
ST034Q05TA	Other students seem to like me. (R)
ST034Q06TA	I feel lonely at school.

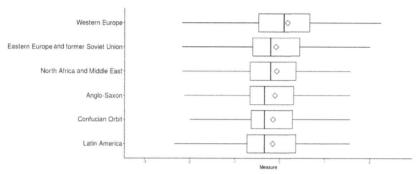

Higher points indicate a stronger sense of belonging; lower points indicate a weaker sense of belonging to school.

Four-point scale: *Strongly agree, agree, disagree,* or *strongly disagree.*

(R) = reverse coded

PANEL B: Test Anxiety (ANXTEST)	

Code	Statement(s)
ST118Q01NA	I often worry that it will be difficult for me taking a test.
ST118Q02NA	I worry that I will get poor <grades> at school.
ST118Q03NA	Even if I am well prepared for a test I feel very anxious.
ST118Q04NA	I get very tense when I study for a test.
ST118Q05NA	I get nervous when I don't know how to solve a task at school.

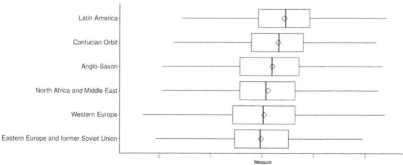

Higher points indicate more test anxiety; lower points indicate less test anxiety.

Four-point scale: *Strongly disagree, disagree, agree,* or *strongly agree.*

Academic studies have established the relationship between a sense of belonging at school and academic motivation (Goodenow and Grady, 1993), and performance (Pittman and Richmond, 2007). Yet as our analysis indicates, there is a substantial gap in academic performance (math, science, and reading scores) between Confucian Orbit and the other clusters, despite students around the world essentially experiencing the same level of well-being at school. What would explain this? The strong disciplinary climate would be one likely candidate, and we add to this that classrooms in East Asia are indeed more 'intensive' and students are under more 'pressure' to perform, but that there are two key reasons that students feel as much at ease as their international peers:

- A more structured and more disciplined classroom environment results in fewer distractions, and therefore more student engagement and focus (Way, 2011). In this sense, students are less likely to fall behind and feel 'out of depth', resulting in more preparedness for examinations.
- There is a great deal of peer support between students, both in terms of the normative pressures to succeed as well as the desire to uplift all students. Despite the Asian classroom fostering a highly competitive environment (i.e. examination success), there is also a value for and enjoyment of co-operation among peers (e.g. Table 3.8, Panel B), that might contribute to an overall more enriching experience. Confucian teachers are, while more strict in general than Western educators, also caring and nurturing, often focussing on a holistic 'picture' of a student.

Student Outlook on Education

In our analysis, two PISA dimensions are used to examine students' outlook on education. The first, epistemological beliefs, refers to the subjective theories about the boundaries and structure of knowledge, and about the nature of *how* knowledge is acquired itself (Trautwein and Lüdtke, 2007). The second, value of co-operation, examines the extent that teamwork is a valued component of student learning style. Together, both dimensions provide a snapshot of the prevailing conditions in schools as they relate to students' information processing strategies, which are shown to have implications for task performance and academic achievement, albeit in varied ways (Ho, 1994; Lodewyk, 2007; Rodriguez and Cano, 2007).

Substantial differences in the way students approach education are often attributed to underlying cultural differences. Notably, the contrast between individualistic and collectivistic cultures have been applied to Western and Eastern societies, respectively, where the former expresses values of independent learning and achievement, and the latter emphasises group-oriented goals (Tweed and Lehman, 2002). While, of course, these classifications are somewhat simplistic, they are nonetheless perhaps how students—more or less—'tick' in the respective clusters.

Students' evaluation of their epistemological beliefs focussed on the importance of critically evaluating information, subjecting knowledge to rigorous tests, and generally accepting that learning is a fluid process. Contrary to the popular discourse that Asian learning is sometimes characterised as 'shallow learning' or defined by 'rote memorisation' (Tan, 2015), our Inter-Ocular Test (IOT) demonstrates that students in the Confucian Orbit do not perceive the critical assessment of knowledge much differently to their peers in the West (i.e. Anglo-Saxon and Western Europe). In addition, as already established, the strong results in science, math, and reading of Confucian Orbit students do not provide any evidence that their understanding of subject matters would indeed be 'shallow' or a result of 'rote learning'. In fact, while the spread in data varies slightly between clusters, the averages are almost identical across the board, and interestingly, the majority of students in the Confucian Orbit and Anglo-Saxon clusters hold stronger epistemological beliefs than the average student from other clusters. A study by Cano (2005) led to two major conclusions that directly apply here: first, students' epistemological beliefs and learning approaches evolve over time, and second, they significantly predict academic achievement.

While the mean for the Confucian Orbit and North Africa and the Middle East are very slightly ahead of the rest (median is identical across the board), this might be attributed to the collectivist nature of their respective cultures. Further, since the value of co-operation, working in teams, or learning in teams is essentially no different to other clusters, the 'issue' of whole class instruction and *chalk and talk* approaches do not appear to have any negative implications for students' beliefs about knowledge (Stevenson and Lee, 1994). Nor does it produce an environment of competition that cannot function through co-operation. This is reflected in Confucianism's emphases on self-betterment *and* relationalism, which cultivates a spirit of taking charge to perform better in the classroom, but also uplifting those around you, simultaneously. Ultimately, with no real identifiable differences between clusters in terms of students' 'processes' for learning, we reiterate that enforcing discipline, and having discipline, within the Confucian Orbit undergirds the strong performance of East Asia.

Spotlight

US Teacher's Open Letter: "Bizarrely Lenient Attitude Toward Disciplining Children"

[A] teacher from South Carolina, said she feels 'exhausted', 'frustrated' and 'ill-supported' by her job and the perils of trying to communicate to parents about their troubled children.

"Not all of you are going to agree with what I've written. Some of you will be downright mad after you read it. As with anything, this doesn't apply to every parent out there. I do have those of you that support me and work with me—you know who you are and you know how immensely grateful I am for you", she clarified before she began. . . .

"Lately, it seems that many parents have adopted a bizarrely lenient attitude toward disciplining children as well as bending over backwards to accommodate their children's every demand. It's unclear what's causing these parents to believe that children should be subject to no limits, no discipline, and no stringent requirements at school. Whatever the cause, these parents are, in fact, doing a terrible disservice to today's young people and to society as a whole. And, they are leaving their children's teachers feeling frustrated, ill-supported, and utterly exhausted".

Ms Axson made note of the 'sky-rocketing' rate 'good teachers' are leaving the profession as proof that things can't continue as they are going.

"If things continue at this pace, no one will be willing to go into teaching at all. The average new teacher these days is lasting a whopping four years before calling it quits. Those seasoned teachers that have witnessed this strange, cultural shift firsthand are dropping like flies, realising they don't have the energy to fight this uphill battle. But, perhaps the saddest thing is that these schools are turning out children who are ill-suited to being constructive, productive members of our society".

"Kids need to learn essential values such as empathy, responsibility, hard work and self-discipline. They must be taught conscientiousness, resilience and integrity. When parents refuse to set limits, give kids consequences, or have appropriate expectations of academic and social performance, students are deprived of the skills and attitudes necessary for their future success. We are essentially robbing them of the greatest gift we can give them".

Ms Axson, a mother-of-three herself, went on to say there are ways to fix the problem and 'clean up the mess we've made', suggesting a handful of ways parents can make a teacher's life easier.

"If we come to you with a problem or write your child up for disrespectful behaviour, don't automatically fight it".

"These kids get into my heart in a way I can't explain to you. I just ask—beg of you—to trust me, support me, and work with me, not against me", she wrote.

"Please quit with all the excuses. If you really want to help your children be successful, stop making excuses for them".

"It's OK for your child to get in trouble sometimes. It builds character and teaches life lessons".

Ms Axson finished her letter—which has since been shared over 4,000 times—by promising parents if they 'let' her, she will give their child 'the best education humanly possible'.

"You and I, together, could be quite the force to be reckoned with, don't you think?"

Source: www.mamamia.com.au/teacher-open-letter-parents-discipline/

Table 3.8 Student Outlook on Education

PANEL A: Epistemological Beliefs (EPIST)

Code	Statement(s)
ST131Q01NA	A good way to know if something is true is to do an experiment.
ST131Q02NA	Ideas in <broad science> sometimes change.
ST131Q03NA	Good answers are based on evidence from many different experiments.
ST131Q04NA	It is good to try experiments more than once to make sure of your findings.
ST131Q05NA	Sometimes <broad science> scientists change their minds about what is true in science.
ST131Q06NA	The ideas in <broad science> science books sometimes change.

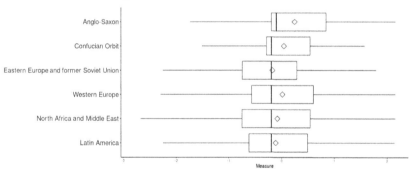

Higher points indicate broader epistemological beliefs; lower points indicate narrower epistemological beliefs.

Four-point scale: *Strongly disagree, disagree, agree,* or *strongly agree.*

PANEL B: Value of Co-operation (CPSVALUE)

Code	Statement(s)
ST082Q01NA	I prefer working as part of a team to working alone.
ST082Q09NA	I find that teams make better decisions than individuals.

(Continued)

Table 3.8 (Continued)

PANEL B: *Value of Co-operation (CPSVALUE)*

Code	Statement(s)
ST082Q13NA	I find that teamwork raises my own efficiency.
ST082Q14NA	I enjoy co-operating with peers.

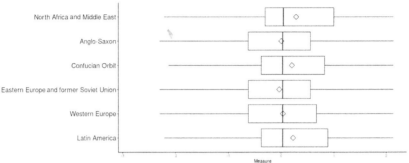

Higher points indicate stronger value for co-operation; lower points indicate weaker value for co-operation.

Four-point scale: *Strongly agree*, *agree*, *disagree*, or *strongly agree*.

Teacher Performance

Teacher performance has been identified in the literature as a key component explaining students' academic performance (Croninger, Rice, Rathbun and Nishio, 2007; Hanushek, 2011). Naturally, this comes as no surprise, notwithstanding there would be a range of definitions and measurement certainly also being challenging, if not controversial: what constitutes 'good' teacher performance, and under which paradigm, or cultural understanding, is it conceptualised?

PISA measures teacher performance on three dimensions used in our research:

- Perceived Feedback;
- Adoption of Instruction;
- Teacher Support in Science Class.

The common pattern among all three dimensions is that the variation—based on these three PISA criteria—is very small, with the largest divergence being on support in science classes (Table 3.9).

Besides the small variations, it is interesting to note that the geographic clusters with the (somewhat) higher scores on feedback, adoption of instruction, and support in science classes are not the ones who also top the 'class' when it comes to academic performance. Perhaps a reasonable

Table 3.9 Teacher Performance

PANEL A: Perceived Feedback (PERFEED)

Code	Statement(s)
ST104Q01NA	The teacher tells me how I am performing in this course.
ST104Q02NA	The teacher gives me feedback on my strengths in this subject.
ST104Q03NA	The teacher tells me in which areas I can still improve.
ST104Q04NA	The teacher tells me how I can improve my performance.
ST104Q05NA	The teacher advises me on how to reach my learning goals.

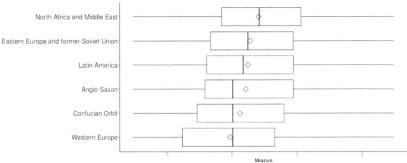

Higher points indicate more perceived feedback; lower points indicate less perceived feedback.

Four-point scale: *Never or almost never, some lessons, many lessons,* or *every lesson or almost every lesson.*

PANEL B: Adaption of Instruction (ADINST)

Code	Statement(s)
ST107Q01NA	The teacher adapts the lesson to my class's need and knowledge.
ST107Q02NA	The teacher provides individual help when a student has difficulties understanding a topic or task.
ST107Q03NA	The teacher changes the structure of the lesson on a topic that most students find difficult to understand.

Higher points indicate a stronger adaption of instruction; lower points indicate a weaker adaption of instruction.

Four-point scale: *Never or almost never, some lessons, many lessons,* or *every lesson or almost every lesson.*

(*Continued*)

Table 3.9 (Continued)

PANEL C: *Teacher Support in Science Class (TEACHSUP)*

Code	Statement(s)
ST100Q01TA	The teacher shows an interest in every student's learning.
ST100Q02TA	The teacher gives extra help when students need it.
ST100Q03TA	The teacher helps students with their learning.
ST100Q04TA	The teacher continues teaching until the students understand.
ST100Q05TA	The teacher gives students an opportunity to express opinions.

Higher points indicate stronger perception of teacher support; lower points indicate weaker perception of teacher support.

Four-point scale: *Every lesson, most lessons, some lessons,* or *never or hardly ever.*

---

explanation for the dispersion would be the disciplined and effective type of instruction in the Confucian Orbit where feedback, adoption, and support are directed at enhancing understanding and ultimately academic performance. Further, it may not necessarily just be about the amount of feedback and support received, but rather *how* it is constructively applied by the student.

It would also be reasonable to assume that humans drawn to the teaching profession would hopefully always have the idealistic aspiration to inspire and help the next generation—but again, the question is about the pedagogical approach that will achieve that goal most effectively (Rockoff, 2004). Not to mention that teachers have different motivations for entering the profession; this has its own implications for attracting the 'right candidates' and maintaining a healthy retention in the profession (Sinclair, Dowson and McInerney, 2006). Western education systems have welfare and integration programmes, but they may not always benefit the majority of learners, and there are few programmes to catalyse the most talented—it's a one-system-fits-all approach, and the problem is that not all students need the same amount of feedback, adaptation, and support. There is a need for segmentation in instruction as is often practiced in East Asia, where peak performing students receive the teacher support they need to excel and less talented students get a different type of teacher support that helps them to catch up. Segmentation of high school students based on academic performance is also not uncommon in central Europe, e.g. Germany and Switzerland.

When looking at teacher performance, perhaps two influencing factors need to also be briefly discussed: the policy environment and parents (Zhao, 2010; Cardona et al., 2009). For the former aspect, there is evidence that overprescribed curriculum and a lack of freedom for teachers in pedagogy (or in other words, no power to discipline students) in some Western societies may hinder teacher performance. For example in the UK,

> teachers' accountability is traced, along with the rise in the audit culture in teaching, and the increase in the power of Ofsted [Office for Standards in Education, Children's Services and Skills is a non-ministerial department of the UK government, reporting to Parliament].
>
> (Perryman, 2006, p. 147)

Perryman titled her paper: "Panoptic Performativity and School Inspection Regimes: Disciplinary Mechanisms and Life under Special Measures", referring to Foucault (1985) who explains 'panoptic' as an experimental laboratory where power, utilised to modify behaviour, is essentially a symbol of 'disciplinary society of surveillance'. What is interesting about Perryman's paper is that discipline, in this case, does not apply to the students, but indeed to the teachers. She outlines that inspections from Ofsted, the 'regime', result in 'panoptic performativity'. "In other words, discipline is targeted at the school and the teaching staff, but not at the students" (Baumann, Tung et al., 2012, p. 3). A "system of intensive inspection regimes" (Perryman, 2006, p. 147) are *de facto* targeted to discipline teachers, but not students. This contrasts to East Asia where teachers do not have such 'straight jackets', but instead are free to apply discipline to students where and as they see fit. Again, the latter approach is found in the geographic cluster with the highest level of academic performance, suggesting that teachers are given freedom to apply discipline, since they, and not the principal or a central inspection regime, know the students best, and can best judge what type of discipline is appropriate and effective. On the other hand, highly—perhaps even overly—regulated systems are more commonly found in the lower academic performance cluster.

Teacher performance is also impacted by parents: are they supportive of the curriculum and pedagogy, or not, and do they even care? When parents practically 'hover' over teachers, they become 'helicopter parents' (Reed,

Duncan, Lucier-Greer, Fixelle and Ferraro, 2016). Naturally, teachers want to have an open and nurturing relationship with parents, but if parents become over-involved and overprotective, then that involvement becomes counterproductive to the teaching and learning environment for students. In the Confucian Orbit, parents like to monitor progress at their children's school, but are more or less always in favour of discipline, with a clear understanding (and acceptance) that it is a necessary precursor to achieving strong academic performance (Watkins and Biggs, 2001). This is in contrast to the West where parents sometimes worry about their offspring experiencing any type of reprimand because they believe it is not the school's place to discipline their child. The spotlight below highlights this reality in the American education system, as well as a growing frustration resulting from the lack of parental support teachers currently face.

In sum, educators are likely to teach best when they are trusted by the 'system' and by parents. Having to worry about 'hovering parents', or a system which limits teachers' authority to run their classroom only undermines and restricts educators from performing their role in preparing today's children for the future. In other words, it is best to recruit teachers with high academic credentials and teaching talent, so they can be trusted by all parties to do the job right, adjusting their style to specific circumstances.

Notes

1. Taoism reflects a notion of 'oneness' and symbolises the natural way. In contrast to Confucianism which stresses self-cultivation by effort, Taoism stresses no action. Instead, "action results in much harm, but quietude results in the fulfilment of authenticity" (Lynn, 1999, p. 164). This philosophy views all life and its element in unity, but also subject to paradox as a cyclical life force that cannot be controlled. 'Life' is beyond the control of the individual, and one should accept their fate as it unfolds.
2. Legalism resembles strong bureaucracy, rule of law, and control. The moral standards of Confucianism are rejected in favour of the power of a system of rules guided by punitive elements (Ames, 1983). Legalism asserts that all humans are not naturally good, but instead born greedy (Watson, 1964), and that mechanisms must be put in place to control action. It stresses the establishment and maintenance of law and order to creating a self-governing system (Witzel, 2012).

References

Alspach, Kyle. "Measured look at uniforms: Alternative to dress code." *The Boston Globe*, 2007.

Ames, Roger T. "Is political Taoism anarchism?" *Journal of Chinese Philosophy* 10, no. 1 (1983): 27–47.

Bandura, Albert. "Social cognitive theory of self-regulation." *Organizational Behavior and Human Decision Processes* 50, no. 2 (1991): 248–287.

Bandura, Albert, and Sebastian Wessels. *Self-efficacy.* New York: W. H. Freeman & Company, 1997.

Baumann, Chris, and Marina Harvey. "Competitiveness vis-à-vis motivation and personality as drivers of academic performance: Introducing the MCP model." *International Journal of Educational Management* 32, no. 1 (2018): 185–202.

Baumann, Chris, and Hana Krskova. "School discipline, school uniforms and academic performance." *International Journal of Educational Management* 30, no. 6 (2016): 1003–1029.

Baumann, Chris, Rosalie L. Tung, and Hamin. "Jade will never become a work of art without being carved: Western versus Chinese attitudes toward discipline in education and society." *Virginia Review of Asian Studies* 10 (2012): 1–17.

Baumann, Chris, Hume Winzar, and Tony Fang. "East Asian wisdom and relativity: Inter-ocular testing of Schwartz values from WVS with extension of the ReVaMB model." *Cross Cultural & Strategic Management* 25, no. 2 (2018): 210–230.

Bechuke, A. L., and J. R. Debeila. "Applying choice theory in fostering discipline: Managing and modifying challenging learners behaviours in South African schools." *International Journal of Humanities and Social Science* 2, no. 22 (2012): 240–255.

Blank, Carmel, and Yossi Shavit. "The association between student reports of classmates' disruptive behavior and student achievement." *AERA Open* 2, no. 3 (2016): 2332858416653921.

Bodine, Ann. "School uniforms, academic achievement, and uses of research." *The Journal of Educational Research* 97, no. 2 (2003): 67–71.

Cameron, Mark. "Managing school discipline and implications for school social workers: A review of the literature." *Children & Schools* 28, no. 4 (2006): 219–227.

Cano, Francisco. "Epistemological beliefs and approaches to learning: Their change through secondary school and their influence on academic performance." *British Journal of Educational Psychology* 75, no. 2 (2005): 203–221.

Cardona, Beatriz, Megan Watkins, and Greg Noble. *Parents, Diversity and Cultures of Home and School.* Perth, NSW: University of Western Sydney, 2009.

Charles, Carol Morgan. *Essential Elements of Effective Discipline.* Boston, MA: Allyn & Bacon, 2002.

Chiu, Ming, and Bonnie Wing Yin Chow. "Classroom discipline across forty-one countries: School, economic, and cultural differences." *Journal of Cross-Cultural Psychology* 42, no. 3 (2011): 516–533.

Chiu, Ming, and Catherine McBride-Chang. "Gender, context, and reading: A comparison of students in 43 countries." *Scientific Studies of Reading* 10, no. 4 (2006): 331–362.

Chua, Amy. *Battle Hymn of the Tiger Mother.* New York: Bloomsbury Publishing, 2011.

Cohen, Jonathan, Libby McCabe, Nicholas M. Michelli, and Terry Pickeral. "School climate: Research, policy, practice, and teacher education." *Teachers College Record* 111, no. 1 (2009): 180–213.

Coughlan, Sean. "Teachers in China given highest level of public respect." *BBC News*, 2013.

Croninger, Robert G., Jennifer King Rice, Amy Rathbun, and Masako Nishio. "Teacher qualifications and early learning: Effects of certification, degree, and experience on first-grade student achievement." *Economics of Education Review* 26, no. 3 (2007): 312–324.

Deci, Edward L., Richard Koestner, and Richard M. Ryan. "Extrinsic rewards and intrinsic motivation in education: Reconsidered once again." *Review of Educational Research* 71, no. 1 (2001): 1–27.

Ding, Meixia, Yeping Li, Xiaobao Li, and Gerald Kulm. "Chinese teachers' perceptions of students' classroom misbehaviour." *Educational Psychology* 28, no. 3 (2008): 305–324.

Doménech-Betoret, F., L. Abellán-Roselló, and A. Gómez-Artiga. Self-efficacy, satisfaction, and academic achievement: The mediator role of students' expectancy-value beliefs. *Frontiers in Psychology* 8 (2017): 1193.

Dowson, Martin, and Dennis M. McInerney. "What do students say about their motivational goals?: Towards a more complex and dynamic perspective on student motivation." *Contemporary Educational Psychology* 28, no. 1 (2003): 91–113.

Evans, David, Michael Kremer, and Muthoni Ngatia. *The Impact of Distributing School Uniforms on Children's Education in Kenya*, 2008.

Fang, Tony. "Yin Yang: A new perspective on culture." *Management and Organization Review* 8, no. 1 (2012): 25–50.

Farh, Jiing-Lih, Gregory H. Dobbins, and Bor-Shiuan Cheng. "Cultural relativity in action: A comparison of self-ratings made by Chinese and US workers." *Personnel Psychology* 44, no. 1 (1991): 129–147.

Finn, Jeremy D. "Withdrawing from school." *Review of Educational Research* 59, no. 2 (1989): 117–142.

Foucault, Michel. *Discipline and Punish: The Birth of Prison*. Harmondsworth: Penguin, 1985, p. 208.

Fwu, Bih-Jen, and Hsiou-Huai Wang. "The social status of teachers in Taiwan." *Comparative Education* 38, no. 2 (2002): 211–224.

Gentile, Elisabetta, and Scott A. Imberman. "Dressed for success? The effect of school uniforms on student achievement and behavior." *Journal of Urban Economics* 71, no. 1 (2012): 1–17.

Goodenow, Carol, and Kathleen E. Grady. "The relationship of school belonging and friends' values to academic motivation among urban adolescent students." *The Journal of Experimental Education* 62, no. 1 (1993): 60–71.

Hanushek, Eric A. "The economic value of higher teacher quality." *Economics of Education Review* 30, no. 3 (2011): 466–479.

Haroun, Ramzi, and Christine O'Hanlon. "Do teachers and students agree in their perception of what school discipline is?" *Educational Review* 49, no. 3 (1997): 237–250.

Harvey, Samuel B., Mark Deady, Min-Jung Wang, Arnstein Mykletun, Peter Butterworth, Helen Christensen, and Philip B. Mitchell. "Is the prevalence of mental illness increasing in Australia? Evidence from national health surveys and administrative data, 2001–2014." *The Medical Journal of Australia* 206, no. 11 (2017): 490–493.

Ho, David Yau-fai. "On the concept of face." *American Journal of Sociology* 81, no. 4 (1976): 867–884.

Ho, David Yau-fai. "Cognitive socialization in Confucian heritage cultures." In *Cross-cultural Roots of Minority Child Development*. London: Psychology Press, 1994, pp. 285–313.

Hue, Ming-Tak. *A Study of the Relationship Between School Guidance and Discipline in Hong Kong Secondary Schools.* PhD diss., Institute of Education, University of London, 2001.

Hue, Ming-Tak. *Preliminary Findings: The Social Construction of Classroom Discipline in Hong Kong Secondary Schools.* Unpublished report, Hong Kong: Hong Kong Institute of Education, 2005.

Hue, Ming-Tak. "Emergence of Confucianism from teachers' definitions of guidance and discipline in Hong Kong secondary schools." *Research in Education* 78, no. 1 (2007a): 21–33.

Hue, Ming-Tak. "The influence of classic Chinese philosophy of Confucianism, Taoism and Legalism on classroom discipline in Hong Kong junior secondary schools." *Pastoral Care in Education* 25, no. 2 (2007b): 38–45.

Hue, Ming-tak, and Wai-shing Li. *Classroom Management: Creating a Positive Learning Environment.* Vol. 1. Hong Kong: Hong Kong University Press, 2008.

Ingersoll, Richard. *Short on Power, Long on Responsibility.* GSE Publications, 2007, p. 129.

Jez, Su Jin, and Robert W. Wassmer. "The impact of learning time on academic achievement." *Education and Urban Society* 47, no. 3 (2015): 284–306.

Juang, Linda P., Desiree Baolin Qin, and Irene J. K. Park. "Deconstructing the myth of the 'tiger mother': An introduction to the special issue on tiger parenting, Asian-heritage families, and child/adolescent well-being." *Asian American Journal of Psychology* 4, no. 1 (2013): 1.

Jung, Kyoung-Rae, Anne Q. Zhou, and Richard M. Lee. "Self-efficacy, self-discipline and academic performance: Testing a context-specific mediation model." *Learning and Individual Differences* 60 (2017): 33–39.

Kim, Joo Yup, and Sang Hoon Nam. "The concept and dynamics of face: Implications for organizational behavior in Asia." *Organization Science* 9, no. 4 (1998): 522–534.

Kim, Su Yeong, Yijie Wang, Diana Orozco-Lapray, Yishan Shen, and Mohammed Murtuza. "Does 'tiger parenting' exist? Parenting profiles of Chinese Americans and adolescent developmental outcomes." *Asian American Journal of Psychology* 4, no. 1 (2013): 7.

Kim, Uichol, and Young-Shin Park. "Indigenous psychological analysis of academic achievement in Korea: The influence of self-efficacy, parents, and culture." *International Journal of Psychology* 41, no. 4 (2006): 287–292.

King, Ronnel B., and Dennis M. McInerney. "Culture's consequences on student motivation: Capturing cross-cultural universality and variability through personal investment theory." *Educational Psychologist* 49, no. 3 (2014): 175–198.

Krskova, Hana, and Chris Baumann. "School discipline, investment, competitiveness and mediating educational performance." *International Journal of Educational Management* 31, no. 3 (2017): 293–319.

Kwon, Young-Ihm. "Early childhood education in Korea: Discrepancy between national kindergarten curriculum and practices." *Educational Review* 56, no. 3 (2004): 297–312.

Lareau, Annette. *Unequal Childhoods: Race, Class, and Family Life.* Berkeley: University of California Press, 2003.

Lee, Jihyun. "Universals and specifics of math self-concept, math self-efficacy, and math anxiety across 41 PISA 2003 participating countries." *Learning and Individual Differences* 19, no. 3 (2009): 355–365.

Lewis, Catherine C. "Cooperation and control in Japanese nursery schools." *Comparative Education Review* 28, no. 1 (1984): 69–84.

Lewis, Catherine C. "From indulgence to internalization: Social control in the early school years." *Journal of Japanese Studies* (1989): 139–157.

Lewis, Catherine C. *Educating Hearts and Minds: Reflections on Japanese Preschool and Elementary Education.* Cambridge: Cambridge University Press, 1995a.

Lewis, Catherine C. "The roots of Japanese educational achievement: Helping children develop bonds to school." *Educational Policy* 9, no. 2 (1995b): 129–151.

Lewis, Catherine C. "The roots of Japanese educational achievement: Helping children develop bonds to school." In W. K. Cummings and P. G. Altbach (Eds.), *The Challenges of Eastern Asian Education: Implications for America.* New York: SUNY Press, 1997, p. 22.

Lewis, Ramon. "Classroom discipline and student responsibility: The students' view." *Teaching and Teacher Education* 17, no. 3 (2001): 307–319.

Lewis, Ramon, Shlomo Romi, Xing Qui, and Yaacov J. Katz. "Teachers' classroom discipline and student misbehavior in Australia, China and Israel." *Teaching and Teacher Education* 21, no. 6 (2005): 729–741.

Lodewyk, Ken R. "Relations among epistemological beliefs, academic achievement, and task performance in secondary school students." *Educational Psychology* 27, no. 3 (2007): 307–327.

Lynn, John R. *A New Translation of the Tao-Te Ching of Laozi as Interpreted by Wang Bi.* New York: Columbia University Press, 1999.

Ma, Xin, Cindy Jong, and Jing Yuan. "Exploring reasons for the East Asian success in PISA." In *PISA, Power, and Policy: The Emergence of Global Educational Governance*, 2013, pp. 225–246.

Maag, John W. "Rewarded by punishment: Reflections on the disuse of positive reinforcement in schools." *Exceptional Children* 67, no. 2 (2001): 173–186.

Martin, Andrew J., Herbert W. Marsh, Dennis M. McInerney, Jasmine Green, and Martin Dowson. "Getting along with teachers and parents: The yields of good relationships for students' achievement motivation and self-esteem." *Journal of Psychologists and Counsellors in Schools* 17, no. 2 (2007): 109–125.

McInerney, Dennis M. "Culture and self-regulation in educational contexts." In *Handbook of Self-Regulation of Learning and Performance.* New York: Routledge, 2011, pp. 442–464.

McInerney, Dennis M., Lawrence A. Roche, Valentina McInerney, and Herbert W. Marsh. "Cultural perspectives on school motivation: The relevance and application of goal theory." *American Educational Research Journal* 34, no. 1 (1997): 207–236.

Miller, Patrick, and Martin Plant. "Truancy and perceived school performance: An alcohol and drug study of UK teenagers." *Alcohol and Alcoholism* 34, no. 6 (1999): 886–893.

Mitchell, Mary M., and Catherine P. Bradshaw. "Examining classroom influences on student perceptions of school climate: The role of classroom management and exclusionary discipline strategies." *Journal of School Psychology* 51, no. 5 (2013): 599–610.

Murray, Richard K. "The impact of school uniforms on school climate." *NASSP Bulletin* 81, no. 593 (1997): 106–112.

Ning, Hoi Kwan, and Kevin Downing. "The reciprocal relationship between motivation and self-regulation: A longitudinal study on academic performance." *Learning and Individual Differences* 20, no. 6 (2010): 682–686.

Oluremi, Fareo Dorcas. "Truancy and Academic Performance of Secondary School students in Southwestern Nigeria: Implications for counselling." *International Journal for Cross-Disciplinary Subjects in Education* 3, no. 2 (2013): 1424–1428.

Pasternak, Rachel. "Discipline, learning skills and academic achievement." *Journal of Arts and Education* 1, no. 1 (2013): 1–11.

Perryman, Jane. "Panoptic performativity and school inspection regimes: Disciplinary mechanisms and life under special measures." *Journal of Education Policy* 21, no. 2 (2006): 147–161.

Pittman, Laura D., and Adeya Richmond. "Academic and psychological functioning in late adolescence: The importance of school belonging." *The Journal of Experimental Education* 75, no. 4 (2007): 270–290.

Reed, Kayla, James M. Duncan, Mallory Lucier-Greer, Courtney Fixelle, and Anthony J. Ferraro. "Helicopter parenting and emerging adult self-efficacy: Implications for mental and physical health." *Journal of Child and Family Studies* 25, no. 10 (2016): 3136–3149.

Riggs, Liz. "Why do teachers quit." *The Atlantic* 10 (2013): 3–5.

Rockoff, Jonah E. "The impact of individual teachers on student achievement: Evidence from panel data." *American Economic Review* 94, no. 2 (2004): 247–252.

Rodriguez, Lourdes, and Francisco Cano. "The learning approaches and epistemological beliefs of university students: A cross-sectional and longitudinal study." *Studies in Higher Education* 32, no. 5 (2007): 647–667.

Romi, Shlomo, and Mira Freund. "Teachers', students' and parents' attitudes towards disruptive behaviour problems in high school: A case study." *Educational Psychology* 19, no. 1 (1999): 53–70.

Shin, Jongho, Hyunjoo Lee, and Yongnam Kim. "Student and school factors affecting mathematics achievement: International comparisons between Korea, Japan and the USA." *School Psychology International* 30, no. 5 (2009): 520–537.

Sinclair, Catherine, Martin Dowson, and Dennis M. McInerney. "Motivations to teach: Psychometric perspectives across the first semester of teacher education." *Teachers College Record* 108, no. 6 (2006): 1132.

Skiba, Russell J., and Reece L. Peterson. "School discipline at a crossroads: From zero tolerance to early response." *Exceptional Children* 66, no. 3 (2000): 335–346.

Stankov, Lazar. "Unforgiving Confucian culture: A breeding ground for high academic achievement, test anxiety and self-doubt?" *Learning and Individual Differences* 20, no. 6 (2010): 555–563.

Steinmayr, Ricarda, and Birgit Spinath. "The importance of motivation as a predictor of school achievement." *Learning and Individual Differences* 19, no. 1 (2009): 80–90.

Stevenson, Harold, and James W. Stigler. *Learning gap: Why our schools are failing and what we can learn from Japanese and Chinese educ.* New York: Simon and Schuster, 1994.

Sullivan, Anna M., Bruce Johnson, Robert Conway, Larry Owens, and Carmel Taddeo. "Punish them or engage them? Teachers' views on student behaviours in the classroom." *Australian Journal of Teacher Education* 39, no. 6 (2012).

Tan, Charlene. "Beyond rote-memorisation: Confucius' concept of thinking." *Educational Philosophy and Theory* 47, no. 5 (2015): 428–439.

Tan, Charlene. "Confucianism and education." *Oxford Research Encyclopedia of Education* (2017): 1–18.

Trautwein, Ulrich, and Oliver Lüdtke. "Epistemological beliefs, school achievement, and college major: A large-scale longitudinal study on the impact of certainty beliefs." *Contemporary Educational Psychology* 32, no. 3 (2007): 348–366.

Tweed, Roger G., and Darrin R. Lehman. "Learning considered within a cultural context: Confucian and Socratic approaches." *American Psychologist* 57, no. 2 (2002): 89.

Watkins, David A., and John Burville Biggs, eds. *Teaching the Chinese Learner: Psychological and Pedagogical Perspectives*. Hong Kong: Hong Kong University Press, 2001.

Watson, Burton. *Han Fei Tzu: Basic Writings*. New York: Columbia University Press, 1964.

Way, Niobe, Sumie Okazaki, Jing Zhao, Joanna J. Kim, Xinyin Chen, Hirokazu Yoshikawa, Yueming Jia, and Huihua Deng. "Social and emotional parenting: Mothering in a changing Chinese society." *Asian American Journal of Psychology* 4, no. 1 (2013): 61.

Way, Sandra M. "School discipline and disruptive classroom behavior: The moderating effects of student perceptions." *The Sociological Quarterly* 52, no. 3 (2011): 346–375.

Weale, Sally (2014), "Culture, not just curriculum," determines east Asian school success. *The Guardian Online*, 9 October 2014, https://www.theguardian.com/world/2014/oct/09/east-asian-school-success-culture-curriculum-teaching. Accessed on 22 February 2018.

Wilkins, Jesse L. M. "Mathematics and science self-concept: An international investigation." *The Journal of Experimental Education* 72, no. 4 (2004): 331–346.

Wilson, John. *Philosophy & Practical Education*. London: Routledge & Kegan Paul, 1977.

Wilson, John. "Corporal punishment revisited." *Cambridge Journal of Education* 32, no. 3 (2002): 409–416.

Witzel, Morgen. "The leadership philosophy of Han Fei." *Asia Pacific Business Review* 18, no. 4 (2012): 489–503.

Wong, Maria Meiha, and Mihaly Csikszentmihalyi. "Motivation and academic achievement: The effects of personality traits and the duality of experience." *Journal of Personality* 59, no. 3 (1991): 539–574.

Woods, Peter R., and David A. Lamond. "What would Confucius do?—Confucian ethics and self-regulation in management." *Journal of Business Ethics* 102, no. 4 (2011): 669–683.

Yang, Jeff. "Do Asian students face too much academic pressure." *CNN Website*, July 2, 2015.

Yang, K. Wayne. "Focus on policy: Discipline or punish? Some suggestions for school policy and teacher practice." *Language Arts* 87, no. 1 (2009): 49–61.

Zhao, Yong. "Preparing globally competent teachers: A new imperative for teacher education." *Journal of Teacher Education* 61, no. 5 (2010): 422–431.

Zimmerman, Barry J. "Self-efficacy: An essential motive to learn." *Contemporary Educational Psychology* 25, no. 1 (2000): 82–91.

4 CDC Over Time

A Simulation Approach

The previous chapters introduced CDC with empirical evidence that indeed discipline drives academic performance, and that the Confucian Orbit has both higher discipline and also higher academic performance levels. A leading authority linking educational efforts and economic growth at Stanford University reminds us that we should "consider the economic returns to a student that follow having greater cognitive skills" (Hanushek, 2011, p. 471). While Chapters 2 and 3 investigated these associations with cross-sectional data, i.e. Programme for International Student Assessment (PISA) data from one point in time (in 2015), this chapter widens our lens to a longer timeframe with data ranging from 2000 to 2018, and thus our analyses presented in this chapter are of a longitudinal nature.

- For our analyses on *education and performance,* we utilise PISA data from 2000 to 2015.
- For our analysis of *competitiveness* over time, we refer to *World Economic Forum* (WEF) data from 2008 to 2018.

In essence, we have data over nearly two decades that allows us to draw conclusions over a relatively long time horizon, given that the quintessential argument for CDC is not least a 'time-effect'—i.e. discipline passed on in schools will ultimately improve a nation's competitiveness over time.

For this chapter, we have three foci:

1. One focus is the aforementioned diachronic perspective, i.e. our longitudinal testing. In this analysis, we are interested in exploring the developments of the CDC dimensions over time. As we have done for the previous analyses in our book, we plot the data, providing illustrations throughout.
2. The second focus is an inclusion of two levels of the M-M-M architecture (Dopfer, Foster and Potts, 2004;[1] House, Rousseau and Thomashunt, 1995), a hierarchy used predominantly in economic

studies consisting of *micro* (i.e. the individual), *meso* (the industry or firm level), and *macro* (the national) level(s). In Chapters 2 and 3, all our data analyses occurred at the individual student level, thus at the micro level of analysis. In this chapter we include one more level of the M-M-M architecture: the macro, or national, level. We aspire to establish a direct association between individual student (micro) level academic performance and national (macro) level of global competitiveness. We want to examine to what degree a nation's competitiveness will increase—over time—when more students can be 'moved' into the elite 15 percent of a nation, in terms of strong academic performance. As previously established in this book, the overarching argument is that such improvements in academic performance are a direct result of high(er) levels of discipline in the classroom, and overall more consistent management of schools.

3. The zenith of our analyses presented in this chapter are our diachronic simulations. The objective of these simulations is to provide a realistic forecast of the (interaction) effects over time on academic performance and on global competitiveness when discipline levels are maintained or enhanced. At the same time, we also demonstrate how academic performance and global competitiveness are likely to decrease when discipline is neglected. Our simulation is categorised along five geographic clusters, in line with our analyses presented in Chapters 2 and 3 where we also apply clusters. In a nutshell, we demonstrate—simulated—effects for changes in discipline standards, with a directly applicable contribution for any cluster (or nation) wishing to improve their performance and competitiveness; expected enhancements can be forecasted when discipline is improved in classrooms; at the same time, likely deteriorations are predicted in performance and competitiveness when discipline is not maintained or enhanced, or even dropped. This is especially crucial for current low-performing clusters with low discipline standards, as our simulations demonstrate.

We start this chapter with longitudinal charts of discipline, academic performance, and competitiveness over time to explore whether there are similar temporal patterns. We next analyse the relationship between discipline and academic performance in 2015, and the relationship between academic performance and national competitiveness over time (2000 to 2018); spanning from the micro student to the macro national level. And we complete this chapter with the aforementioned simulation scenarios: what happens to a nation's competitiveness if school discipline increases or decreases, respectively. In our conclusion for this chapter we reflect on the 'natural ceilings' for each CDC dimension. The sky is not always the limit, as we will explore.

Diachronic Analysis of Discipline and Academic Performance

Chapters 2 and 3 have revealed that the Confucian Orbit stands out with high levels of discipline and academic performance, higher than the other geographic clusters in our analysis. While those tests reflect the discipline and performance in 2015, they do not tell us to what degree these patterns will emerge over time. In order to understand 'history' looking over the two past decades, we next analysed discipline and academic performance with a temporal perspective. Such an analysis provides us with a better understanding of whether the strong performance of the Confucian Orbit in 2015 is indeed a consistent and sustainable pattern, or just a matter of chance.

We have plotted the longitudinal analysis of discipline and academic performance in Figure 4.1. Comparing panels A to C, we observe a clear pattern/trend over time, namely the Confucian Orbit having the lowest percentage of students perceiving a low disciplinary climate (Panel A), yet indeed the Confucian Orbit students indicating the highest level of discipline standards (Panel B), and Panel C tells us that the academic performance of the Confucian Orbit students is the highest of all geographic clusters.

From our temporal analysis of discipline and academic performance one can comfortably conclude that the strong discipline standards and academic performance of the Confucian Orbit is consistent and of a sustainable nature; or in other words, 2015 was no outlier. In fact, we learn from the analysis of the discipline charts that the standards have indeed improved over time (Panels A and B). In 2000, discipline standards in the Confucian Orbit were—perhaps surprisingly—low to begin with, but improved dramatically over the next four PISA testing cycles. As previously mentioned, there has been a time when, for example in Japan with the *Yutori* education approach, East Asia slightly moved towards a more Western permissive style of education, but has since largely returned to original standards and pedagogic approach. Such reforms and 'experimentations' with education policies in the East at the time (Kim, 2004) could explain the initially lower discipline scores for the Confucian Orbit. In addition, PISA has included new countries into their testing of students, and that included China where discipline standards are also high.

Diachronic Analysis of Elite Performers

Achievement scores are not normally distributed across the countries and over time, so the averages are misleading. A better measure of achievement within the countries and within the cultural regions is the proportion of students who have achieved above a minimum level. We followed

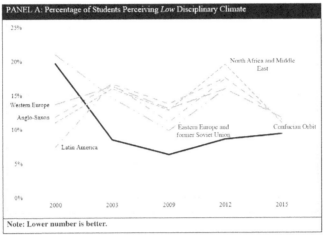

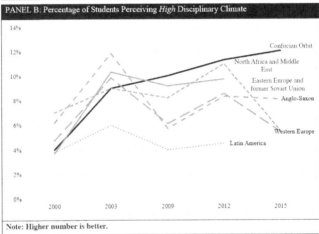

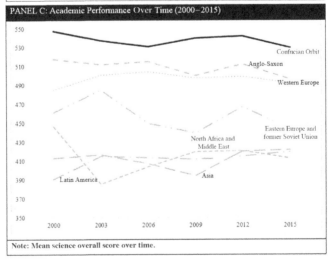

Figure 4.1 Discipline and Performance Over Time (2000 to 2015)

McKinsey and Company's report (2017) and selected those students who achieved a science score above 650 and called them 'Elite' students, and we selected those who achieved a science score below 400 and called them 'Low'-performing students, visualised in Figure 4.2. Across all

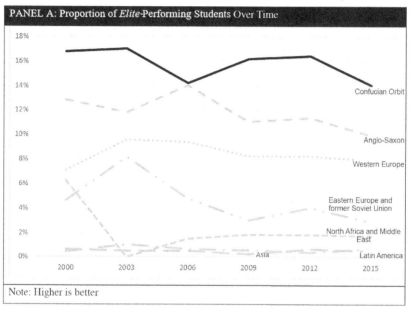

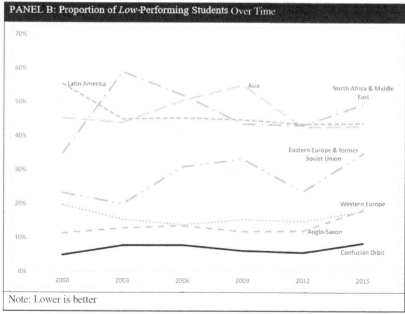

Figure 4.2 Proportion of Elite and Low-Performing Students Across Clusters Over Time

countries/societies, the Elite group was the top-performing 10 percent of respondents; the lowest-performing students were the bottom 10 percent. The distribution within each country of course is quite different. As we would expect, the proportions of Elite and Low-performing students are correlated with the means, but the correlations are not high, reinforcing the observation that the spread of scores is different for each country. Also, as expected, we can see that the developed economies, Western Europe and Anglo-Saxon cultures, perform well compared with other regional groups. The highest-performing cultural group is the Confucian Orbit, which here includes Japan, Hong Kong, and Korea.

Global Competitiveness Over Time

For this next analysis, we included competitiveness, the third dimension of our CDC framework. We have already established that discipline drives academic performance, with the Confucian Orbit strongest on all dimensions, and as just established in this chapter, we also observe this pattern over time. We now extend our analysis to explore whether the Confucian Orbit would also be more competitive than other parts of the world, presumably not least because of their strong academic performance and discipline passed on in education, resulting in self-discipline and a strong work ethic in the workforce.

Competitiveness is often referred to as the global competitiveness of a nation, in other words, how strong a nation (or society) is in comparison to other nations. The *World Economic Forum* (WEF) in Davos, Switzerland, has created a generally accepted measurement of competitiveness, captured by the Global Competitiveness Index (GCI) based on 12 pillars (Schwab and Sala-i-Martin, 2014). We have provided an overview of the 12 pillars and a cursory summary of definitions of competitiveness in Chapter 1.

We found a similar pattern for competitiveness over time (Figure 4.3) as we found for discipline and academic performance: the Confucian Orbit has ranked highest since 2008 until 2018. In other words, for the past decade, according to WEF, Confucian Orbit nations/societies are strongest in terms of their global competitiveness.

Dissecting the GCI, we can understand why the Confucian Orbit ranks high or highest; China, Japan, Korea, Taiwan have all focussed on improving the 12 pillars during their rapid economic developments:

1. Institutions;
2. Infrastructure;
3. Macroeconomic Environment;
4. Health and Primary Education;
5. Higher Education and Training;
6. Goods Market Efficiency;
7. Labour Market Efficiency;

8. Financial Market Development;
9. Technological Readiness;
10. Market Size;
11. Business Sophistication;
12. Innovation Technological.

When we combine the results from our longitudinal analyses of discipline, academic performance, and competitiveness, we can see that the pattern over the past two decades is by and large consistent with the Confucian Orbit in the highest ranked position. Throughout our book we have made the argument, and one that is now empirically supported, that better disciplined students perform better academically, and that this in turn shapes a nation's competitiveness. While we find that this pattern holds true for countries within the Confucian Orbit, it is important to note that our link between school discipline and national performance would also depend on how they are linked at the intermediary: that is the role of organisations, firms, and the employees within them. We do not measure this organisational (meso) level in our model—due to a lack of available data—but we comfortably make inferences about strong discipline and work ethic that is learned in the school environment, as being transferrable to the workforce, thus having a positive effect on competitiveness and productivity.

In fact, we follow a stream of researchers who consider the traditional values imparted by Confucianism as having a strong and positive influence

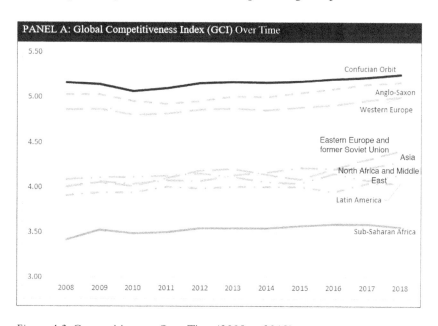

Figure 4.3 Competitiveness Over Time (2008 to 2018)

on how businesses are run, organisations are managed, and employees behave—which has come to be popularised as *Confucian Dynamism*. Hofstede and Bond (1988) originally conceptualised Confucian Dynamism as the difference between dynamic and future-oriented dimensions and static traditional-oriented dimensions. Lin and Ho (2009) adapted the measure in their comparison of Chinese societies, and focussed on specific items such as:

1. I am always careful not to do anything inappropriate;
2. I never forget my goals even in the face of adversity;
3. I avoid offending others;
4. I respect elders.

In essence, the measures focus on being cautious and deliberate in one's conduct with not only others, but how one goes about getting things done. Not unlike our research, such studies and many more (e.g. Franke, Hofstede and Bond, 1991; Lam, 2003; Redding, 1990) consider Confucian Dynamism as a cultural driving force for the unprecedented economic growth of some countries in the region, and have focussed on how aspects including those values (i.e. 'spirit' to doing things or how relationships are managed) listed above can, and have been, successfully utilised as a tour de force in beating the competition on a global stage. While competition, in a conventional sense, might be associated with aggressive tactics or hostile rivalry, the Confucian approach to 'competing' (and winning) would perhaps be best characterised as taking slow and steady steps through conservative action over time.

Many studies that probe this link between Confucianism and performance or competitiveness describe specific ethics (Ip, 2009), business practices (Tsai, Young and Cheng, 2011), and approaches to human resource development and management (Wang, Wang, Ruona and Rojewski, 2005) that help facilitate a type of 'success' at the organisational (meso) level. There is a great deal of merit in all that has been said in relation to Confucian Dynamism at the meso level, and we add to this body of research by demonstrating that some of these 'best practices' are the product of discipline established in the home and school environments, and cultivated throughout an individual's formative years—as evidenced by the performance within the Confucian Orbit.

In the context of organisations or simply work, the types of attributes that might perhaps be 'manifestations' of having had been disciplined, and thus possessing self-discipline could easily be reflected in Robertson and Hoffman's (2000) conceptualisation of Confucian Dynamism:

1. Managers must be persistent to accomplish objectives;
2. There is a hierarchy to on-the-job relationships and it should be observed;
3. A good manager knows how to economise;

4. It is important to have a conscience in business;
5. Personal stability is not critical to success in business;
6. Respect for tradition hampers performance;
7. The exchange of favours and gifts is not necessary to excel;
8. Upholding one's personal image makes little difference in goal achievement.

In other words, while these features are often associated with Confucian culture directly, or are considered to be a 'natural tendency' of those who exist under the influence of Confucian societies, our research points in the direction that these attributes are shaped by an overarching discipline or manner in which individuals are moulded from an early age. That is, enforcing the discipline that helps individuals realise these potentialities for success is, in essence, our interpretation of Confucian Dynamism. Consistent with our discussions from previous chapters, Confucianism is about self-betterment and being malleable to adapt, change, and evolve according to the situation in an effort to *improve*; this does not exist in isolation, but instead requires an individual to be subjected to change, and to embrace it equally. Thus it is an attitude to succeed that is shaped at the individual level, and carried on through management practices at the organisational level, that have allowed the Confucian Orbit to maintain a relatively stable position at the 'top of the ladder' in global competitiveness over time (Figure 4.3). We include Fang's (2014, p. 78) list of 'Confucian competitive strategies' as a way to illustrate the way in which discipline under Confucianism might be applied in business:

1. The importance of strategies;
2. Transforming an adversary's strength into weakness;
3. Engaging in deception to gain a strategic advantage;
4. Understanding contradictions and using them to gain an advantage;
5. Compromising;
6. Striving for total victory;
7. Taking advantage of an adversary's or competitor's misfortune;
8. Flexibility;
9. Gathering intelligence and information;
10. Grasping the interdependent relationship of situations;
11. Patience;
12. Avoiding strong emotions.

Academic Performance and Global Competitiveness Over Time

The literature has long explored the interplay of education and economic performance of some sorts. In fact, there is a large body of literature on the drivers of academic performance, and also on how academic performance impacts economic performance or competitiveness. We cluster the literature into three categories, and list relevant literature in chronological order:

Investigations in Relation to Determinants of Academic Performance

- Schooling years and schooling quality (Barro and Lee, 1996);
- Teacher quality and academic achievement (Rivkin, Hanushek and Kain, 2005);
- Teacher performance-related pay and PISA achievement (Woessmann, 2011);
- Increasing government school expenditure and declining performance (Jensen, Reichl and Kemp, 2011);
- Efficiency of public spending on educational performance (Agasisti, 2014).

Investigations in Relation to Education as a Determinant of Economic Performance

- Capital formation by education (Schultz, 1960);
- Investment in humans, technological diffusion, and economic growth (Nelson and Phelps, 1966);
- Education expansion and expenditures per student and the effects of growth in Asia (Keller, 2006);
- Investment in primary, secondary, and higher education and the effects on economic growth (Keller, 2006);
- Economic value of higher teacher quality (Hanushek, 2010);
- Public expenditures on education, human capital, and growth (Annabi, Harvey and Lan, 2011);
- Education determining a nation's health and educational outcomes (Siddiqi, Kawachi, Berkman, Hertzman and Subramanian, 2012);
- Education and economic growth (Barro, 2013);
- Government spending on education and growth of human capital accumulation (Dissou, Didic and Yakautsava, 2016).

Investigations in Relation to Education as a Determinant of Competitiveness

- Knowledge, skills, and competitiveness (Mayhew and Keep, 1999);
- Education reform raising economic competitiveness (Sahlberg, 2006);
- National economic competitiveness and human capital (Sabadie and Johansen, 2010);
- Education and competitiveness (BenDavid-Hadar, 2013);
- Secondary education explaining competitiveness and vice versa with 'alternative causal directions' (Baumann and Winzar, 2016);
- School discipline, investment, competitiveness, and mediating educational performance (Krskova and Baumann, 2017).

The overarching conclusion from our cursory review of the relevant literature presented in the above three categories is that—in one way or another—education has a positive association with economic performance and also competitiveness. Traditionally, the focus had been on economic performance such as GDP or GDP growth, with research dating back to the 1960s. Only over the past two decades have scholars turned to exploring how education benefits a country's competitiveness. This association, is, of course, a 'chicken or egg causality dilemma'—which ones come first?

Baumann and Winzar (2016) explored the power of secondary education explaining competitiveness and found that education combined with industrialisation (or industrial development) explains 30 percent of changes in competitiveness, or indeed 53 percent when cultural effects were added to their 'education-driven model'. Crucially, that study also tested for the 'vice versa' constellation, or what the authors labelled 'alternative causal direction' (p. 21). What emerged was a 'competitiveness-driven model' suggesting that education explains 18 percent of improvements of competitiveness. A conclusion that can be drawn from this 'alternative causal direction' testing would be that indeed both directions 'work', but that the effect of education on competitiveness is stronger than vice versa, in line with the modelling approach followed in the analysis reported in our CDC study.

Figure 4.4 shows the association between the percentage of elite students (i.e. the top 15 percent of a country/society) in the year 2000 with that same country's/society's GCI, or Global Competitiveness Index in the year 2018. In other words, this analysis spans over 18 years, visualising the 'interplay' of education and competitiveness over nearly two decades. What the figure makes obvious is that there are—in essence—two groups:

1. **High % of elite students in 2000 and high GCI in 2018:** When a country/society has a high proportion of their students in the top-performing academic performance category, then longer term, it will also have a high GCI. Examples are Japan, Hong Kong, and Korea, but also Western countries like Switzerland and the Netherlands.
2. **Low % of elite students in 2000 and low GCI in 2018:** When a country/society has a low proportion of their students in the top-performing academic category, then longer term, it will also have a low GCI. Examples are Albania and Argentina.

While there are the above two 'extreme' categories, there are also many cases 'in between', e.g. Iceland with relatively a low percentage of students in the top-performing category in 2000, but nonetheless with a mid-range GCI in 2018.

Regardless of any outliers in the graph, the overall pattern is clear—the more students a country/society can 'move' to the elite segment of their students, the more competitive it will be longer term. Well-educated and 'driven' school leavers will do better at tertiary studies, and will also perform well in the workforce later on. This also means that there is

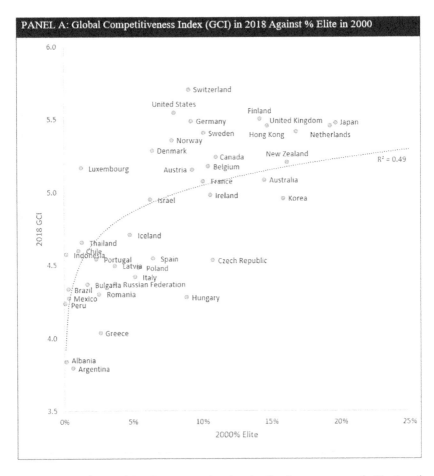

Figure 4.4 Relationship Between Academic Performance and National Competitiveness (2000 to 2015/2018)

indeed a long-term effect. We have modelled an 18-year time span in Figure 4.4, but likely the effect would be even stronger over longer time periods. This warrants further investigation.

Predictive Model of Educational Achievement and Global Competitiveness

Logically, changes to education can take some time to percolate through to productivity in the workforce, efficiency of infrastructure, and efficacy in management practices. The available data from the OECD and the WEF gave us a period of 18 years to measure education effects. We ran a two-stage least squares regression model of lagged proportion of

Elite performers from the PISA data set against the latest, 2018, Global Competitiveness Index measures for the same countries. The proportions were Z-transformed to make the percentage measures linear. Two-stage regression is appropriate when not all influential variables are available for inclusion in the model, and when we can apply one or more instrumental variables that are highly correlated with the independent variable. Here, we regressed Z-Elite_2000 against GCI_2018, and instrumental variables were GCI_Infrastructure_2018 and Z-Elite_2015. The result was a regression model with R-square of 0.54. The resulting regression equation was:

model-prediction-GCI: GCI_2018 = 6.176 + 0.733*Z-Elite_2000

The equation is illustrated in Figure 4.4 *Global Competitiveness Index in 2018 Against % Elite in 2000*. Note how the Z-transformation gives a non-linear relationship between the two measures. Percentage of Elite performers is readily transformed into Z-scores with the NORM.INV function in Excel and Z-scores back into percentages with the NORM. DIST function. We can see that some countries perform above the regression line and others perform below. These distances are residuals in the regression model. A forecast of future values should take those residuals into account. If we assume that residuals are country-specific variations from the model, due to technological differences, culture, natural resources, or geography, then we can apply these to a prediction model.

Forecast GCI = model-prediction-GCI + CountryResidual

With the regression model and country-specific adjustment, we can use the model to predict future GCI with a change in percentage of students in the Elite levels, as in Table 4.1.

In the forecasting model shown in Figure 4.1 we have Global Competitive Index measures for 2018, and % Elite school performers in 2000, 18 years earlier. Let's see what happens if we improve the proportion of Elite by one percentage point in all countries.

- Japan, with the highest proportion of elite performers (19.7%) has a GCI of 5.473. If this %Elite rises to 20.7% then forecast GCI becomes 5.499, an improvement of 0.026 GCI points.
- The United States, with %Elite of 8% and GCI of 5.554, the highest in the sample. If the US improved %Elite to 9%, then GCI improves to 5.591, up by 0.047 GCI points.
- Indonesia has the lowest level of Elite performers in our sample with about 0.1%, and GCI of 4.571. If educational attainment can be improved to 1.1% then GCI improves to 5.100, an improvement of 0.529 points.

Table 4.1 Predicting the Effect of Changing % of Elite Performers

Country	2018 GCI	2000 % Elite	Change % Elite to . . .	Forecast-GCI	Improvement	Relative Improvement
Japan	5.473	19.7%	20.7%	5.499	0.026	1.6%
Netherlands	5.455	19.3%	20.3%	5.481	0.026	1.6%
United Kingdom	5.415	16.8%	17.8%	5.443	0.029	1.8%
New Zealand	5.204	16.2%	17.2%	5.234	0.029	1.8%
Korea	4.958	15.9%	16.9%	4.988	0.030	1.8%
Hong Kong	5.456	14.7%	15.7%	5.488	0.031	1.9%
Australia	5.084	14.5%	15.5%	5.116	0.031	2.0%
Finland	5.501	14.2%	15.2%	5.533	0.032	2.0%
Canada	5.243	11.0%	12.0%	5.280	0.038	2.4%
Ireland	4.980	10.6%	11.6%	5.018	0.039	2.4%
Belgium	5.178	10.5%	11.5%	5.217	0.039	2.4%
Sweden	5.408	10.1%	11.1%	5.448	0.040	2.5%
France	5.076	10.1%	11.1%	5.116	0.040	2.5%
Austria	5.156	9.3%	10.3%	5.199	0.042	2.6%
Germany	5.488	9.2%	10.2%	5.531	0.043	2.7%
Switzerland	5.704	9.1%	10.1%	5.747	0.043	2.7%
United States	5.544	8.0%	9.0%	5.591	0.047	2.9%
Norway	5.355	7.8%	8.8%	5.402	0.048	3.0%
Spain	4.546	6.5%	7.5%	4.601	0.055	3.4%
Denmark	5.286	6.4%	7.4%	5.341	0.055	3.4%
Israel	4.949	6.2%	7.2%	5.005	0.056	3.5%

Poland	4.483	5.4%	6.4%	4.545	0.063	3.9%
Italy	4.418	5.1%	6.1%	4.483	0.065	4.0%
Iceland	4.707	4.8%	5.8%	4.775	0.068	4.2%
Latvia	4.496	3.7%	4.7%	4.578	0.082	5.1%
Greece	4.036	2.7%	3.7%	4.140	0.104	6.5%
Portugal	4.541	2.4%	3.4%	4.654	0.113	7.1%
Thailand	4.657	1.3%	2.3%	4.828	0.171	10.6%
Luxembourg	5.167	1.2%	2.2%	5.342	0.175	10.9%
Indonesia	4.571	0.1%	1.1%	5.100	0.529	32.9%

An interesting property of the model is that the range of GCI values is reduced when all countries improve their education outcomes. Higher-performing countries go up, but lower-performing countries go up much more. This is presented in the Relative Improvement column in Table 4.1. For us, it implies that improved education makes a country more competitive over time, but we see decreasing marginal returns. We also see that top-performing countries do not lose their superiority, but lower-performing countries improve their situation greatly, and still retain their relative position in a ranking of indicators.

Wheel of Competitiveness

Figure 4.5 shows our newly introduced 'wheel of competitiveness', illustrating how a nation (or perhaps an organisation, an individual) that is competitive will also perform better, and that in turn leads to more competitiveness, and that in turn again leads to higher performance levels, etc. This illustration is an attempt to visualise the results from this chapter where we explore how competitiveness and performance interact. In the centre of our wheel of competitiveness we place discipline, *de facto* a moderator on the association between competitiveness and performance and then in turn on competitiveness on performance.

The big challenge for a nation in the lower performance/competitiveness sphere is how to 'enter' this wheel in an upward spiral so that their

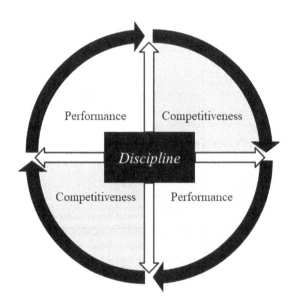

Figure 4.5 Wheel of Competitiveness

performance would increase competitiveness and so on. If their initial performance is low, it is not easy to gain on competitiveness in the first place. The same is true for competitiveness as a starting point: when a nation only has a low level of competitiveness, then it will be challenging to lift performance in every sense—from academic performance in education, to economic performance, to effective government management, reliable logistics and transport systems, and so forth.

Ultimately, this 'game' is not least about the availability (and allocation) of resources, e.g. research and development (R&D) investments, and indeed investment in education at all levels. It is—to a degree—a chicken-and-egg dilemma. A nation that is resource-rich has the means to further increase their competitiveness and ultimately improve performance, and thus further enhance their competitiveness. But a nation without those funds available to do so depends on foreign aid (and/or foreign direct investment, or FDI) to make the wheel of competitiveness spin, initially, and also spin faster and more sustainably (almost certainly in economics terms, but also environmentally).

What the study from our CDC modelling overall suggests is that indeed discipline in education passed on to the next generation as self-discipline and work ethic drives performance and competitiveness, in one way or another. In our 'wheel of competitiveness' we place discipline in the centre, and as a moderator between competitiveness and performance. How the mechanics would work specifically—in statistical testing—we can only infer from our simulations presented in this chapter; more work is needed in this area. Regardless, discipline is, in one way or another, a direct driver of performance and competitiveness. Conceptually and statistically, it could (also) act as a moderator, or as a multiplier. Multiplier in the sense that investments made into a nation's education system result in better outcomes when 'coupled' with discipline (as we have established in Chapters 2 and 3).

Longer-term, as previously alluded to, there would be 'spill-over' effects, i.e. high discipline levels at school lead to better academic performance, and that discipline also transfers into adult life as a driver of performance at the workplace. But this all begins at the individual level, where instilling the right form of discipline is imperative to help the wheel spin, and grow or maintain its momentum. This also means that, for any country, better/ high(er) levels of discipline will act as a moderator in the competitiveness to performance wheel and 'speed up' the quality and spinning of the wheel of competitiveness to performance, and so on.

While we only model one aspect of the discipline and competitiveness link in this study, namely the relationship between school discipline, academic performance, and national competitiveness, we implore other researchers to consider the other relationships of this multi-level, multi-faceted phenomenon. We illustrate this relationship in Figure 4.6, as a conceptual model, where the relationship between a nation's culture (the societal

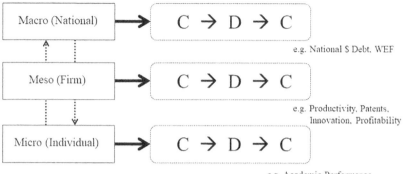

Figure 4.6 Conceptual Model of CDC at Multiple Levels

norms and values) in turn shapes its view on discipline, and ultimately driving competitiveness. This relationship operates at each level—the micro, meso, and macro—producing a cyclical or bi-directional effect. That is, it operates in a bottom-up *and* top-down fashion, simultaneously, where individual performance has a spill-over effect to the organisational level, affecting national productivity; similarly, how a nation is organised at the macro level—its institutional frameworks—directly impact the criteria by which businesses and schools operate. Due to the lack of available data, we only model the relationship between the micro (individual) and macro (national) levels in this study, but a crucial missing link is an explanation for how individual discipline and performance drives organisational performance (increased productivity, patents, innovations, profitability), which in turn affects national competitiveness.

Simulation: Discipline and Academic Performance and National Competitiveness

Here, we combine two prediction models and apply them at the regional level: (1) the prediction model shown in Figure 4.1 forecasts the effects of changes to a number of Elite academic performers on the Global Competitive Index for each country; (2) a similar model forecasts the effects of perceived Discipline on the number of Elite academic performers in each country. The combined model then lets us predict the effects of changes to perceived Discipline on GCI over time.

The following simulation gives predicted results with gross percentage changes in the proportion of students who perceive a high level of disciplinary climate. For example, if a cohort has 5.5 percent high disciplinary climate, a 2 percent decrease will be 3.5 percent disciplinary climate. As we saw in Table 4.1, we recognise that competitiveness is a relative construct, so we present the change in relative scores for %elite and for Global Competitive Index, or GCI.

The model assumes that no change in Discipline, or anything else will maintain the *status quo*, and there is no change in GCI. A decrease of, say, two percentage points among all regional groups would see a GCI decrease of 1.9 percent in Western Europe and decreases of 1.7 percent and 3.5 percent in Anglo-Saxon cultures and Confucian Orbit cultures, respectively. Similarly, a 5 percent increase in perceived high disciplinary climate will lead to increases of between 2.6 percent and 3.6 percent in relative GCI. All of that is intuitively straightforward. The interesting result is when one group sees an increase in disciplinary climate while others drop. In the final sub-table, we see what happens if, say, countries in the Confucian Orbit increase in disciplinary climate by 2 percent points while those in the West drop by 2 percent points. The result is a 3.7 percent difference in relative GCI between Western Europe and the Confucian Orbit.

Of course, we should treat these forecasts with some healthy scepticism. These are point estimates with fairly large error terms. Two-stage least-squares R^2 for the Discipline to %Elite path is 0.18, and two-stage least-squares R^2 for the %Elite to GCI path is 0.54. True values for any one country are likely to vary considerably and, of course, structural changes over time can affect outcomes.

Effects of Overall Reduction in Discipline

	% Points Discipline Change	*Relative % Elite Change*	*Relative GCI Change*
Confucian Orbit	–2.0%	–10.6%	–3.5%
Anglo-Saxon	–2.0%	–4.2%	–1.7%
Western Europe	–2.0%	–3.0%	–1.9%

Effects of No Change in Discipline

	% Points Discipline Change	*Relative % Elite Change*	*Relative GCI Change*
Confucian Orbit	0.0%	0.0%	0.0%
Anglo-Saxon	0.0%	0.0%	0.0%
Western Europe	0.0%	0.0%	0.0%

Effects of Overall Increase in Discipline

	% Points Discipline Change	*Relative % Elite Change*	*Relative GCI Change*
Confucian Orbit	2.0%	5.8%	1.8%
Anglo-Saxon	2.0%	3.4%	1.3%
Western Europe	2.0%	2.2%	1.2%

Effects of Large Overall Increase in Discipline

	% Points Discipline Change	*Relative % Elite Change*	*Relative GCI Change*
Confucian Orbit	5.0%	12.1%	3.6%
Anglo-Saxon	5.0%	7.6%	2.8%
Western Europe	5.0%	4.8%	2.6%

Effects of Increase in Discipline in Confucian Orbit and Decrease Elsewhere

	% Points Discipline Change	*Relative % Elite Change*	*Relative GCI Change*
Confucian Orbit	2.0%	5.8%	1.8%
Anglo-Saxon	−2.0%	−4.2%	−1.7%
Western Europe	−2.0%	−3.0%	−1.9%

Take Home Messages From Diachronic CDC Analyses and Simulations

The 'take home' messages from this chapter centred around the dimensions of our simulations: there are time effects, there are effects within the M-M-M architecture, and there are segmentation issues (e.g. the elite performing students vis-à-vis the middle or low performers).

Naturally, it is not easy for a nation or a geographic cluster to 'climb' the ladder, i.e. to progress from a weak performer to a peak performer. At the same time, it is also not necessarily easy to stay on top. Based on our simulation, perhaps surprisingly, it is actually easier to stay on top on this instance rather than moving up, which may contrast other areas of competition (see our 'wheel of competitiveness' in Figure 4.5). This contrasts to many other fields where competition and competitiveness are crucial. For example, in sports, there is a biological 'clock' when a human peak performs, with over time natural deterioration, whereas in music, a classical pianist may get better over time, but a rock band or pop singer will only have his/her time for a little while when being at the top of the charts. Brands may sustain over time (e.g. Coca-Cola, Nestlé, Qantas, and KLM, IBM), yet many disappear after their 'due date', sometimes due to mismanagement, and/or massive 'missed' disruptive innovation opportunities as well as challenges (e.g. Pan American, Eastern, Swissair, Kodak). For nations, the challenge is to maintain or increase their global competitiveness, as captured by the WEF. We found in our testing that indeed the strong performers are also the ones who constantly innovate and thus remain competitive and perform strong over time. For low-performing nations, the upward hill is precisely that—i.e. a massive challenge. We have demonstrated that one way forward is to focus on discipline in schools to (1) improve academic performance of their students and (2) pass on work ethic and drive/motivation over time into the workforce. Ultimately, discipline is then not least a driver of a nation's global competitiveness.

For all the dimensions explored in our book, especially when conducting the simulations of different scenarios over time, an important question is to what degree there are *natural ceilings* for the three CDC and related dimensions?

- **Confucianism:** Naturally, culture such as Confucianism is not (directly) transferable to other cultural settings/nations. Each nation has their own cultural heritage and wants to maintain/protect such. However, some cultural elements or traits could perhaps be integrated into other societies. An example could be the striving for constant betterment as is common under Confucianism. Asian migrants have indeed 'transferred' Confucianism into their new places of residence and passed on Confucian values such as discipline to their children and that has indeed resulted in peak academic performance in Western schools beyond the local averages (Fuligni, 1997; Kao, 1995). At the same time, there is no natural ceiling for the CDC dimension of Confucianism as such, and in this study, we did not measure Confucianism on a scale (as we have for the other dimensions). That is not to say that this can't be done—we have indeed published measurements of Confucianism (Viengkham, Baumann and Winzar, 2018), but for the purpose of this book, we 'captured' culture by the clustering of nations/societies.
- **Discipline:** There would be a natural ceiling for this dimension. In PISA, the range for discipline measures is normalised so that it ranges from –2.4 to +1.9, with an average of about zero and standard deviation of about one. To a degree, it is a matter of 'the higher, the better'. More disciplined students allow better and more effective, perhaps also more deep and clearer, teaching and learning. Low levels result in distractions for teachers and students, and learning is shallow or generally poor. While there are clearly no benefits of low levels of discipline, there is a question about a possible maximum level. Presumably there is a point of diminishing returns as our simulations also suggest. For example, if there is too

much discipline, then there are no more additional benefits, and teaching and learning could no longer be constructive if discipline is 'overdone', or applied unnecessarily. Key is finding the healthy 'high' level of a disciplined classroom environment that results in a focussed learning environment for students to learn and grow. Our simulations have given some indications where this optimal point could be.

- **Academic Performance:** To some degree, naturally, this is 'the higher, the better' situation, at least in principle. At the same time, not everyone in any given classroom has the same talent and therefore the same potential for growth in math, reading, and science, or any other subject for that matter. Regardless, if and as we propose, a disciplined environment allows each and every student to reach their potential, then that would be the desired level of academic performance to aspire towards. The PISA scores for math, science, and reading generally are scaled to range from about 200 to 800, with a mean of about 460 and standard deviation of 100. In this study, we followed McKinsey and Co's report (2017) and defined 'Elite' students as those who achieved a science score above 650, and we defined 'Low'-performing students as those who achieved a science score below 400.

- **Competitiveness:** This dimension is similar to academic performance in that 'the more the better' principle applies. The World Economic Forum data ranges from 2.87 to 5.86 for the Global Competitiveness Index. At the national level, there is quite a massive spread on the 12 WEF pillars measured when comparing the countries/societies included in WEF. In a relative sense, for each nation/society, their performance and improvement per WEF pillar has to be viewed (and managed) in relation to their history, their current stage of industrial development, and naturally also, in relation to their potential. For competitiveness, there is not really a concern whether or not there is a 'theoretical' natural ceiling, but rather in which direction the individual 12 pillars will—or can be—move(d) for each nation/society. To some degree they naturally correlate, e.g. a nation that has top-notch infrastructure often also has solid health and primary education, and efficient labour markets and generally high scores on all the 12 WEF pillars. So we are looking at gradual, 'nuanced' improvements.

Prior research (see e.g. Jensen et al., 2011; Keller, 2006; Krskova and Baumann, 2017) established an association between funding for education and educational performance in one way or another. Naturally, educators would always support a call to politicians for additional funding for their schools and students, for their own training and so on, but this also begs the question to what degree there would also be a natural ceiling of academic performance even when additional funding is invested, new technology used, more and better discipline applied, etc. There is likely no easy answer to a near philosophical question, but most likely where some kind of a natural ceiling would be as we have discussed for CDC dimensions above.

Figure 4.7 depicts an asymptotic non-linear curve with an s-shape for the relationship between investment in education and achievement level. An s-shaped curve indicates that the association starts with slow growth; it takes time for additional funds to be effective, for new teaching material and techniques to be used, new pedagogical approaches to be implemented, new testing to occur, etc. There are 'teething problems', resistance by some, and new 'things' that need trial and error. But post this phase, there would be exponential growth when the additional investment funds 'kick in'—teachers and students use the new material more effectively and efficiently. There is a midpoint/inflection point, however, a turning point where additional funds no longer have a strong exponential effect; things slow down. At one stage, any additional funding only has a very limited additional learning/achievement effect; that is where the curve reaches stabilisation, or the 'upper asymptote'. If we were to borrow terminology and wisdom from the 'Optimal Investment Theory', then we would be looking at 'incremental returns on investments' with a challenge to find the *optimal* investment 'point', or the amount where the investment in education results in the best possible academic performance/achievement level.

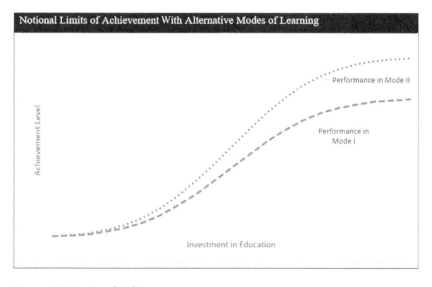

Figure 4.7 Limits of Achievement

While the curve in Figure 4.7 is probably—more or less—realistic for most nations/societies, the curve itself can be moved upwards when a more radical change occurs, e.g. ground-breaking new technology is used in instruction, massive improvements in curriculum and/or pedagogy, or on the topic of CDC, when discipline standards are improved *and* investment in education increased. Figure 4.7 shows these effects as performance in mode I, i.e. the baseline; and performance in mode II with the dramatic change. Either way, there is an upper asymptote where additional funding for education no longer results in additional achievement levels or better academic performance.

Spotlight

Biology of Competitiveness

Baumann and Harvey (2018) found evidence for the important role of competitiveness in driving human performance. They suggested cross-disciplinary studies on evolutionary biological sciences (and their scientific constructs of competition) with educators focussing on academic performance with this broad research question:

RQ1. Is there a biological drive to compete and to learn?

If the question is whether competitiveness is a biological drive, then this is incontrovertibly true: it is one of the cornerstones of natural selection. Without competition, survival is impossible in the long term: performance is built into all genomes. However, whether competitiveness is an essential, or desirable, characteristic of learning, education, and advancement opens a particular question unique to sentient animals and therefore asks new questions about Darwinism. Is there a conscious competition to discover and imprint new skills? Humans, and maybe other mammals with large brains, might respond to their self-awareness by competing for new skills as a means to an end—survival. But even then, this behaviour might be so strongly coded into our genomes that it is not a matter of culture but rather, an unconscious act just like other basic biological drives in humans. It could be that other higher primates are a better model to test this question because they benefit from learning and yet one avoids the complexity of human memory, consciousness of long timeframes and culture.

Modern, technologically driven societies have constructed a culture that says competition in most endeavours is good. Does this competition in the cerebral process of learning spring from some inner, genetically determined imperative? Knowing that humans are long-lived and their culture sustains beliefs for generations, the rewards for learning are amplified and the drive to compete for the opportunity to learn is greater than for any other species. However, overt competition is much less apparent in indigenous societies where there are benefits of high levels of cooperation (altruism). Of course, many argue that this is not altruism in its purest sense but simply an individual defending one's own genes, or those genes defending themselves. In other words, there is an equilibrium between 'aggressors' and 'helpers' in human societies that is influenced by longevity, memory, generational investment and culture. If one applies this thinking to competitiveness in learning and education, it would suggest an equilibrium is also required—the entrepreneur versus the dilettante if you like. If this were not the case, we might live in amongst a 'super race' of giant intellects that would, deliberately or not, exclude all competitors—no libraries, no publishing, no conferences etc. If it were so, there would be few good deeds to be seen unless a new skill, and a competitive advantage lay at the end of the journey. Mercifully, that does not yet describe any societies.

Source: Brian Atwell, Professor of Biological Sciences, Macquarie University, 2018

Appendix

These pages show summary data from the PISA 2015 survey, showing summary scores for reading, mathematics, and science academic performance, and disciplinary climate, in science classes. These are followed by summary figures for the Global Competitiveness Indicators published by the World Economic Forum.

PISA 2015 Reading Score

	Mean	Standard Deviation	Minimum	Maximum	Percentile 25	Percentile 75
Albania	405.52	87.27	120.53	680.69	346.65	466.76
Algeria	349.48	62.69	126.74	577.65	306.95	389.34
Argentina (Ciudad Autónoma de Buenos Aires)	472.83	81.75	209.37	670.84	419.59	531.32
Australia	491.60	98.12	126.23	783.85	423.53	563.53
Austria	486.02	94.18	174.99	736.57	421.23	556.83
Belgium	501.77	93.83	133.64	743.78	436.73	573.87
Brazil	404.45	88.71	89.94	712.65	340.23	465.74
B-S-J-G (China)	505.82	98.43	125.65	778.08	441.30	576.99
Bulgaria	434.68	107.15	10.96	760.29	352.23	518.44
Canada	514.12	84.91	203.18	800.82	456.02	575.69
Chile	475.54	83.52	179.79	710.41	415.71	537.44
Chinese Taipei	495.69	87.93	126.82	745.42	439.72	559.57
Colombia	436.05	82.16	134.71	688.42	377.05	495.11
Costa Rica	427.12	72.31	184.56	696.49	378.50	475.15
Croatia	487.78	84.42	245.61	731.25	428.62	550.39
Czech Republic	498.40	97.02	140.83	739.01	430.18	571.13
Denmark	487.26	85.32	195.43	730.09	427.68	549.03
Dominican Republic	362.38	78.55	98.51	630.28	306.82	415.82
Estonia	520.82	81.80	229.92	741.84	466.02	579.68
Finland	527.65	87.53	72.86	749.70	474.27	590.74
France	503.67	105.22	187.16	785.62	429.89	583.29

(Continued)

(Continued)

	PISA 2015 Reading Score					
	Mean	Standard Deviation	Minimum	Maximum	Percentile 25	Percentile 75
FYROM	348.09	88.37	72.24	637.14	284.54	409.02
Georgia	404.06	96.01	72.68	693.31	338.62	471.22
Germany	512.16	92.88	179.66	763.59	449.21	579.74
Greece	476.80	88.44	123.39	711.21	416.57	542.83
Hong Kong	528.85	79.01	237.42	724.44	481.14	584.48
Hungary	477.25	89.80	173.31	724.49	412.64	543.85
Iceland	482.42	92.66	134.93	778.87	421.11	550.56
Indonesia	403.84	67.62	182.11	643.50	356.60	449.52
Ireland	520.75	81.07	234.66	751.92	465.90	578.56
Israel	482.28	106.46	115.70	780.04	407.59	563.98
Italy	492.88	83.93	196.97	743.06	436.66	554.01
Japan	516.25	85.76	190.54	760.96	461.47	577.85
Jordan	411.54	84.83	65.04	650.85	358.10	472.34
Korea	516.71	90.06	211.39	784.19	459.59	583.31
Kosovo	339.75	70.34	106.93	565.30	290.21	389.59
Latvia	488.93	77.37	237.90	720.62	437.97	544.66
Lebanon	352.39	106.91	74.73	722.28	273.62	428.65
Lithuania	465.55	88.47	90.66	726.21	403.03	531.70
Luxembourg	482.29	101.01	185.72	742.01	408.16	560.52
Macao	508.76	76.82	218.81	717.24	458.76	563.80
Malta	451.88	112.15	58.48	748.88	375.15	533.36
Mexico	428.99	71.22	180.05	672.25	378.99	479.51
Moldova	417.19	90.18	112.21	714.65	353.43	481.52
Montenegro	424.39	87.01	137.42	668.74	362.00	487.15
Netherlands	504.95	95.82	189.43	769.87	439.67	576.30

New Zealand	509.96	98.45	161.21	760.30	442.83	581.89
Norway	513.25	92.23	54.31	812.03	454.13	579.95
Peru	399.09	83.97	134.64	664.13	335.39	459.69
Poland	506.54	83.33	168.70	735.05	450.56	567.55
Portugal	486.57	87.64	205.08	720.64	423.00	552.25
Puerto Rico (USA)	416.35	88.70	168.90	676.14	353.50	477.53
Qatar	402.32	104.80	102.39	750.24	322.89	480.79
Romania	434.33	87.22	144.94	722.93	373.81	494.00
Russian Federation	495.45	79.74	209.61	748.73	440.51	554.19
Singapore	526.93	93.58	208.80	779.07	463.81	596.19
Slovak Republic	454.57	98.03	134.04	714.21	388.72	527.10
Slovenia	485.94	87.87	146.45	727.66	424.19	550.47
Spain	499.84	80.14	216.57	724.92	448.24	557.75
Sweden	500.19	94.94	152.21	761.06	437.62	570.41
Switzerland	488.92	90.74	197.25	781.59	425.79	556.48
Thailand	420.25	81.83	166.76	669.71	360.39	477.47
Trinidad and Tobago	427.46	96.57	126.08	711.87	356.95	499.25
Tunisia	361.56	73.24	119.78	609.81	310.31	410.38
Turkey	425.42	74.53	138.95	665.64	373.85	478.22
United Kingdom	495.13	87.08	173.63	804.88	434.29	557.33
United States	496.63	93.56	184.84	768.25	433.16	564.05
Uruguay	438.44	90.97	171.80	722.83	372.34	503.59
Spain (regions)	501.58	80.34	204.01	755.13	448.83	560.39
United Arab Emirates	433.99	99.37	70.80	743.14	360.92	507.38
USA (Massachusetts)	524.83	88.05	195.97	754.54	470.51	585.20
USA (North Carolina)	499.45	90.33	226.15	755.60	434.58	567.03
Vietnam	489.08	64.88	116.68	697.06	444.80	533.22

Reading Overall by Country

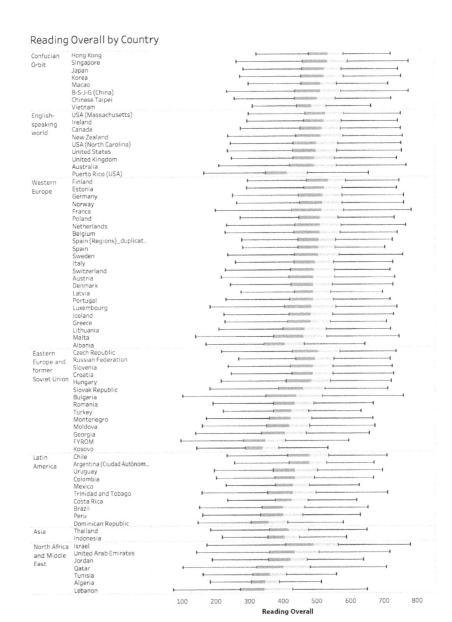

Figure A4.1 Distributions—Reading Overall

PISA 2015 Math Score

	Mean	Standard Deviation	Minimum	Maximum	Percentile 25	Percentile 75
Albania	412.85	76.55	150.37	675.92	358.17	465.92
Algeria	358.85	58.35	173.23	616.05	319.19	393.35
Argentina (Ciudad Autónoma de Buenos Aires)	454.27	80.50	172.37	691.29	399.69	512.27
Australia	482.84	87.82	201.55	779.51	419.51	545.69
Austria	498.85	87.81	182.83	758.58	435.24	561.64
Belgium	510.32	91.29	198.92	793.25	445.48	579.29
Brazil	374.39	77.24	113.37	711.67	318.97	421.57
Bulgaria	443.19	89.53	154.06	732.07	375.31	508.47
Canada	504.52	78.61	225.52	792.65	449.58	559.73
Chile	442.20	83.53	182.37	690.74	380.65	503.90
Chinese Taipei	539.72	97.17	108.15	817.21	474.65	610.19
Colombia	397.38	69.73	174.69	672.41	347.07	444.89
Costa Rica	400.19	60.94	199.20	638.79	356.39	440.88
Croatia	464.98	81.68	200.59	726.38	405.51	521.33
Czech Republic	502.56	87.22	217.71	769.59	439.44	564.26
Denmark	497.61	78.53	249.64	730.25	440.58	554.64
Dominican Republic	331.25	61.78	128.79	604.12	288.39	369.99
Estonia	520.85	74.45	283.46	747.75	468.18	573.70
Finland	511.87	75.73	201.87	737.36	461.73	565.55
France	496.57	89.28	162.56	770.75	432.75	563.76
Georgia	406.26	86.65	73.50	686.11	347.53	465.09
Germany	508.74	83.40	239.28	765.73	451.31	567.73
Greece	461.69	81.39	163.97	710.12	404.13	520.88

(Continued)

(Continued)

PISA 2015 Math Score

	Mean	Standard Deviation	Minimum	Maximum	Percentile 25	Percentile 75
Hong Kong	550.72	82.28	244.82	795.08	497.88	609.75
Hungary	484.73	86.10	211.60	770.34	423.92	545.59
Iceland	488.79	85.72	219.15	769.58	428.06	551.28
Indonesia	393.03	72.55	168.35	676.35	340.76	438.18
Ireland	503.41	74.36	208.07	728.78	452.22	554.64
Israel	471.64	96.40	177.99	770.69	401.21	543.59
Italy	499.79	83.94	221.57	813.69	441.31	559.51
Japan	532.51	82.17	201.10	758.20	477.58	590.71
Jordan	382.94	76.06	50.32	651.93	333.02	435.01
Korea	523.39	92.69	177.78	792.41	461.31	589.89
Kosovo	356.83	68.28	135.60	642.18	309.79	402.07
Latvia	484.22	70.36	253.13	737.85	435.42	533.37
Lebanon	401.54	92.71	107.66	739.10	332.68	466.00
Lithuania	474.02	80.83	200.31	734.17	415.77	531.58
Luxembourg	486.45	87.97	241.57	760.11	419.51	551.89
Macao	543.90	73.14	184.44	792.50	495.23	596.57
Malta	483.53	102.51	78.67	761.00	413.39	559.18
Mexico	413.20	67.23	186.45	679.63	366.03	459.67
Moldova	419.90	80.79	154.24	691.27	362.31	475.85
Montenegro	416.49	78.25	145.69	680.82	359.70	470.64
Netherlands	513.91	86.49	232.85	806.54	453.49	578.24
New Zealand	495.83	85.77	230.01	765.83	434.17	557.12
Norway	501.10	78.66	210.82	749.02	447.00	557.12
Peru	387.90	75.47	115.18	646.99	333.70	440.25

Poland	505.28	81.08	151.14	746.32	447.50	561.19
Portugal	480.95	90.69	162.44	755.43	412.42	547.50
Puerto Rico (USA)	382.39	70.58	197.05	619.83	332.51	426.69
Qatar	402.34	91.65	129.43	728.64	332.81	464.59
Romania	444.01	78.99	214.37	691.05	386.71	497.80
Russian Federation	494.84	74.84	221.94	720.22	442.08	548.47
Singapore	556.28	89.91	262.75	826.34	494.44	621.75
Slovak Republic	477.01	88.96	171.43	764.83	417.73	541.07
Slovenia	494.42	82.23	235.40	778.21	434.58	553.40
Spain	490.55	77.62	223.01	774.87	437.60	546.50
Sweden	493.60	83.10	202.20	776.01	436.28	553.34
Switzerland	519.37	88.50	221.12	793.55	455.83	583.96
Thailand	428.79	83.11	169.25	719.03	368.78	482.16
Trinidad and Tobago	416.30	90.06	143.54	728.11	351.03	480.26
United Arab Emirates	428.10	88.05	118.97	732.92	363.19	488.80
Tunisia	366.60	73.36	142.72	682.26	315.38	411.44
Turkey	415.80	73.63	192.09	676.35	363.35	466.52
FYROM	368.68	84.59	105.26	721.12	310.05	423.18
United Kingdom	491.50	81.07	114.47	754.24	434.09	548.80
United States	468.75	82.61	192.29	723.09	409.88	526.96
Uruguay	420.27	81.18	190.06	712.05	360.14	476.83
B-S-J-G (China)	541.34	95.82	159.48	812.95	475.61	612.63
Spain (regions)	492.98	76.13	221.88	736.25	440.27	548.16
USA (Massachusetts)	498.61	78.93	204.35	713.33	448.55	552.76
USA (North Carolina)	470.63	80.53	216.39	732.65	410.82	527.79
Vietnam	496.64	75.12	220.91	764.97	442.31	547.86

Mathematics Overall by Country

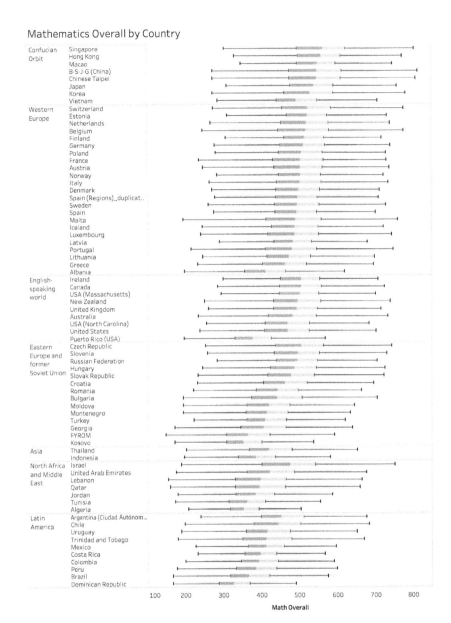

Figure A4.2 Distributions—Mathematics Overall

	PISA 2015 Science Score					
	Mean	Standard Deviation	Minimum	Maximum	Percentile 25	Percentile 75
Albania	427.03	73.44	193.78	664.49	374.26	478.73
Algeria	375.46	60.46	155.60	612.24	333.54	410.62
Argentina (Ciudad Autónoma de Buenos Aires)	472.14	79.97	201.74	684.06	415.67	530.51
Australia	498.75	100.71	215.11	802.02	423.73	572.82
Austria	496.85	93.25	226.01	772.96	427.52	565.11
Belgium	505.43	96.20	198.05	786.66	435.04	578.99
Brazil	398.44	81.15	146.95	718.98	338.77	450.58
Bulgaria	448.03	97.14	189.85	748.39	373.38	522.05
Canada	516.31	87.47	225.54	795.29	455.10	579.64
Chile	465.12	84.87	218.37	704.61	400.55	529.09
Chinese Taipei	530.60	96.30	218.19	799.37	465.62	601.84
Colombia	424.30	75.33	204.34	702.79	369.16	476.70
Costa Rica	419.75	64.74	226.46	679.09	373.10	463.46
Croatia	476.49	84.99	237.76	751.41	413.67	536.43
Czech Republic	503.54	94.37	218.62	759.17	432.98	573.78
Denmark	486.44	91.10	190.00	814.40	420.40	552.77
Dominican Republic	334.72	66.90	156.36	626.98	287.02	373.79
Estonia	535.64	85.38	265.29	775.17	476.72	597.71
Finland	531.57	91.93	234.43	793.90	468.36	598.68
France	498.76	97.82	216.58	750.15	426.95	573.29
Georgia	413.01	85.52	180.29	717.25	351.07	471.51
Germany	512.21	95.54	206.72	792.95	442.76	581.90

(Continued)

(Continued)

	PISA 2015 Science Score					
	Mean	Standard Deviation	Minimum	Maximum	Percentile 25	Percentile 75
Greece	463.69	86.04	212.71	715.65	399.39	527.01
Hong Kong	525.61	76.32	256.71	746.96	479.08	579.44
Hungary	484.73	90.17	210.46	753.52	418.41	551.44
Iceland	473.72	87.23	203.22	726.41	408.97	536.43
Indonesia	409.28	63.35	225.68	640.90	363.61	449.84
Ireland	502.55	85.32	212.61	764.43	443.96	562.49
Israel	469.54	102.12	187.24	758.65	392.45	546.13
Italy	492.38	85.03	192.52	750.17	430.84	555.09
Japan	538.77	89.67	244.57	805.71	476.84	604.16
Jordan	411.81	78.30	124.26	635.43	356.69	467.53
Korea	515.20	91.43	231.51	791.42	451.72	582.46
Kosovo	372.75	64.43	200.72	616.25	326.31	414.15
Lebanon	390.80	84.90	159.22	698.46	328.18	448.71
Latvia	491.22	77.03	260.61	729.89	437.10	545.58
Lithuania	468.23	87.54	166.57	742.78	402.58	530.69
Luxembourg	483.51	97.02	218.80	792.38	408.28	556.21
Macao	528.64	77.67	258.08	782.85	476.51	584.19
Malta	469.89	112.28	101.47	765.07	387.37	552.76
Mexico	420.33	66.33	218.25	659.37	373.24	465.47
Moldova	427.84	80.55	177.43	686.51	370.08	484.19
Montenegro	409.74	80.32	149.47	704.64	351.34	463.82
Netherlands	510.65	97.46	253.72	809.62	437.57	584.73
New Zealand	513.75	100.40	215.84	796.69	440.49	586.51

Norway	497.84	92.63	189.28	773.13	431.93	563.02
Peru	397.68	72.20	171.92	654.08	343.37	445.92
Poland	502.18	86.27	168.50	755.87	439.21	562.74
Portugal	489.69	89.53	232.80	758.41	420.78	556.35
Puerto Rico (USA)	408.27	80.75	218.08	637.81	347.68	462.62
Qatar	417.87	94.37	177.74	758.06	344.18	483.82
Romania	435.43	74.25	177.80	684.31	381.35	484.77
Russian Federation	486.40	78.58	257.92	743.98	429.58	542.82
Singapore	546.68	100.87	235.22	835.62	477.07	622.05
Slovak Republic	462.65	94.79	172.84	766.29	394.00	531.55
Slovenia	494.50	91.08	231.15	774.08	426.69	560.90
Spain	497.19	83.11	245.45	723.03	440.00	556.64
Sweden	492.99	98.21	197.29	795.91	422.68	564.09
Switzerland	502.06	94.72	183.92	777.04	431.58	574.00
Thailand	433.94	84.02	218.78	690.60	370.12	490.80
Trinidad and Tobago	424.87	88.40	156.64	708.55	356.42	488.49
United Arab Emirates	437.54	94.90	133.43	728.58	365.90	505.12
Tunisia	386.35	59.03	222.27	624.36	343.88	424.06
Turkey	421.91	73.20	234.21	681.43	367.35	473.74
FYROM	380.85	77.12	135.92	663.39	325.14	430.33
United Kingdom	502.91	93.42	203.58	806.14	432.79	571.19
United States	495.82	94.38	193.73	817.77	425.37	565.76
Uruguay	437.02	83.09	212.02	708.12	373.16	496.64
B-S-J-G (China)	528.06	95.40	185.79	790.28	461.79	600.05
Spain (regions)	499.35	83.09	198.27	745.84	440.32	560.32
USA (Massachusetts)	527.19	92.87	254.05	775.17	464.94	593.81
USA (North Carolina)	501.91	92.43	250.20	741.14	431.92	571.11
Vietnam	525.70	70.74	311.26	770.66	473.88	574.72

Science Overall by Country

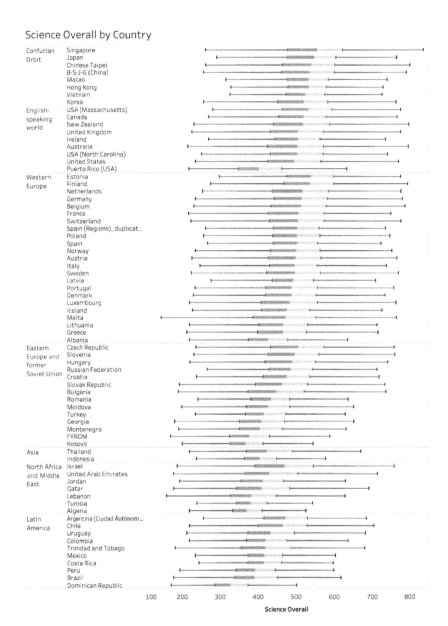

Figure A4.3 Distributions—Science Overall

	Mean	Standard Deviation	Minimum	Maximum	Percentile 25	Percentile 75
Albania						
Algeria	-0.1167	0.9066	-2.4162	1.8837	-0.7475	0.6558
Argentina (Ciudad Autónoma de Buenos Aires)	-0.0901	0.8345	-2.4162	1.8837	-0.6873	0.5529
Australia	-0.2357	1.0361	-2.4162	1.8837	-0.8964	0.4541
Austria	0.2548	1.0864	-2.4162	1.8837	-0.5154	1.0389
Belgium	-0.1415	1.0158	-2.4162	1.8837	-0.7968	0.5529
Brazil	-0.2243	0.9722	-2.4162	1.8837	-0.8747	0.3993
Bulgaria	-0.1867	0.9891	-2.4162	1.8837	-0.8747	0.4541
Canada	-0.0043	1.0242	-2.4162	1.8837	-0.6873	0.6605
Chile	-0.0910	0.8587	-2.4162	1.8837	-0.6688	0.5252
Chinese Taipei	0.1811	0.8969	-2.4162	1.8837	-0.2683	0.6605
Colombia	-0.0028	0.8804	-2.4162	1.8837	-0.5803	0.5954
Costa Rica	0.1278	0.9156	-2.4162	1.8837	-0.5148	0.8033
Croatia	-0.0482	0.8916	-2.4162	1.8837	-0.6315	0.5529
Czech Republic	-0.1866	1.0385	-2.4162	1.8837	-0.8747	0.5529
Denmark	0.0065	0.9622	-2.4162	1.8837	-0.6002	0.6605
Dominican Republic	0.0213	1.0136	-2.4162	1.8837	-0.6847	0.7001
Estonia	-0.0675	0.9060	-2.4162	1.8837	-0.6676	0.5529
Finland	-0.1057	0.8813	-2.4162	1.8837	-0.7211	0.4046
France	-0.2653	0.9584	-2.4162	1.8837	-0.8964	0.3363
Georgia	0.3521	0.8614	-2.4162	1.8837	-0.1424	0.9373
Germany	0.0548	0.9386	-2.4162	1.8837	-0.5803	0.7011
Greece	-0.1949	0.8442	-2.4162	1.8837	-0.7413	0.3363

(Continued)

Science Disciplinary Climate (WLE) (PISA 2015)

(Continued)

| | Science Disciplinary Climate (WLE) (PISA 2015) | | | | | |
	Mean	Standard Deviation	Minimum	Maximum	Percentile 25	Percentile 75
Hong Kong	0.3572	0.9345	-2.4162	1.8837	0.0039	0.9828
Hungary	-0.0822	0.9899	-2.4162	1.8837	-0.7439	0.5529
Iceland	0.0171	0.9529	-2.4162	1.8837	-0.5803	0.5952
Indonesia	0.2148	0.8490	-2.4162	1.8837	-0.3843	0.8351
Ireland	0.0946	1.0287	-2.4162	1.8837	-0.5803	0.8934
Israel	-0.0205	1.0673	-2.4162	1.8837	-0.7391	0.6605
Italy	-0.0316	0.9126	-2.4162	1.8837	-0.6647	0.6558
Japan	0.8516	0.9326	-2.4162	1.8837	0.2829	1.8837
Jordan	-0.0900	0.9533	-2.4162	1.8837	-0.7217	0.5529
Korea	0.6240	0.9174	-2.4162	1.8837	0.0039	1.1892
Kosovo	0.5562	0.8912	-2.4162	1.8837	0.0039	1.1892
Latvia	-0.1682	0.9128	-2.4162	1.8837	-0.7439	0.4046
Lebanon	-0.0991	0.8666	-2.4162	1.8837	-0.6873	0.4541
Lithuania	0.0467	1.0579	-2.4162	1.8837	-0.6620	0.7048
Luxembourg	-0.1185	1.0955	-2.4162	1.8837	-0.8504	0.6558
Macao	0.1598	0.7690	-2.4162	1.8837	-0.2336	0.6558
Malta	-0.0134	0.9906	-2.4162	1.8837	-0.6676	0.7001
Mexico	0.0510	0.8777	-2.4162	1.8837	-0.5407	0.6558
Moldova	0.3797	0.7673	-2.4162	1.8837	0.0039	0.9373
Montenegro	0.0685	1.0430	-2.4162	1.8837	-0.6087	0.8079
Netherlands	-0.0982	0.8049	-2.4162	1.8837	-0.6062	0.2884
New Zealand	-0.1609	1.0443	-2.4162	1.8837	-0.8504	0.5529
Norway	0.1373	0.9307	-2.4162	1.8837	-0.4176	0.7011

Peru	0.1268	0.8546	-2.4162	1.8837	-0.4176	0.6605
Poland	-0.0451	0.9237	-2.4162	1.8837	-0.6326	0.5529
Portugal	0.1069	0.9939	-2.4162	1.8837	-0.5436	0.8351
Puerto Rico (USA)	0.0830	0.9563	-2.4162	1.8837	-0.5454	0.7006
Qatar	-0.0670	1.0235	-2.4162	1.8837	-0.7439	0.5952
Romania	0.2478	0.8219	-2.4162	1.8837	-0.3015	0.8934
Russian Federation	0.3093	1.0171	-2.4162	1.8837	-0.2683	0.9828
Singapore	0.1829	0.8999	-2.4162	1.8837	-0.3506	0.8351
Slovak Republic	-0.1251	1.0050	-2.4162	1.8837	-0.7968	0.5529
Vietnam	0.4208	0.6654	-2.4162	1.8837	0.0039	0.8934
Slovenia	-0.1003	1.0642	-2.4162	1.8837	-0.8428	0.6145
Spain	-0.0729	0.9503	-2.4162	1.8837	-0.7211	0.5952
Sweden	0.0145	0.9513	-2.4162	1.8837	-0.6030	0.6558
Switzerland	0.0544	1.0358	-2.4162	1.8837	-0.6614	0.8351
Thailand	0.3309	0.8405	-2.4162	1.8837	-0.0604	0.8934
Trinidad and Tobago	-0.0465	0.9180	-2.4162	1.8837	-0.6873	0.5540
United Arab Emirates	0.0309	1.0306	-2.4162	1.8837	-0.6873	0.7187
Tunisia	-0.4177	0.8508	-2.4162	1.8837	-0.9769	0.0039
Turkey	-0.1349	0.9648	-2.4162	1.8837	-0.7224	0.3949
FYROM	0.2165	0.8861	-2.4162	1.8837	-0.3200	0.8934
United Kingdom	-0.0443	1.0439	-2.4162	1.8837	-0.7439	0.6558
United States	0.2908	1.0143	-2.4162	1.8837	-0.3506	0.9383
Uruguay	-0.1004	0.9693	-2.4162	1.8837	-0.7439	0.5529
B-S-J-G (China)	0.3594	0.9510	-2.4162	1.8837	-0.0454	0.9373
Spain (regions)	-0.0812	0.9628	-2.4162	1.8837	-0.7393	0.5529
USA (Massachusetts)	0.5143	0.9730	-2.4162	1.8837	0.0039	1.1892
USA (North Carolina)	0.0760	1.0283	-2.4162	1.8837	-0.5831	0.8351

Discipline in Science by Country

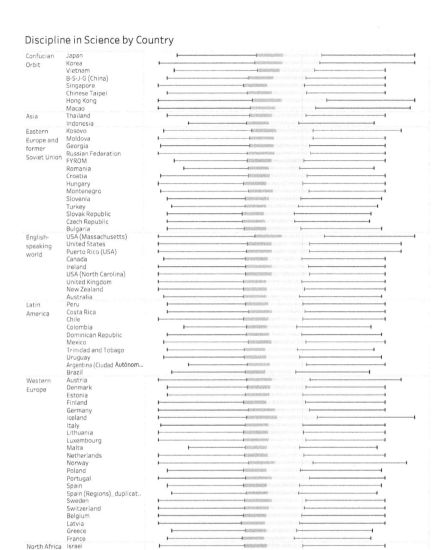

Figure A4.4 Distributions—Disciplinary Climate in Science Classes

Competitiveness

Global Competitiveness Figures for All 12 Pillars for 2018

Row Labels	1st Pillar: Institutions	2nd Pillar: Infrastructure	3rd Pillar: Macroeconomic Environment	4th Pillar: Health and Primary Education	5th Pillar: Higher Education and Training	6th Pillar: Goods Market Efficiency	7th Pillar: Labour Market Efficiency	8th Pillar: Financial Market Development	9th Pillar: Technological Readiness	10th Pillar: Market Size	11th Pillar: Business Sophistication	12th Pillar: Innovation	Global Competitiveness Index
Albania	3.878	3.562	4.595	6.237	4.768	4.432	3.964	3.809	4.071	2.990	3.902	3.199	4.185
Algeria	3.629	3.562	4.634	5.766	3.952	3.639	3.266	3.057	3.358	4.778	3.317	2.941	4.066
Argentina	3.277	3.852	3.377	5.889	4.996	3.436	3.292	3.103	4.321	4.878	3.822	3.302	3.951
Armenia	4.058	3.853	4.135	5.995	4.421	4.699	4.401	3.878	4.086	2.788	3.986	3.308	4.191
Australia	5.352	5.267	5.674	6.523	5.877	4.876	4.685	5.453	5.718	5.133	4.854	4.515	5.192
Austria	5.151	5.725	5.523	6.402	5.677	4.893	4.487	4.577	5.971	4.589	5.577	5.026	5.247
Azerbaijan	4.649	4.540	4.796	5.718	4.463	4.797	5.007	3.843	4.554	3.973	4.439	3.997	4.690
Bahrain	5.040	5.067	3.977	6.224	4.986	4.981	4.552	4.305	5.568	3.307	4.494	3.604	4.539
Bangladesh	3.390	2.918	4.903	5.220	3.102	4.115	3.601	3.602	2.764	4.719	3.704	2.848	3.906
Belgium	5.017	5.419	4.867	6.627	5.820	5.183	4.469	4.682	5.936	4.788	5.418	4.951	5.225
Benin	3.526	2.308	3.938	4.692	3.130	3.665	4.412	3.362	2.389	2.659	3.303	3.027	3.472
Bhutan	4.800	3.644	4.583	5.420	4.005	4.164	4.730	4.010	3.212	1.935	3.833	3.235	4.100
Bosnia and Herzegovina	3.093	3.303	4.817	5.973	3.981	3.701	3.494	3.497	4.270	3.147	3.467	2.716	3.869
Botswana	4.364	3.639	6.094	4.829	3.839	4.214	4.517	4.041	3.627	2.955	3.691	3.189	4.304
Brazil	3.354	4.114	3.443	5.411	4.205	3.791	3.682	3.700	4.568	5.692	4.119	3.209	4.135

(Continued)

(Continued)

Row Labels	1st Pillar: Institutions	2nd Pillar: Infrastructure	3rd Pillar: Macroeconomic Environment	4th Pillar: Health and Primary Education	5th Pillar: Higher Education and Training	6th Pillar: Goods Market Efficiency	7th Pillar: Labour Market Efficiency	8th Pillar: Financial Market Development	9th Pillar: Technological Readiness	10th Pillar: Market Size	11th Pillar: Business Sophistication	12th Pillar: Innovation	Global Competitiveness Index
Brunei Darussalam	4.429	4.315	5.147	6.315	4.471	4.344	4.441	3.748	4.488	2.890	3.692	3.230	4.515
Bulgaria	3.481	4.061	5.723	5.801	4.618	4.322	4.255	4.144	5.135	3.924	3.819	3.317	4.463
Burundi	3.198	2.123	3.587	4.785	2.616	3.744	4.257	2.805	2.112	1.780	3.270	2.753	3.215
Cambodia	3.393	3.139	4.637	5.261	2.883	4.173	4.424	4.089	3.423	3.381	3.577	2.908	3.932
Cameroon	3.480	2.254	4.445	4.772	3.521	3.936	4.138	3.620	2.634	3.399	3.516	3.246	3.651
Canada	5.431	5.702	5.127	6.602	5.770	5.151	5.429	5.436	5.880	5.435	4.979	4.669	5.349
Cape Verde	3.936	3.502	4.136	5.849	4.057	4.007	3.674	3.213	3.796	1.556	3.444	3.077	3.760
Chad	2.641	1.899	4.398	3.623	2.301	3.013	3.777	2.733	1.964	2.824	2.848	2.577	2.989
Chile	4.535	4.783	5.384	5.816	5.254	4.652	4.417	4.922	5.212	4.541	4.261	3.456	4.709
China	4.419	4.657	5.999	6.212	4.781	4.549	4.548	4.229	4.183	7.000	4.514	4.136	5.002
Colombia	3.211	3.770	4.827	5.526	4.504	4.033	3.985	4.636	4.344	4.758	4.066	3.268	4.288
Congo, Democratic Rep.	3.203	2.332	3.454	4.254	2.748	3.591	4.340	3.043	2.498	3.215	3.178	2.812	3.270
Costa Rica	4.248	4.248	4.546	6.245	5.132	4.379	4.219	4.445	4.932	3.453	4.499	3.655	4.497
Croatia	3.455	4.647	4.849	6.130	4.545	4.043	3.767	3.647	5.039	3.617	3.793	2.937	4.191
Cyprus	4.180	5.107	4.192	6.212	4.858	4.896	4.530	3.439	5.521	2.899	4.154	3.416	4.299
Czech Republic	4.165	4.605	6.232	6.402	5.249	4.660	4.488	4.799	5.497	4.494	4.609	3.871	4.774
Denmark	5.458	5.511	6.222	6.408	5.972	5.114	5.195	4.873	6.093	4.289	5.418	5.134	5.391
Dominican Republic	3.048	3.300	5.100	5.073	3.934	3.907	3.617	3.569	3.710	3.887	3.779	2.781	3.865

Ecuador	3.053	4.118	4.345	5.907	4.251	3.651	3.408	3.337	3.603	3.920	3.594	2.897	3.914
Egypt	3.939	4.131	2.588	5.536	3.597	4.149	3.221	3.887	3.453	5.078	3.788	2.917	3.903
El Salvador	2.748	3.970	4.466	5.310	3.485	3.963	3.429	4.152	3.444	3.257	3.600	2.564	3.768
Estonia	5.038	5.092	6.072	6.430	5.523	5.089	5.016	4.852	5.912	3.105	4.363	4.039	4.850
Ethiopia	3.832	2.709	4.874	4.772	2.767	3.715	4.193	3.405	2.357	3.888	3.508	3.202	3.782
Finland	6.163	5.391	5.487	6.896	6.178	5.151	4.778	5.543	5.981	4.164	5.264	5.689	5.489
France	4.842	6.101	4.820	6.393	5.409	4.680	4.349	4.530	5.899	5.747	5.249	4.888	5.180
Gambia	4.307	3.638	2.417	4.195	3.438	4.505	4.640	4.040	3.222	1.529	4.069	2.928	3.605
Georgia	4.200	4.186	5.103	5.788	4.021	4.513	4.392	4.059	4.264	3.088	3.669	2.794	4.279
Germany	5.301	5.964	6.100	6.519	5.695	5.267	5.030	5.033	6.169	6.001	5.646	5.649	5.655
Ghana	4.034	3.252	2.644	4.547	3.673	4.295	4.296	3.781	3.563	3.772	4.091	3.403	3.723
Greece	3.654	4.887	3.701	6.096	4.872	4.124	3.725	2.494	4.802	4.278	3.936	3.266	4.022
Guatemala	3.325	3.818	4.935	4.971	3.667	4.520	3.849	4.899	3.437	3.750	4.199	3.196	4.085
Guinea	3.416	2.432	4.122	3.541	2.913	4.258	4.364	4.600	2.969	2.448	4.060	3.574	3.475
Haiti	2.659	1.790	4.848	4.807	2.650	3.030	3.894	2.454	2.217	2.598	2.640	2.078	3.216
Honduras	3.205	3.244	5.044	5.514	3.562	4.045	3.485	4.462	3.256	3.149	3.753	2.928	3.917
Hong Kong	5.693	6.702	6.281	6.381	5.700	5.736	5.593	5.512	6.167	4.802	5.381	4.532	5.532
Hungary	3.455	4.360	5.131	5.647	4.331	4.378	4.207	4.309	5.095	4.334	3.683	3.364	4.327
Iceland	5.455	5.560	5.939	6.584	5.792	4.785	5.208	4.217	6.166	2.461	4.872	4.664	4.993
India	4.443	4.223	4.538	5.503	4.310	4.472	4.146	4.373	3.116	6.431	4.487	4.094	4.587
Indonesia	4.270	4.524	5.717	5.425	4.517	4.591	3.908	4.503	3.863	5.728	4.556	4.019	4.682
Iran, Islamic Rep.	3.718	4.353	5.153	6.037	4.708	4.039	3.300	3.016	3.615	5.237	3.678	3.344	4.270
Ireland	5.347	5.106	5.770	6.478	5.848	5.347	4.872	3.990	5.969	4.497	5.160	4.705	5.158
Israel	4.940	5.398	5.244	6.344	5.444	4.816	4.900	5.074	6.172	4.294	5.257	5.795	5.312
Italy	3.504	5.374	4.244	6.393	4.959	4.409	3.674	3.051	5.092	5.588	4.918	3.985	4.542

(Continued)

(Continued)

Row Labels	1st Pillar: Institutions	2nd Pillar: Infrastructure	3rd Pillar: Macroeconomic Environment	4th Pillar: Health and Primary Education	5th Pillar: Higher Education and Training	6th Pillar: Goods Market Efficiency	7th Pillar: Labour Market Efficiency	8th Pillar: Financial Market Development	9th Pillar: Technological Readiness	10th Pillar: Market Size	11th Pillar: Business Sophistication	12th Pillar: Innovation	Global Competitiveness Index
Jamaica	3.940	4.094	3.937	6.106	4.378	4.395	4.454	4.571	4.123	2.782	4.259	3.354	4.247
Japan	5.411	6.340	4.303	6.604	5.381	5.236	4.783	4.887	6.006	6.068	5.733	5.369	5.495
Jordan	4.503	4.340	3.778	5.640	4.524	4.508	3.970	3.988	4.294	3.623	4.326	3.593	4.297
Kazakhstan	4.028	4.201	4.168	5.948	4.572	4.293	4.566	3.305	4.627	4.546	3.562	3.220	4.350
Kenya	3.817	3.462	3.574	4.756	3.800	4.355	4.705	4.161	3.707	3.797	4.345	3.846	3.977
Korea	4.043	6.082	6.628	6.344	5.336	4.974	4.181	3.901	5.648	5.527	4.908	4.783	5.072
Kuwait	4.049	4.263	5.599	5.611	3.912	4.163	3.594	4.075	4.271	4.394	3.974	2.972	4.429
Kyrgyzstan	3.438	3.045	4.378	5.697	4.010	4.205	3.690	3.752	3.238	2.779	3.260	2.676	3.896
Lao PDR	4.015	3.266	3.806	5.189	3.466	4.278	4.561	3.891	2.991	3.063	3.746	3.225	3.914
Latvia	3.764	4.403	5.770	6.113	4.955	4.419	4.474	4.051	5.269	3.244	4.071	3.222	4.398
Lebanon	3.183	2.786	2.460	5.764	4.321	4.399	3.741	3.887	4.353	3.630	4.243	3.401	3.845
Lesotho	3.874	2.489	3.814	2.967	3.030	4.289	3.832	2.389	2.583	2.110	3.564	2.837	3.195
Liberia	3.520	2.410	3.339	3.169	2.496	4.015	4.143	3.703	2.225	1.548	3.487	2.786	3.080
Lithuania	4.134	4.654	5.610	6.197	5.163	4.573	4.332	4.101	5.624	3.615	4.354	3.725	4.584
Luxembourg	5.742	5.681	6.275	6.206	4.747	5.519	5.012	4.965	6.457	3.342	5.233	4.990	5.232
Madagascar	3.022	1.994	4.142	4.768	2.906	3.936	4.344	3.100	2.524	2.988	3.347	3.082	3.405
Malawi	3.499	1.789	2.187	4.749	2.662	3.792	4.465	3.548	2.275	2.646	3.271	2.705	3.114
Malaysia	4.978	5.458	5.443	6.317	4.866	5.108	4.717	4.955	4.904	5.086	5.146	4.672	5.174
Mali	3.331	2.825	4.070	3.087	3.015	4.000	3.760	3.365	2.856	2.976	3.550	3.195	3.330
Malta	4.472	4.774	5.847	6.566	5.158	4.876	4.680	4.369	5.893	2.681	4.576	3.826	4.648

Mauritania	2.933	2.100	4.639	4.165	1.902	3.110	3.328	2.129	2.239	2.514	2.708	2.325	3.089
Mauritius	4.486	4.802	4.687	6.068	4.646	4.888	4.398	4.379	4.524	2.820	4.491	3.361	4.523
Mexico	3.198	4.304	5.167	5.689	4.109	4.317	3.771	4.508	4.209	5.672	4.274	3.409	4.435
Moldova	3.205	3.741	4.530	5.398	4.089	4.065	3.939	3.083	4.623	2.680	3.359	2.641	3.992
Mongolia	3.370	3.113	4.369	5.591	4.510	3.954	4.234	2.999	4.177	2.996	3.305	2.987	3.899
Montenegro	3.900	4.156	3.705	5.906	4.542	4.363	4.179	4.238	4.865	2.277	3.628	3.169	4.145
Morocco	4.204	4.416	4.905	5.631	3.580	4.426	3.582	3.929	3.811	4.337	3.985	3.142	4.244
Mozambique	3.055	2.471	1.863	3.594	2.253	3.798	3.899	2.769	2.869	3.095	3.164	2.800	2.886
Namibia	4.395	4.211	4.017	4.774	3.325	4.180	4.595	4.210	3.628	2.868	3.769	3.243	3.991
Nepal	3.575	2.613	5.589	5.677	3.443	3.968	3.899	3.912	2.767	3.368	3.392	2.758	4.018
Netherlands	5.757	6.438	6.077	6.692	6.089	5.500	5.067	4.628	6.344	5.102	5.690	5.552	5.662
New Zealand	6.066	5.453	6.062	6.619	5.965	5.301	5.474	5.813	6.092	3.937	4.935	4.690	5.369
Nicaragua	3.243	3.583	5.095	5.548	3.419	3.878	3.851	3.567	3.060	3.012	3.224	2.468	3.950
Nigeria	3.168	2.037	3.512	2.998	3.104	4.069	4.599	3.701	2.978	4.984	3.684	2.849	3.300
Norway	5.822	5.043	6.640	6.592	5.879	4.983	5.107	5.188	6.121	4.433	5.369	5.006	5.404
Oman	4.960	4.905	4.704	5.901	4.402	4.528	3.504	4.161	4.507	4.057	3.951	3.262	4.310
Pakistan	3.527	3.034	4.031	4.144	2.995	3.983	3.367	3.644	2.982	4.946	3.806	3.381	3.669
Panama	3.820	4.901	6.115	5.643	4.015	4.600	4.146	4.995	4.376	3.586	4.366	3.415	4.437
Paraguay	2.997	2.625	5.186	5.083	3.443	4.173	3.770	3.804	3.229	3.344	3.485	2.672	3.711
Peru	3.215	3.775	5.355	5.439	4.104	4.278	4.271	4.511	3.725	4.454	3.810	2.849	4.223
Philippines	3.505	3.429	5.822	5.629	4.591	4.025	4.018	4.187	3.804	4.970	4.102	3.347	4.351
Poland	3.843	4.699	5.195	6.215	4.978	4.555	4.139	4.171	4.895	5.173	4.114	3.395	4.594
Portugal	4.400	5.593	4.036	6.435	5.092	4.702	4.351	3.255	5.736	4.334	4.366	4.001	4.567
Qatar	5.604	5.834	5.933	6.250	5.008	5.224	4.894	4.707	5.413	4.383	5.021	4.682	5.106
Romania	3.703	3.822	5.250	5.486	4.409	4.143	3.972	3.740	4.780	4.612	3.467	3.085	4.277
Russian Federation	3.747	4.927	5.027	5.995	5.124	4.209	4.333	3.447	4.548	5.898	3.966	3.547	4.642

(Continued)

(Continued)

Row Labels	1st Pillar: Institutions	2nd Pillar: Infra- structure	3rd Pillar: Macro- economic Environ- ment	4th Pillar: Health and Primary Education	5th Pillar: Higher Education and Training	6th Pillar: Goods Market Efficiency	7th Pillar: Labour Market Efficiency	8th Pillar: Financial Market Develop- ment	9th Pillar: Techno- logical Readiness	10th Pillar: Market Size	11th Pillar: Business Sophisti- cation	12th Pillar: Inno- vation	Global Compe- titiveness Index
Rwanda	5.418	3.392	4.344	5.339	3.236	4.679	5.371	4.515	3.243	2.641	4.089	3.647	4.349
Saudi Arabia	5.010	5.202	4.872	6.032	4.872	4.597	4.103	4.157	4.941	5.442	4.505	3.728	4.827
Senegal	3.900	3.138	4.481	4.295	3.444	4.201	3.912	3.668	3.253	3.057	3.776	3.460	3.809
Serbia	3.422	4.087	4.610	6.023	4.554	3.956	3.964	3.561	4.194	3.719	3.516	3.108	4.141
Seychelles	3.774	4.552	4.599	5.966	3.916	4.281	4.103	3.267	4.153	1.450	3.854	2.940	3.796
Sierra Leone	3.296	2.579	3.239	4.289	2.543	3.711	3.723	3.168	2.456	2.221	3.236	2.684	3.198
Singapore	6.085	6.544	5.982	6.761	6.266	5.765	5.791	5.657	6.089	4.781	5.216	5.283	5.706
Slovak Republic	3.512	4.287	5.404	6.097	4.535	4.481	4.006	4.550	5.084	4.078	4.187	3.329	4.334
Slovenia	4.051	4.804	5.229	6.493	5.372	4.639	4.102	3.449	5.365	3.412	4.376	3.982	4.477
South Africa	3.807	4.310	4.523	4.466	4.060	4.483	3.963	4.355	4.582	4.914	4.491	3.796	4.321
Spain	4.097	5.877	4.351	6.294	5.197	4.513	4.209	4.006	5.676	5.421	4.624	3.718	4.700
Sri Lanka	3.805	3.800	4.269	6.155	4.232	4.195	3.298	3.783	3.161	4.204	4.094	3.416	4.084
Swaziland	4.016	3.220	3.279	3.631	3.236	3.873	4.073	3.767	2.607	2.212	3.449	2.399	3.354
Sweden	5.590	5.563	6.439	6.410	5.588	5.227	4.875	5.135	6.302	4.662	5.634	5.498	5.519
Switzerland	5.935	6.255	6.575	6.783	6.074	5.498	5.940	5.290	6.390	4.687	5.892	5.821	5.858
Taiwan, China	4.850	5.705	6.327	6.484	5.635	5.256	4.728	4.896	5.739	5.220	5.130	5.106	5.327
Tajikistan	4.413	3.337	4.100	5.749	4.310	4.339	4.588	3.487	2.951	2.774	3.867	3.577	4.136

Country													
Tanzania	3.846	2.774	4.596	4.284	2.626	3.902	4.291	3.519	2.640	3.810	3.683	3.223	3.711
Thailand	3.796	4.700	6.226	5.511	4.564	4.721	4.258	4.439	4.481	5.237	4.372	3.464	4.723
Trinidad and Tobago	3.493	4.322	3.843	5.929	5.104	4.090	4.013	4.188	4.864	3.156	4.065	2.975	4.090
Tunisia	3.777	3.826	3.945	5.952	4.091	3.953	3.093	3.390	3.727	3.861	3.673	3.072	3.930
Turkey	3.846	4.472	5.097	5.600	4.777	4.484	3.389	3.819	4.423	5.499	3.993	3.315	4.418
Uganda	3.481	2.486	4.593	4.642	2.762	3.877	4.642	3.723	2.902	3.443	3.623	3.268	3.698
Ukraine	3.209	3.947	3.523	6.023	5.087	4.036	4.011	3.108	3.833	4.485	3.722	3.368	4.107
United Arab Emirates	5.934	6.264	5.630	6.262	5.049	5.618	5.174	4.761	5.811	4.940	5.284	4.579	5.297
United Kingdom	5.517	5.959	4.649	6.466	5.479	5.285	5.436	5.027	6.329	5.753	5.583	5.094	5.507
United States	5.325	6.010	4.509	6.328	6.120	5.472	5.644	5.727	6.235	6.860	5.774	5.820	5.853
Uruguay	4.551	4.665	4.258	5.774	4.619	4.277	3.528	4.093	5.337	3.332	3.793	3.145	4.146
Venezuela	2.179	2.629	2.435	5.323	4.558	2.756	2.724	3.102	3.021	4.376	3.025	2.555	3.228
Vietnam	3.794	3.902	4.587	5.809	4.075	4.147	4.349	3.979	3.983	4.912	3.669	3.306	4.356
Yemen	2.674	1.831	2.849	4.677	2.247	3.436	2.996	2.177	2.041	3.148	2.944	2.418	2.875
Zambia	3.721	2.444	3.682	4.361	2.922	4.169	3.858	3.664	2.899	3.349	3.615	3.168	3.518
Zimbabwe	3.246	2.660	3.194	4.693	3.115	3.457	3.721	3.165	2.741	2.798	3.187	2.547	3.320

Note

1. See Figure 1. The analytical structure of a meso trajectory in Dopfer et al. (2004), page 273, for a helpful illustration of the three-level architecture.

References

Agasisti, Tommaso. "The efficiency of public spending on education: An empirical comparison of EU countries." *European Journal of Education* 49, no. 4 (2014): 543–557.

Annabi, Nabil, Simon Harvey, and Yu Lan. "Public expenditures on education, human capital and growth in Canada: An OLG model analysis." *Journal of Policy Modeling* 33, no. 6 (2011): 852–865.

Barro, Robert J. "Education and economic growth." *Annals of Economics and Finance* 14, no. 2 (2013): 301–328.

Barro, Robert J., and Jong Wha Lee. "International measures of schooling years and schooling quality." *The American Economic Review* 86, no. 2 (1996): 218–223.

Baumann, Chris, and Hume Winzar. "The role of secondary education in explaining competitiveness." *Asia Pacific Journal of Education* 36, no. 1 (2016): 13–30.

Baumann, Chris, and Marina Harvey. "Competitiveness vis-à-vis motivation and personality as drivers of academic performance: Introducing the MCP model." *International Journal of Educational Management* 32, no. 1 (2018): 185–202.

BenDavid-Hadar, Iris. "Education in times of fiscal constraints and globalization." *International Journal of Educational Management* 27, no. 7 (2013): 762–774.

Dissou, Yazid, Selma Didic, and Tatsiana Yakautsava. "Government spending on education, human capital accumulation, and growth." *Economic Modelling* 58 (2016): 9–21.

Dopfer, Kurt, John Foster, and Jason Potts. "Micro-meso-macro." *Journal of Evolutionary Economics* 14, no. 3 (2004): 263–279.

Fang, T. "Understanding Chinese culture and communication: The yin yang approach." In B. Gehrke & M.-T. Claes (Eds.), *Global leadership practices: A cross-cultural management perspective* (pp. 171–187). Houndmills: Palgrave Macmillan, 2014.

Franke, Richard H., Geert Hofstede, and Michael H. Bond. "Cultural roots of economic performance: A research note." *Strategic Management Journal* 12, no. S1 (1991): 165–173.

Fuligni, Andrew J. "The academic achievement of adolescents from immigrant families: The role of family background, attitudes, and behavior." *Child Development* 68, no. 2 (1997): 351–363.

Hanushek, Eric A. *Education Production Functions: Developed Countries Evidence.* Amsterdam: Elsevier (Economics of Education), 2010, pp. 132–136.

Hanushek, Eric A. "The economic value of higher teacher quality." *Economics of Education Review* 30, no. 3 (2011): 466–479.

Hofstede, Geert, and Michael Harris Bond. "The Confucius connection: From cultural roots to economic growth." *Organizational Dynamics* 16, no. 4 (1988): 5–21.

House, Robert, Denise M. Rousseau, and Melissa Thomashunt. "The Meso paradigm-a framework for the integration of micro and macro organizational-behavior." *Research in Organizational Behavior: An Annual Series of Analytical Essays and Critical Reviews* 17 (1995): 71–114.

Ip, Po Keung. "Is Confucianism good for business ethics in China?" *Journal of Business Ethics* 88, no. 3 (2009): 463–476.

Jensen, Ben, Julian Reichl, and Andrew Kemp. "The real issue in school funding: An analysis of increasing government school expenditure and declining performance." *Australian Economic Review* 44, no. 3 (2011): 321–329.

Kao, Grace. "Asian Americans as model minorities? A look at their academic performance." *American Journal of Education* 103, no. 2 (1995): 121–159.

Keller, Katarina R. I. "Education expansion, expenditures per student and the effects on growth in Asia." *Global Economic Review* 35, no. 1 (2006): 21–42.

Kim, Jeong Won. "Education reform policies and classroom teaching in South Korea." *International Studies in Sociology of Education* 14, no. 2 (2004): 125–146.

Krskova, Hana, and Chris Baumann. "School discipline, investment, competitiveness and mediating educational performance." *International Journal of Educational Management* 31, no. 3 (2017): 293–319.

Lam, Kit-Chun Joanna. "Confucian business ethics and the economy." *Journal of Business Ethics* 43, no. 1–2 (2003): 153–162.

Lin, Liang-Hung, and Yu-Ling Ho. "Confucian dynamism, culture and ethical changes in Chinese societies—A comparative study of China, Taiwan, and Hong Kong." *The International Journal of Human Resource Management* 20, no. 11 (2009): 2402–2417.

Mayhew, Ken, and Ewart Keep. "The assessment: Knowledge, skills, and competitiveness." *Oxford Review of Economic Policy* 15, no. 1 (1999): 1–15.

McKinsey and Company Report. *Drivers of Student Performance: Insights From Asia*, 2017. https://www.mckinsey.com/industries/social-sector/our-insights/drivers-of-student-performance-asia-insights

Nelson, Richard R., and Edmund S. Phelps. "Investment in humans, technological diffusion, and economic growth." *The American Economic Review* 56, no. 1/2 (1966): 69–75.

Redding, G. *The Spirit of Chinese Capitalism*. Berlin: Walter de Gruyter & Co., 1990.

Rivkin, Steven G., Eric A. Hanushek, and John F. Kain. "Teachers, schools, and academic achievement." *Econometrica* 73, no. 2 (2005): 417–458.

Robertson, Christopher J., and James J. Hoffman. "How different are we? An investigation of Confucian values in the United States." *Journal of Managerial Issues* (2000): 34–47.

Sabadie, Jesus Alquezar, and Jens Johansen. "How do national economic competitiveness indices view human capital?" *European Journal of Education* 45, no. 2 (2010): 236–258.

Sahlberg, Pasi. "Education reform for raising economic competitiveness." *Journal of Educational Change* 7, no. 4 (2006): 259–287.

Schultz, Theodore W. "Capital formation by education." *Journal of Political Economy* 68, no. 6 (1960): 571–583.

Schwab, Klaus, and Xavier Sala-i-Martin. "The global competitiveness report 2013–2014." *World Economic Forum*. Full Data Edition, 2014.

Siddiqi, Arjumand, Ichiro Kawachi, Lisa Berkman, Clyde Hertzman, and S. V. Subramanian. "Education determines a nation's health, but what determines educational outcomes? A cross-national comparative analysis." *Journal of Public Health Policy* 33, no. 1 (2012): 1–15.

Tsai, Terence, Michael N. Young, and Bor-shiuan Cheng. "Confucian business practices and firm competitiveness: The case of Sinyi real estate." *Frontiers of Business Research in China* 5, no. 3 (2011): 317.

Viengkham, Doris, Chris Baumann, and Hume Winzar. "Confucianism: Measurement and association with workforce performance." *Cross Cultural & Strategic Management* 25, no. 2 (2018): 337–374.

Wang, Jia, Greg G. Wang, Wendy E. A. Ruona, and Jay W. Rojewski. "Confucian values and the implications for international HRD." *Human Resource Development International* 8, no. 3 (2005): 311–326.

Woessmann, Ludger. "Cross-country evidence on teacher performance pay." *Economics of Education Review* 30, no. 3 (2011): 404–418.

5 Conclusions and Outlook on CDC

In this book we introduce CDC: Confucianism, Discipline, and Competitiveness. We argue that they are related constructs, or to be more precise, that under Confucianism, discipline is a key 'ingredient' of education, and that in turn drives academic performance, and that in turn drives competitiveness. In one sentence, this is what our book is all about—and in a total of five chapters, we argue our case with large empirical databases: Programme for International Student Assessment (PISA) data from the Organisation for Economic Co-operation and Development (OECD) and the World Economic Forum's (WEF) Global Competitiveness Index (GCI).

A famous quote during the emergence of Japan's economic boom states that "Japanese and American management is 95 per cent the same and differs in all important respects" (Pascale and Athos, 1981, p. 85). Forty years on with evidence from CDC we add that it is the Confucian-driven discipline through education that makes all the difference.

In essence, our book is not least a 'follow up' from Amy Chua's book titled *Battle Hymn of the Tiger Mother* (2011). The American Yale Law School professor had also written books on democracy and globalisation, but her book on 'tiger mom' parenting was by far her most influential, and also not the least uncontroversial. Chua's approach to parenting was shocking to some from a permissive Western pedagogical standpoint, but then again, many (also in the West) were clearly tempted to agree with her points, and of course in East Asia, the book was largely applauded from a Confucian point of view.

Chua's book argued for a rather strict parenting style, founded in anecdotal evidence through sharing her own experiences as a mother while raising her two daughters. No doubt her approach has made her two daughters, Sophia and Lulu, successful, notwithstanding that the book contains little or no empirical evidence that discipline would indeed be a contributing factor to performance at large. Importantly, however, both her daughters supported her mother's parenting style outlined in her bestselling book with public endorsements on television shows and in the media; both have become well rounded individuals in their own right, and attribute that outcome not least to their upbringing, and the value of hard work and discipline instilled in them from an early age. A recent interview with Chua's eldest daughter, a Harvard senior at the time, revealed her appreciation for her mother's strict disciplinarian approach, commenting that as a result, "I don't slack—and that's part of Tiger Mom".[1]

Amy Chua has long since turned her fame into an 'enterprise'—she has written more books, has set up her own website (http://battlehymnofthetigermother.com/), and she appears on various television networks (e.g. CNN, Fox). She is also a regular contributor to online and print media. The *Boston Globe* had this to say about her book, putting her contribution in context of changed global market dynamics:

> The cultural divide Chua so brilliantly captures is one we stand to witness more and more in our globalized age, after all; and what with Asia and Asian achievement looming ever larger in the American imagination, the issues inherent in *Battle Hymn [of the Tiger Mother]* are as important as they are entertaining.

Further, her controversial, though evidently successful approach to parenting has garnered commentary in the West that not only resurfaced the longstanding debate on 'strict versus fair' disciplinarian approaches, but has also put into perspective how many felt about where discipline was heading:

> In a poll on the *Wall Street Journal* website regarding Chua's response to readers, two-thirds of respondents voted that the "Demanding Eastern" parenting model is better than the "Permissive Western" model. Allison Pearson wondered the following in The Daily Telegraph: "Amy Chua's philosophy of child-rearing may be harsh and not for the fainthearted, but ask yourself this: is it really more cruel than the laissez-faire indifference and babysitting-by-TV which too often passes for parenting these days?"
>
> (https://en.wikipedia.org/wiki/Battle_
> Hymn_of_the_Tiger_Mother)

The academic domain has also not been bypassed by the debate around Amy Chua's memoir. The *Asian American Journal of Psychology* published a Special Issue on Tiger Parenting, Asian-Heritage Families, and Child/Adolescent Well-Being in 2013 where the editorial "deconstruct[ed] the myth of the 'tiger mother'" (Juang, Qin and Park, 2013):

- Studies have indeed found that Asian-heritage parents are more authoritarian when compared with European American parents.
- Korean American parenting *ga-jung-kyo-yuk* (which is more or less home preparation for a competitive world through parents and

relatives) is a blend of authoritarian and authoritative parenting types, thus Korean traditional parenting does not entirely match the (previously introduced) Western Baumrind typology of parenting. Koreans combine an authoritative style, warmth, and good communication within the family. They also have unique cultural disciplinary parenting practices.

- Hmong (a Chinese minority group) American adolescents have positive impressions about their parents, describing their mothers as supportive, loving, openly communicative, and showing warmth, contrasting stereotypes of Asian American parents as tiger parents.
- The special issue also found evidence that Asian mothers have "broader goals for their children beyond academic success, including being happy, self-sufficient, and socially and emotionally well adjusted".
- The special issue also revealed that "many (including Chua) may have an 'outdated' view of Chinese parenting. Immigrants may be even more traditional than their non-immigrant counterparts in the heritage countries, and in some ways, immigrants may continue to operate on a frozen and mummified notion of their heritage culture".
- The special issue found "evidence that Asian-heritage parenting can evince positive outcomes in both the academic and psychosocial domains. And that to do so, Asian-heritage parents are employing parenting practices that emphasise nurturance and warmth as well as developing a bicultural parenting style that blends values from both their heritage culture and the mainstream American culture".
- The editorial concludes that tiger parenting is often defined as harsh, demanding, and emotionally unsupportive; strict, controlling, and demanding high academic achievement of their children. There is equally evidence that "that Asian-heritage parents are also warm, supportive, and loving toward their children, which has not been emphasized (and perhaps even de-emphasized) in the literature".

Chua's book was on parenting, and as we have outlined throughout our book chapters, the pedagogical literatures of parenting and school education 'tango', they intertwine—one borrows from the other and vice versa—as we have demonstrated in our discussions. As the debate around Chua's book also highlights, there are effects of globalisation and global migration impacting upbringing and formal education, for example Asian Americans introducing Confucian and other cultural traits into the Western education landscape, a notion we will return to in our research implications.

Our study was based on school education, more precisely reflecting middle or high school levels (students aged 15 years, surveyed through PISA testing). As a framework to argue our case, and to provide empirical evidence from the OECD's publicly available PISA data, and the WEF data sets on global competitiveness, we posed two fundamental questions at the onset of our research project: *firstly*, does discipline drive academic performance and competitiveness? *Secondly*, could it be that under Confucianism, discipline is stronger, and therefore drives performance and competitiveness to be higher in the Confucian Orbit?

We structured our book into five chapters, with the following foci of analysis: Chapter 1 being the introduction, and Chapter 5 the conclusion:

- In *Chapter 2*, we addressed the question: *could school discipline be a driver of academic performance?* Analysing PISA 2015 data, we utilise Structural Equation Modelling (SEM) and compare the resulting model across six geographic clusters.
- In *Chapter 3*, we looked at discipline and academic performance under the microscope. We wanted to explore whether under Confucianism, discipline standards are higher, with associated stronger academic performance. We again used the 2015 PISA data set. This time we applied a new technique called 'Inter-Ocular Testing (IOT)' where we plotted the distribution of each dimension per geographic cluster. This allowed for a visual comparison in addition to mean and median statistics.
- In *Chapter 4*, we looked at CDC over time, offering a diachronic perspective. Applying longitudinal testing, we wanted to examine discipline standards and academic performance over time, comparing geographic clusters. In the same chapter we 'zoomed' in on the 'elite' academic performers vis-à-vis low-performing students over time. The ultimate dependent variable of CDC is competitiveness, so another test presented in Chapter 4 explored competitiveness over time for seven geographic clusters. Following our narrative that discipline is a driver of academic performance, and performance in turn a driver of competitiveness, we explored how academic performance associates with national competitiveness over time. Last but not least, we wanted to offer a simulation with forecasted effects on academic performance and competitiveness when discipline standards are maintained, enhanced or dropped.

We shall not repeat all the results from our study in this conclusion chapter—please refer to the chapter numbers above on where to find the fine-tuned discussions. However, the overarching induction[2] from our study is the demonstration of very similar, if not identical, mechanisms on how discipline does indeed drive academic performance. We did demonstrate these effects for all six geographic regions or in other words, globally.

What makes the big difference is the cultural setting, or the national culture that is reflected in a nation's educational setting, their policies, their teacher education, their philosophy, and how they run their educational institutions, how schools apply discipline in everyday classes. Our study clearly shows that discipline standards around the world are markedly different, and that such differences are not least the explanation why some geographic regions peak perform academically, while others are somewhere in the middle, and others indeed under-perform.

Confucianism is one of the cultural dimensions that stands out in our research—the Confucian Orbit has the highest standards in discipline with the equally highest academic performance. In one way or another, such performance also transforms into sustainable global competitiveness over time.

When we looked at the literature on discipline, we found that a number of helpful and applicable definitions and understandings exist (please see our summary Chapter 1, Table 1.2), and while we ourselves started to understand the concept of discipline better during the course of the research project presented in this book, we came up with an advancement of how discipline could be viewed, could be defined, and we subsequently introduced a new categorisation of discipline (Chapter 3, Figure 3.3).

We offer suggestions and recommendations based on our empirical analyses and simulations that are practical, tangible, with realistic outcomes, especially our breakdown of the discipline dimensions, *de facto* what we label: 'taxonomy of discipline dimensions'. In essence, our approach offers another lens to understanding discipline as made up of a set of criteria, for which there are consequences for non-compliance (e.g. bad behaviour, lack of respect, talking out of turn, unpunctuality). Additionally, we include non-performance as a discipline issue, or a dimension of discipline as it is viewed and practiced in the Confucian Orbit. This is pivotal since traditionally, in Western understanding, underperformance is no (longer a) discipline matter; instead it is often seen as a matter for counselling and support programmes. This is in contrast to how an education within the Confucian Orbit would view or treat failure, or underperformance; under Confucianism, students are viewed in essence as capable (i.e. have the ability) of performing, with solid growth potential. It is the educator's role to guide the student to performance, to betterment, to growth. That also means that Confucianism is less forgiving for poor performance. The one who does not complete their homework, or does not do well on a test, did poorly because they did not try their hardest—and subsequently require discipline as a 'wake-up call'—perhaps even a reminder that they can do better—and this can take many forms throughout the Confucian Orbit. Regardless of the specific type of discipline, this approach does seem to work in the Confucian Orbit with their demonstrated peak academic performance, providing further evidence that East Asian education has a solid understanding (and practice) "that both intrinsic and extrinsic motivation are significantly associated with academic performance, . . . that [there is] the combined importance of intrinsic and extrinsic motivation (carrot and stick) in driving performance" (Baumann and Harvey, 2018, p. 185). The final question for this project is now what our findings mean for theory, for practice, and for future research. We offer some key implications following.

Theoretical Implications

The study reported in this book is not least inspired by the original work conducted by Baumann and Krskova (2016). This follow-up provides a detailed extension with more recent and updated data, and importantly, with Inter-Ocular Testing (IOT) (i.e. plotting the data) and simulation. The theoretical foundation for our work is best summarised in the Contextual Theoretical Foundation for CDC spotlight:

Spotlight

Contextual Theoretical Foundation for CDC

Academic research has long aspired to explain differences in academic performance and soon it became clear that education also links, in one way or another, to economic performance. Researchers started to put such research in a global context (e.g., Hanushek, 2003; Keep and Mayhew, 1999; Porter, 1990; Sahlberg, 2006) with comparisons of diverging pedagogic theory and respective academic results. There are a number of theories at play when dealing with performance, academic, and economic. Going back in history, as far back as Adam Smith in his *Wealth of Nations* from 1776, issues of abilities and talents contributing to countries' capital were being discussed, suggesting an association between education and economic performance. In the 1960s, Schultz argued in his *Capital Formation by Education Theory* (Schultz, 1960) that education should be treated as an investment in nations and his *Human Capital Theory* (Schultz, 1961) explains why some nations have progressed both in terms of educational performance and subsequent economic progression.

Source: Baumann and Krskova (2016)

Our study advances the understanding of drivers of academic performance and competitiveness, and we extend the narrative since traditionally, education was tested as driver of gross domestic product (GDP) in the literature (e.g. Barro and Lee, 1996; Vessman and Hanushek, 2007; Keller, 2006), but not competitiveness. Competitiveness is multi-faceted and multi-dimensional, made up of the WEF 12 pillars (Chapter 1,

Figure 1.6) and thus captures a broader range of social and economic indicators than GDP alone.

From the literature it has been suggested that academic achievement has some link with parenting styles (e.g. Dornbusch, Ritter, Leiderman, Roberts and Fraleigh, 1987; Leung, Lau and Lam, 1998; Shumow, Vandell and Posner, 1998; Spera, 2005), overall suggesting that authoritative parenting results in better adjustment to school environment with higher levels of performance (Aunola, Stattin and Nurmi, 2000). Our contribution to theory is perhaps most aligned with the work by Pellerin (2005), applying parental styles to school discipline. Pellerin's work is based on the foundation of Baumrind's prominent parenting typology (indifferent, permissive, authoritarian, and authoritative). The findings from our research point in the direction that indeed discipline drives performance and ultimately national level competitiveness, suggesting that the authoritative approach to pedagogy, characterised by both high demandingness and high responsiveness, has a role to play in the overall well-being and progression of a country.

While we offer cultural differences as a plausible explanation for the differences on how discipline is viewed and practiced in schools, we offer a visualisation of discipline in action, or rather 'consequences for non-compliance' across clusters (discussed in Chapter 3). The aim is to better advocate for improvements to discipline standards, ultimately considering more severe consequences for non-compliance with poor manners, misbehaviour, infringement with uniform or dress code requirements, unpunctuality, and possibly poor performance (i.e. not trying hard enough). While these dimensions are already well-cultured discipline dimensions in the Confucian Orbit, in other words, students are effectively disciplined for non-compliance with these discipline dimensions, this approach could also be adopted more globally, including the West and Anglo-Saxon societies that generally subscribe to a more permissive pedagogy. Our empirical testing suggests that if or when the bar is lifted in terms of discipline, it would result in generally better performance. We suggest that this notion should also be incorporated into future theoretical and conceptual work in the field of education/pedagogy, i.e. discipline should be included in conceptual, empirical, and philosophical research as a fundamental part of education.

Our study does suggest that the Confucian Orbit has the highest levels of discipline, and this is rooted in the cultural traditions and interpretation of Confucianism. Confucianism views holistic human betterment as a key objective of education and socialisation, with discipline being an integral part of that educational spirit. Discipline dimensions have recently been explored and empirically tested in a revised construct measurement of Confucianism—which examined the pedagogical aspects of the tradition, alongside its relational and transformative aspects. Interestingly, the study found that discipline was viewed as less important for the two clusters which had the largest proportion of respondents with exposure to Western education, i.e. had previously studied outside of East Asia (Viengkham, Baumann and Winzar, 2018).

Our work and theoretical contribution should be viewed in historical context, or in other words, one should look at the development of discipline over time. Recently, it has been proposed that there was an 'Evolution of institutional approach to education' (Baumann, Hamin and Yang, 2016) where East Asia and the West initially *converged* up until the Neo Institutional phase (around the 1970s), but clearly *diverged* during the Postmodernist era (i.e. late twentieth century until present times). In essence, East Asia has long been driven by Confucianism (i.e. for the past 2,500 years) with progression to Confucian Dynamism during the East Asian economic progression (Japan, Taiwan, Korea, Mainland China; also Singapore and Hong Kong, and more recently, Vietnam). During that progression, the region upgraded their infrastructure in education (schools and universities in East Asia are often technologically highly advanced: Korea has the fastest Internet in the world; blackboards have been replaced by interactive whiteboards; students are 'connected'), updated their curriculum (not seldom inspired by Western school material), and, this is crucial for our argument presented in this book, principally maintained the authoritarian approach to education (Table 5.1). Maintaining their Confucian pedagogical approach with a focus on school discipline not least contributed to their progression to top world standard education, as evidenced by their peak academic performance such as PISA and also the university sector.[3] In fact, of the most recently released global university rankings by *World University Rankings 2019*, around 13 percent of the top 110 institutions come from East Asia, the Confucian Orbit more specifically, including:

Rank	University	
22	Tsinghua University	China
31	Peking University	China
36	University of Hong Kong	Hong Kong
42	The University of Tokyo	Japan
46	Hong Kong University of Science and Technology	Hong Kong
55	Chinese University of Hong Kong	Hong Kong
63	Seoul National University (SNU)	South Korea
65	Kyoto University	Japan
82	Sungkyunkwan University (SKKU)	South Korea
93	University of Science and Technology of China	China
101	Zhejiang University	China
102	Korea Advanced Institute of Science and Technology (KAIST)	South Korea
105	Fudan University	China
110	City University of Hong Kong	Hong Kong

As previously alluded to, some have argued that the disciplined approach to education in East Asia might have rather hindered creativity and innovation, but this argument is not supported by the newest university overall ranking, nor by the *Annual Reuters' Ranking of the World's Most Innovative Universities* (2018), an objective ranking based on empirical data (patent filings, research paper citations, advancing science, inventing new technologies, powering new markets). With 46 universities in the USA, two from Canada, and 27 universities in Europe, traditionally Western universities rank high on innovation; Stanford University, Massachusetts Institute of Technology (MIT) and Harvard University top the list. Yet, Asia features 23 universities, the highest ranking being:

11	Korea Advanced Institute of Science and Technology (KAIST)	South Korea
13	Pohang University of Science and Technology (POSTECH)	South Korea
20	University of Tokyo	Japan
22	Osaka University	Japan
26	Kyoto University	Japan
34	Seoul National University (SNU)	South Korea

It has to be noted that the innovative researchers contributing to the above-listed East Asian universities have largely experienced a Confucian (note, all top Asian universities are in the Confucian Orbit) disciplined approach to education during their schooling and upbringing, indeed stricter at the time than it is now, and it appears that precisely that experience has resulted in largely inquiring minds that now drive innovation.

It should also be noted that East Asian universities often have relatively strict rules about attendance and behaviour, for example a leading university in South Korea featured in the top global rankings above, enforces clear consequences for not fulfilling required class attendance, with academic performance being very strong at that Korean institution. In contrast, there is evidence of low attendance at lectures and tutorials at some Western tertiary institutions, for example at one Australian institution "attendance rates at lectures across campus drop to 30 per cent of enrolment after the first two weeks of semester" (Cleary, 2016). It should be noted that poor attendance was found across campus: "The quality or size of the facility or the teaching made no difference, nor did the lecturer". A lack of discipline was not only found in terms of being absent from lectures, but also in terms of not regularly engaging with the material itself: "About 10 per cent of students downloaded lectures towards the end of semester". This also means that technology alone may not solve a decline in discipline standards.

Western universities have in many cases become quite multicultural. At American Ivy League universities (i.e. hence highly research intensive institutions), we observe a strong representation of Asian Americans (e.g. Chinese, Japanese, Korean), triggering a debate on the drivers of Asian students in the West. A recent article in the *Asian American Journal of Psychology* offered a summary of this debate (see spotlight).

Spotlight

Is There Such a Thing as Asian Culture? Unveiling Asian American Achievement

In their recently published paper in the *Asian American Journal of Psychology*, sociologists Min Zhou and Jennifer Lee examine the reasons behind the extraordinary socioeconomic achievement of Asian Americans.

Asian Americans exhibit the highest median household income and highest level of education of all U.S. racial groups, even surpassing native-born White Americans. At 5.5 percent of the U.S. population, Asian Americans are highly visible in Ivy League universities and prestigious public universities, where they account for 20 to 40 percent of the student body.

Pundits, journalists, and some scholars have attributed their socioeconomic achievement to cultural values or traits—such as the emphasis on hard work, career development, marriage, parenthood, and family cohesion—that they characterize as innately Asian. This 'culture of success' thesis is merely the antithesis of the popular and highly contested 'culture of poverty' argument.

Zhou and Lee challenge the culture of success antithesis head on. They argue that there is no such as a thing as Asian culture. Rather, culture has structural roots. What seem to be common cultural patterns among Asian Americans emerge from the structural circumstances of contemporary immigration.

The prevailing cultural explanation fails to consider the pivotal role of U.S. immigration law, which ushered in a new stream of highly-educated, highly-skilled Asian immigrants. The authors call this unique circumstance 'hyper-selectivity', defined as an immigrant group arriving in the U.S. with a significantly higher percentage of college graduates than that of the adult populations in both receiving and sending countries.

The opposite is 'hypo-selectivity' referring to an immigrant group arriving in the U.S. with a significantly lower percentage of college graduates than that of the adult populations in both sending and receiving countries.

Hyper-selectivity has profound consequences for the socioeconomic attainment of not only immigrants but also their children.

The authors examine several critical consequences of hyper-selectivity that affect Asian Americans' socioeconomic achievement:

- starting points
- success frame

- ethnic capital
- stereotype promise

Their analysis is based on a qualitative study of adult children of Chinese, Vietnamese, and Mexican immigrants in metropolitan Los Angeles.

Chinese are the largest Asian ethnic group in the U.S. and Los Angeles. They are also among the most hyper-selected of Asian immigrant groups. Vietnamese are the largest Asian refugee group in the U.S. Although they arrived with severe structural disadvantages, the Vietnamese are nonetheless highly selected, rather than hyper-selected. Mexicans are the largest immigrant group in the country (accounting for 30 percent of U.S. immigrants) and also the largest immigrant group in Los Angeles. Their sheer size—combined with their disadvantaged status as a hypo-selected group—often puts them in the spotlight of policy debates about immigration and comprehensive immigration reform.

The authors find that the hyper-selectivity of contemporary immigration positively influences the educational trajectories and outcomes of the children of immigrants beyond individual family or parental socioeconomic characteristics, resulting in group-based advantages. In particular, the children of Chinese immigrants begin their quest to get ahead from more favorable starting points, are guided by a more constricting success frame, and have greater access to ethnic capital to support the success frame than those of other immigrant groups such as Mexicans.

In turn, these group-based advantages help the children of Chinese immigrants, including those from working class families, excel in school. The desirable educational outcomes produce stereotype promise—the boost in performance that comes with being favorably perceived and treated as smart, high-achieving, hard-working, and deserving—that benefits not only the hyper-selected group members, like the Chinese, but also other group members who may not be hyper-selected but are racialized as Asian, such as the Vietnamese.

Zhou and Lee conclude that Asian culture is not innate, but is remade from selective Asian immigration. Children of highly educated immigrants begin their quest to get ahead from more favorable starting points, have greater access to ethnic capital to support a success frame, and benefit from positive societal perceptions and stereotypes.

The authors caution that, while the so-called positive stereotypes enhance the academic performance of Asian American students, the same stereotypes hinder them as they pursue leadership positions in the workplace. Asian American professionals face a bamboo ceiling—an invisible barrier that impedes their upward mobility much like the glass ceiling does for women—pointing to an Asian American achievement paradox.

Source: Zhou, M. and Lee, J. (2017). Hyper selectivity and remaking of culture: Understanding the Asian American achievement paradox. *Asian American Journal of Psychology*, 8(1), 7–15

Table 5.1 The Evolution of Institutional Approaches to Education: East Vis-à-Vis West

	Original Institution	*Neo Institution (1970+)*	*Postmodernist Era (Late 20th Century)*
East Asia	*Confucianism* based on Confucius (551–479 BCE)	*Confucian Dynamism*	Authoritarian/ authoritative approach to education
West	*Calvinism* based on Calvin (1509–1564)	*Protestant Work Ethic* (PWE)	Shift to Permissive Education approach
Institutional Character	Philosophy and *religion* on how to *order the State* and spiritual life	*Convergence:* Ideology and values in an economic context were similar in the post-war era in East Asia and the West	*Divergence:* education (schools, colleges, universities) passes on diverging values in East Asia vis-à-vis Western institutions
Common Denominators	Value of education Humility Filial piety Harmony in human relationships	Hard work Internal motivation Respect Saving resources Willingness to serve	*East Asia:* focus on performance, discipline, and respect *West:* focus on playful learning, freedom of expression

Source: Adapted from Baumann et al. (2016)

Historically, it should be understood that the West has not always followed the permissive approach to education that is common now. Quite on the contrary: the Protestant Work Ethic (PWE) has/had long resulted in a rather authoritarian way in which schools were run, but during the emergence of the '*Antiautoritäre Erziehung*' (a somewhat strong form of permissive education) in the 1960s and 1970s in the Germanic geographic region, there was a departure from traditional pedagogy. Table 5.1 summarises this evolution which is a reflection of these institutional changes (i.e. when culture changes, then institutions change their practice, and this will result in different discipline and performance outcomes in the case of education). At the risk of oversimplification, the Western *Weltanschauung* has changed, whereas the Confucian *Weltanschauung* has remained more stable/traditional.

Practical Implications

We designed our CDC research not least based on the premise that the high school students being educated today will face numerous complexities, and a rapid rate of change in the wider world. Employment will become less stable and more precarious. This has probably always been true to some degree, but the challenges must have always been greatest during the transitional periods from one 'Industrial Revolution' to the next phase;

we are now at the onset of the fourth Industrial Revolution. The aim of education is to pass on technical skills, knowledge, and inspiration (among other 'abilities'; naturally also aspiration, morals, and values deemed important to society). Societies place a premium on socialising individuals with the 'tools' to cultivate sustain throughout their lives, and education is the vehicle through which this is achieved. Naturally, one outcome of education with such aspirations would result in academic performance as a student, and economic performance in adult life, not least 'work ethic' formed though discipline at school (Baumann et al., 2016). To some degree both education and work careers have become more competitive, and this trend might further intensify over time. Therefore, education *should* encourage graduates to be competitive in an increasingly competitive landscape. This starts with recognising that competitiveness is directly linked to education and discipline. With that narrative in mind, we designed our CDC framework and designed our study in a way that we can ultimately explain precisely that: what drives competitiveness, our dependent variable (or the phenomena we want to explain).

One of the main statistical tools we employed for this research, and which we report on in Chapter 2, are regressions from Structural Equation Modelling (SEM), which allowed us to explain some phenomena, and also to predict it. We also used that approach to forecast future outcomes in simulations per geographic cluster in Chapter 4. We 'predicted' outcomes where, hypothetically, discipline standards in a nation's education system are improved—an approach that is both practical and cost-effective (i.e. no massive additional resources are required, unlike infrastructure upgrades for example), and thus also realistic. Indeed, Krskova and Baumann (2017) have established that discipline is more effective in driving performance than additional investments in education. All that is required is effectively changing school policy, and for teaching staff to increasingly focus on, and act upon, the discipline dimensions (i.e. our new 'taxonomy of discipline dimensions') outlined in this book. Of course any implementation of such 'drastic' change would require the support of multiple stakeholders, and as our analysis has indicated for the case of Confucian Orbit, discipline works best where there is co-operation between teachers and parents as well (i.e. mutual support in achieving these goals).

We categorise the role of parents in relation to their engagement with their children's education and their view on school discipline, inspired by Baumrind (1991), as the following three groups, EDP, EPP, and DIP. We label these categories as the Parent-Engagement-School-Discipline taxonomy, or PESD:

- EDP: Parents are *engaged* and favour a disciplined approach to education;

- EPP: Parents are *engaged* and favour a permissive, less-disciplined approach to education;
- DIP: Parents are *disengaged* and are indifferent about disciplined approach to education.

The first category of our new taxonomy, *Engaged Discipline Parents (EDP)*, would be the predominant type in the Confucian Orbit, i.e. parents of an authoritative nature that are engaged with their offspring's education, and are in favour of teachers following a disciplined approach to education. This may not least contribute to strong academic performance.

The second category, *Engaged Permissive Parents (EPP)* would be the type not uncommon in Western societies perhaps, where parents are engaged with their children's education, but are in favour of teachers not applying discipline. The term 'helicopter parenting' (Reed, Duncan, Lucier-Greer, Fixelle and Ferraro, 2016) has emerged in the literature and in the popular press. Parent's involvement can be 'over the top', surpass a supportive role to 'too involved', a near intruding role. Not only can helicopter parenting ultimately result in mental health issues for children longer term (e.g. depression, anxiety as adults), but parents' over-engagement/protection can also hinder teachers to apply necessary discipline at school when teachers constantly have to 'fear' parent's complaints or legal action (legal aspects are beyond the scope of our research, yet of course the degree the law permits/encourages or hinders discipline in schools is another angle that warrants exploration).

DIP, or *Disengaged Indifferent Parents*, our third category, also not uncommon in Western upbringing, is where parents are *disengaged* and are therefore indifferent about a disciplined approach to education. The German language has coined that category as '*Schlüsselkinder*', i.e. children that are given a key to their home so they can leave/enter without parental supervision (but also without affection and a 'have a good day hug'), and this means that the children are—by and large—unsupervised before and after school when at home. For this category, the lack of parental support could likely be compensated at school with a more disciplined (and caring, nurturing, benevolently) approach, guiding students to academic performance, passing on good manners/behaviour and societal values ('politeness').

Our simulations have shown what happens when discipline is maintained, increased or decreased per geographic cluster in terms of its impact on academic performance and on competitiveness. And they paint a very clear picture: for each cluster, it is evident that the best way forward in education is to enhance school discipline in order to improve academic performance and ultimately global competitiveness.

Global competitiveness is not least characterised by the gig economy that we have discussed in our introduction chapter: more and more workers are no longer in stable employment situations, but instead 'hop' from gig to gig to make ends meet; many dream of someday becoming the next Bill Gates (founder of Microsoft) or Mark Zuckerberg (founder of Facebook). Expanding on the information presented in Figures 5.1 and 5.2, In a gig economy, the discipline elements we have introduced (e.g. behaviour, punctuality, performance) are likely becoming more important rather than during times of stable employment. In the latter, employees have workers' rights and enjoy job protection even when performance slips. In the gig economy, in contrast, workers are likely to be affected by a number of personal choices or habits that would sometimes go unchecked in the traditional employment setting: tardiness, poor manners, inconsistent performance, and even poor dress or uniform standards, are all factors that could hinder someone from keeping or getting their next 'gig'. This is worsened by the reality that it is both easy and convenient to seek a replacement of a 'gig worker' if the first one doesn't work out. We reiterate through our research that the new economic reality does *not* call for the abolishment of good school discipline standards—but quite the opposite: based on the associations

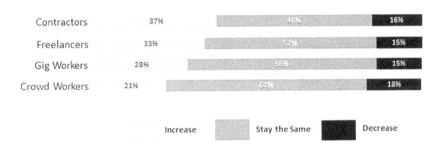

Figure 5.1 The Future of Work Arrangements

Source: Adapted from Deloitte Insights (www.deloitte.com/insights)—2018 Industry Report on Global Human Capital Trends

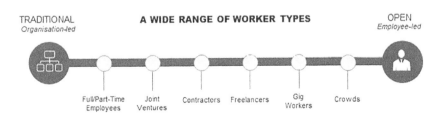

Figure 5.2 Range of Worker Types

Source: Adapted from Deloitte Insights (www.deloitte.com/insights)

between discipline, performance and competitiveness we have established in this research, discipline is likely to become an even more important asset, if not skill, for the future to employability.

So what should, or rather *can*, schools and teachers do? We have provided as a starting point a very clear list of 'check points' for school policy and application of discipline in the classroom. In essence, these are areas that teachers should focus on and 'enforce' policy and guidelines, with particular emphasis on clear consequences when a standard or expectation has not been met (non-compliance). Many of them are discipline dimensions that are practically 'common sense' and have/had been practiced in education for centuries, but with the changes to a more permissive education model, in some cases, have 'dropped off the radar'. For this to work, educators must not only set a clear standard and communicate their expectations to students, but also diligently and *consistently* enforce discipline when they are not met. Our study demonstrates that better discipline by and large results in better performance and competitiveness; and though we have mainly applied our discussion to the Confucian Orbit, our empirical analysis indicates that, most importantly, it is also possible for the non-Confucian clusters.

Spotlight

Taxonomy of Discipline Dimensions

- Behaviour, conduct, and deportment
- Manners
- Respect for teachers, education, and other students
- Punctuality
- Uniform/dress standard
- Academic performance
- Homework (e.g. checks by teachers for completion)

Our call to maintain or increase discipline levels is not in contrast to instilling students with a fire for creativity, a zest for knowledge, learning to work in groups (mastering collaboration and team dynamics), and learning to interact on a one-on-one basis or being able to solve problems on their own. Students need to learn how to apply theory to practice, and also to take on mentorship roles of their own (e.g. mentoring junior students), need exposure to project-based learning and resource management, notwithstanding that in many cases, the younger generation is faster than their teaching staff in accessing online material and data. Then again, an (overly) permissive approach to education may not foster these skills at the same level as a more disciplined approach can, as evidenced by the high math, reading, and science results in the Confucian Orbit with high discipline levels in contrast to lower performance levels in less disciplined educational settings.

It is impossible to precisely predict the work environment future generations will face, at least not without a massive margin for error. Today, people are already becoming more and more inundated with distractions, via new technologies and platforms. However, a glance at industry and consulting reports, in corroboration with our own results, allows us to anticipate a few key points. Sigelman (2017) in a *Burning Glass* study found that data and analytics professionals have a need for basic curriculum skills that are taught in a nation's education system, such as writing (part of PISA reading skills), problem-solving (part of PISA science and math skills), and research as well as a capability of working in a team. *Deloitte's 2018 Global Human Capital Trends Survey* also recognises complex problem-solving, cognitive abilities as well as social skills as key capabilities for future workforces, indicating that the current cohort of students will need a hybrid of skills and knowledge for future employability; not least also beyond technical competency, but also a healthy dose of (self-) discipline.

> As technology advances, skills are becoming obsolete faster than ever. But—contrary to conventional wisdom—the greatest value now lies beyond purely technical skills. In fact, the most valuable roles are those that enable machines to pair with skilled, cross-disciplinary thinkers to innovate, create, and deliver services.
>
> (Deloitte's 2018 Global Human Capital Trends Survey, p. 41)

In fact, another Deloitte report on the twenty-first century career titled *Catch the Wave* indicates that traditional STEM subjects (reflected in PISA testing) will become *more* important for future workforces, with an extension to STEAM (science, technology, engineering, and math; with the extension to include art).

Spotlight

Deloitte's Look Into the Future Job World

Will You Still Hire Me Tomorrow?

In early 2016, our colleagues at Deloitte UK looked at Oxford University's noted study predicting which jobs would disappear over the next 20 years. They mapped these jobs against the O*NET job skills required in both the 'disappearing jobs' and the 'growing jobs', identifying a set of 40+ 'essentially human sills' that are becoming ever more important in the workforce. The findings clearly point in this direction:

- **Brains over brawn:** In absolute terms, knowledge of specialist STEM subjects is 40 percent more important than the physical abilities of strength, endurance, flexibility, or the ability to manipulate objects.
- **Social and cognitive skills:** A 10 percent increase in cognitive abilities contributes to a 12 percent increase in median hourly earnings.
- **STEM and STEAM continue to grow:** By 2039, math and science knowledge is expected to increase in importance by 8 percent, leading to approximately 4.5 million new STEM-enabled jobs to be created globally, including engineers, scientists, IT and digital professionals, economists, statisticians, and teachers.

Source: Adapted from Deloitte's report on careers for the twenty-first century: *Catch the Wave*, p. 70

Research Implications

Based on our research exploring the CDC framework reported in this book, we now offer seven areas for further research.

1. **Local vis-à-vis immigrant students:** In our study, we used the PISA data to capture school discipline and academic performance. We did not separate students with an immigration background to local students—we treated all country samples as representative of each country. Given the large sample size of approximately 500,000 cases globally, and with large country samples ranging from 51,553 to 166,956 (see the Chapter 4 Appendix for a sample overview), such effects may be largely nullified. Nevertheless, future research should explore such differences and establish to what degree students with a Confucian background (e.g. Chinese, Japanese, Korean) also peak- or out-perform local students in the West and/or Anglo-Saxon schools. It would also be interesting to test for how long or for how many generations Confucian background parents pass on their values to their offspring. What is the attrition rate of cultural adaption? Research could also explore 'reverse' effects, or in other words, do students from non-Confucian backgrounds improve self-discipline, academic performance, and competitiveness when they are studying in the Confucian Orbit, and how many generations are required to result in tangible effects?
2. **Segmentation and effects over time:** Beyond Confucianism, other segmentation criteria for analysis could be used, for example following the approach we have presented in our simulation (see

Chapter 4) where we have grouped students according to their academic performance, e.g. low and elite performance. More work in this sphere is needed to better understand the effects of discipline on performance per segment. What are the specific mechanisms of discipline on each segment and in each geographic cluster? This research approach in mind, future research might also wish to probe the effects of discipline over time, e.g. under which conditions does strict discipline at school and/or home result in equally high levels of self-discipline in adult life (and there are multiple combinations to be researched)? A further point of inquiry would be to consider whether discipline standards and performance might be different across school types within a country; while we have just used PISA data for each country as a whole in our analysis, different types of discipline might be enforced across different school types—charter, religious, military academy, or selective—which might drive performance differently. Indeed, schools have the role to not only educate, but to also 'build character', therefore a comparison across school types would be necessary for a more comprehensive picture.

3. **School discipline vis-à-vis (self-)discipline:** There is a recent stream of research exploring the role of self-discipline and self-regulation as predictors of academic achievement (Zimmerman and Kitsantas, 2014), self-control and academic achievement (Stadler, Aust, Becker, Niepel and Greiff, 2016), and self-discipline as an indicator of learning (Gorbunovs, Kapenieks and Cakula, 2016). Even more recently, Jung, Zhou, and Lee (2017) explored the role of self-efficacy and self-discipline on academic performance. It would indeed be fascinating to explore this research stream more, for example what specifically is the association between discipline experienced at school and at home in the transformation into self-discipline and self-regulation. Could it be that there are different trajectories for different segments of disciplined individuals, i.e. lower disciplined students who become more disciplined benefiting more, whereas those who are already highly disciplined reach a point of diminishing return?

4. **Rules of engagement—effective 'tools' to discipline students:** Besides the convergence or divergence of students migrating to other parts of the world, another, and not unequally important, research question centres around the types of consequences most effective to discipline students. No doubt, such a research stream would be controversial—but that is not to say it would not be quite crucial to explore. What type of discipline 'tools' work best, and under what circumstances? And for which 'infringement'? What type of discipline do they use in the Confucian Orbit vis-à-vis in the West and elsewhere? The range would be from time-outs to reprimanding, to extra homework, detention or suspension, to physical consequences (Wilson, 2002).

Each may have pros and cons—and each must be understood in the cultural setting, e.g. Confucianism. One interesting research question would also be to explore the role of school uniforms in the context of school discipline, with embryotic research suggesting that indeed uniformed students are also better behaved (Baumann and Krskova, 2016).

5. It may be fair to conclude that in the West, generally discipline 'tools' have been taken away from teachers more and more, with legal restrictions to how students can actually (or not) be disciplined; as we have flagged in our review of the literature, this lack of power is not least a 'push out' factor for teachers to defect the profession in the West. Crucially, this move towards a permissive approach to education (or laissez-faire) has, as we have demonstrated in our work reported in this book, also been accompanied with low(er) discipline levels, and perhaps alarmingly, with lower academic performance. In the Confucian Orbit, the law is not always clear cut about how teachers are permitted to discipline students, but public opinions are often clear and rooted in Confucian tradition, i.e. strict discipline is better than the opposite approach.

6. On the note of legal issues, the rules of engagement for teachers to discipline students and how is, as discussed in detail, a cultural reflection for a country/society. However, institutions may be driven by culture, and teaching staff have to obey the law and follow school policy. In that sense if countries wanted to 'tighten' school policy on discipline, then that would also require an update on the law actually permitting teachers to apply appropriate discipline.

7. **Competitive Productivity (CP):** In our research we have viewed and measured competitiveness at the macro level, in other words at the national level. How competitive is a nation in global context, i.e. relative to other nations? We have established that education (or academic performance of high schoolers) indeed has a positive effect on national competitiveness over time. Future work could extend the modelling of competitiveness to include the competitiveness of an individual (see Baumann and Harvey, 2018; Baumann, Cherry and Chu, 2019), or at the micro level. This would make the unit of analysis more 'streamlined' in the CDC framework since then, all measurement would occur at the same micro level without 'crossing' over to other levels of the M-M-M architecture. Naturally, both approaches to modelling do have merit—the measurement and modelling depends on the research question to be addressed, i.e. should the model test how micro-level academic performance drives national (macro) level competitiveness as we have demonstrated, or do we want to explore further how academic performance drives micro-level (individual) competitiveness?

8. In 2013, Baumann and Pintado's introduction of *Competitive Productivity* (or CP) was detached from the identification of a specific macro, meso, or micro-level perspective: "Competitive Productivity is in essence both an attitude and a behaviour directed at outperforming the competition through pragmatism" (p. 9). More recently, CP has been conceptualised at the M-M-M levels (Baumann et al., 2019) with a proposed definition of CP at the micro level: "Individual Competitive Productivity (ICP) is both an attitude and behaviour directed at outperforming the competing individuals, and past performance through pragmatism". Future research on the CDC framework and model could 'replace' national level competitiveness with ICP as the ultimate dependent variable. In sum, the proposed research direction in this regard would explore to what degree discipline drives academic performance and ICP. Such a model could be tested with direct effects of discipline on ICP, and mediated effects of discipline on ICP via academic performance.

9. **The digitalisation of education:** The transformation of educational resources to an online platform bring with it many opportunities for learning and engagement, but also a number of promising avenues for research on its effects on discipline and performance (Krumsvik, 2009). While digitisation (i.e. process of converting information from physical to digital format, such as scanning a document) has been around for decades, digit*alisation* is the emerging wave of experiencing traditional classroom learning through an online platform. The entire process is delivered through one digital system, from information disbursement, communication with teachers and peers, to ICT-based examinations. The digital revolution has produced radical changes not only in the accessibility to education; such as resources, personalisation, and tools for learning, but also affects 'what the students get out of it' beyond technical knowledge (Enhuber, 2015). Whereas in traditional classroom settings, teachers have more 'control' and students receive more 'direct' feedback via verbal and non-verbal instruction, this dynamic is essentially eliminated online, notwithstanding that instructors can monitor online activity (and inactivity) of students. Substantial research could be focussed on what this means for discipline, in at least two ways.

- First, in societies where discipline is strictly enforced in the classroom (i.e. Confucian Orbit) and plays an integral role in preparing students for the future, whole digitalisation of education would essentially reduce the delivery and efficacy of discipline as a tool in producing 'correct behaviours'.
- Second, successful application of online education will be contingent upon students having a degree of self-discipline to keep atop of their workload in what essentially becomes independent study; to

what degree does self-discipline need to pre-exist for this to work, or how might self-discipline evolve from this, are questions to be considered. This research direction is not least inspired by work on the 'Virtual Generation' (Proserpio and Giola, 2007) that concluded: "Although the technology was well known by the students, nobody bothered to use it" (p. 73).

10. **The value of discipline in life and society:** Perhaps the final research question offered in our book shall be on the *overall* value of discipline, discipline in other areas of life. In our work we focussed on an educational setting, but there would be cases to be made that discipline also plays a role in other areas of life—or in other words, (self-) discipline learned as a child and youth is also beneficial in adult life. Could it be that more disciplined individuals are better in dealing with monetary matters, e.g. have higher savings rates? Tung and Baumann (2009) found precisely such evidence with the Chinese having significantly higher saving rates than Caucasians in Australia and Canada, for instance. Could discipline also contribute to crime and terrorism, two problems mushrooming in Western societies, but areas better under control in the Confucian Orbit? There could be an even wider spread application of solid (self-) discipline, for example with better disciplined individuals having better (healthier) nutrition and diet, and more exercise. Could discipline also be a contributing factor to preserve national cultures (given that Confucianism sustained over 2,500 years)? In other words, there is a very large area with depth and width to be explored in relation to discipline from many angles beyond what we have researched in our book.

Outlook on CDC

Our research, in simple terms, points towards the changing dynamics in global performance, from education to competitiveness. It has been argued that this twenty-first century will be the Asian century, following on from the British Empire and American dominance in the past two centuries. Key roles in that Asian century will be played by the East Asian societies, with China being the largest in term of population and economic powers:

A seismic change that has occurred in the last quarter of the twentieth century is the meteoric rise of China, the world's most populated nation. In the late 1970s, China was one of the poorest countries on earth; yet within the course of three short decades, it has become the most 'cash rich' nation and has assumed the status of the world's banker.

(Tung, 2013)

Tung has categorised and titled two of her thoughts/sections in that same book chapter as follows, and those two headings seem to capture important trends during the Asian Century:

- From 'West leads East' to 'West meets East';
- Awareness of the need to understand and perhaps learn from Asia.

With the changed dynamics and market as well as political power, we are now also demonstrating with the results from the research presented in our book, that the changes may well include education (i.e. pedagogy) and competitiveness.

Just as the motto for China after its humiliating defeat by Western powers in the mid-nineteenth century was 'to learn from the West to defeat the West', in light of the rise of Asia and the emerging markets it appears that the West has finally awakened to the need to understand and perhaps learn from Asia. As Hexter and Woetzel have observed (2007, p. 7): "As China emerges into the world economy, best practices there will become best practices globally. More products developed in China will become global products; more industrial processes developed in China will become global processes".

Source: Tung, R. L. (2013). 16 The future of East Asian management. *Managing Across Diverse Cultures in East Asia: Issues and challenges in a changing globalized world*, 263

Our research has shown that the Confucian Orbit, at the centre of the Asian Century, has emerged as the strongest when it comes to academic performance, and this is not least a result of a Confucian-driven disciplined approach to education. Given that, by now, East Asian firms have taken over traditional Western brands/firms (e.g. Volvo, Jaguar, Gategroup, SR Technics) with a change of Western management to East Asian management practices, it is not unlikely that the West will also look more closely at the East Asian recipe of high academic performance. As we have outlined in our Introduction (Chapter 1), the UK has adopted Chinese math books (so curriculum, more broadly), and it is not unlikely that the West and other parts of the world may also 'eyeball' East Asian pedagogy and potentially adopt the stricter discipline common in Confucian schools. As we have discussed previously throughout the book, for discipline to be 'effective' in the sense of mobilising students to improve their performance, consistency across the school and home environments is necessary. In other words, ideally, there needs to be a 'mutual support' of sorts between teachers and parents regarding their vision of discipline, and how it should be used to promote performance. This is something we see within the Confucian Orbit, where goals relating to students' learning goals are established and thus clear standards and expectations for achieving them are set early on. Discipline is a tool used to empower students, not only in guiding them towards the correct actions, but also instilling in them an ability to moderate their own behaviours for success (i.e. self-discipline and work ethic). While we used PISA data on school discipline to capture the classroom environment in schools, we did not have data on the student's home environment (in terms of discipline). However, it would be reasonable to assume that there could be two end points, at the most extreme, on a scale that depicts students' upbringing in their formative years which contributes to an understanding of academic performance.

We put forth that there is a culminating/additive (if not multiplying) effect of how individuals are disciplined at home, and how they are disciplined at school, which shapes a likely outcome regarding their approach and performance in school, and later, the workforce. Or as Baumann, Tung, and Hamin (2012, p. 2 and forward) put it:

> Understanding how people in different cultures view obedience and how they are disciplined in their respective academic institutions has tremendous implications for how people are managed in organizations and how they react to authority/discipline in the workplace and in society at large.

We think about this dynamic like chain links: authoritarian approaches to discipline represent a strong and solid link (+), whereas permissive approaches represent a weak and hollow link (–). If authoritarian approaches are consistent at home and school, we would see this double strength (++) manifest in higher levels of performance and self-discipline, because there are clear demands and an understanding of how to achieve them. Conversely, when permissive approaches are consistent at home and school, the weak links multiply (—), resulting in low performance, a lack of self-discipline—a result most evident when there is lack of direction or 'push' across both contexts. In circumstances where are inconsistencies between disciplinary approaches between the home and school environment, such as authoritarian at home and permissive at school, or vice versa, we might expect to see an outcome somewhere in between. Naturally, this categorisation is speculative and needs to be verified in future research. There is evidence of growing disciplinary problems (e.g. low lecture and tutorial attendance rates at the tertiary level) and a plateauing of academic performance (higher failure rates for entry level courses) reported from some tertiary institutions (Cleary, 2016), which points towards our suggested framework presented in Table 5.2.

Table 5.2 Chain Link Reaction of Permissive Vis-à-Vis Authoritarian Parental and School Environment

Home Environment	School Environment	Likely Outcome for Tertiary Education and/or Workforce
Authoritarian	Authoritarian	High level of self-discipline and high performance
Authoritarian	Permissive	. . . .
Permissive	Authoritarian	. . . .
Permissive	Permissive	Low level of self-discipline and low performance

What would also be interesting to explore would be the role of discipline at the tertiary level. Naturally, by and large the dimensions we have outlined would presumably not only drive the academic performance of 15-year-olds (so the PISA testing age) and other school aged children, but indeed also 18-year-old university entrants, and beyond. Starting class on time, having students' attention, working hard on their assignments, preparing for exams, having no disruption in lectures and tutorials would no doubt also be factors driving tertiary academic performance, and this could yet be explored. Factoring in different levels of maturity (or age), of course the consequences for non-compliance would differ between school and university, e.g. some form of punishment for school children for misbehaving, but what 'tools' do universities have to discipline their students? We have previously alluded to relatively low attendance rates at lectures and tutorials at some Western universities, and while this may not likely increase academic performance, it could perhaps be an outcome of lowered discipline standards passed on to students at school level. In Thailand, for example, university students wear 'school' uniforms to classes, and this could be a contributing factor for better behavioural standards on campus. In Western societies, before universities became 'mainstream' (i.e. tertiary level education attainment levels now reaching roughly 50 percent of 25–64 year olds[4]) there is little evidence that academic nor behavioural standards would have increased. There could be the previously alluded to economic forces (when education turns into a 'business') to let behavioural and performance standards 'slip' in order not to deter students (or 'customers'), and these dynamics certainly warrant detailed future exploration.

In our research, we have outlined scenarios for each geographic cluster (in Chapter 4) with consequences for school discipline maintained, increased, or decreased. We anticipate very direct effects on academic performance, and longer term, also effects on a nation's global competitiveness.

One East Asian country that has real-life experience with relaxing education policy is Japan, in this could be a warning for other Confucian Orbit societies potentially drifting towards a Western style permissive approach to education—in the case of Japan, it did not work. In the early 1980s, the country introduced the *Yutori* education, or 'cushiony' education, resulting in what is referred to as the *Yutori* generation, i.e. the 'lazy generation' that grew up under that policy. The change of school policy at the time was aimed at reducing stress for students, but soon was widely criticised by teaching staff, politicians, and a number of employers, disappointed with the lack of work ethic seen in that generation. Not least was Japan alarmed by disappointing international competition results of their students. The policy was subsequently abolished in the mid-2000s and has been replaced by a 'back to the roots' change—longer hours, fewer rest periods, and shifting extra-curricular activities back to regular subjects. Japan also increased the number of English vocabulary to be mastered by students, a number that was lowered during *Yutori* education. Two spotlights, '*Yutori* Education' and 'Impact of *Yutori* Education', outline the nature of *Yutori* education and its outcome.

Spotlight—*Yutori* Education

Cautionary Tale: The Yutori 'Cushion' Pedagogy Experience in Japan

In 1996, when the 15th Central Council for Education (中央教育審議会 *Chūō Kyōiku Shingikai*) was asked about what the Japanese education of the 21st century should be like, it submitted a report suggesting 'the ability to survive' should be the basic principle of education. 'The ability to survive' is defined as a principle that tries to keep the balance of intellectual, moral, and physical education.

In 1998, the teaching guidelines were revised to reflect the council's report. 30% of the curriculum was cut and 'time for integrated study' in elementary and junior high school was established. It was a drastic change.

The School Curriculum Council stated its goals in a report.

To enrich humanity, sociability, and the awareness of living as a Japanese within international society.

1. To develop the ability to think and learn independently.
2. To inculcate fundamental concepts in children at an appropriate pace while developing their individuality.
3. To let every school form its own ethos.

Around 1999, a decline in the academic abilities of university students became a serious concern. Elementary and secondary education started to be reconsidered. This trend focused criticism on the new teaching guidelines and aroused controversy.

Source: https://en.wikipedia.org/wiki/Yutori_education

Spotlight—Impact of *Yutori* Education

Japanese School Reforms Fail to Make Grade

The engineered super-humans were supposed to make Japan stronger, but the government experts who created them miscalculated. Now the beasts are running amok, threatening to destroy the country they were designed to save.

The plot of a blood-soaked manga comic? Not exactly. It is the story of the last decade of Japanese education policy—at least according to the many critics who believe it has been a damaging failure.

The supposed monsters are young Japanese, and the policy that is said to have ruined them is *yutori* education.

Yutori means comfort or breathing space. It became a catch-all term for a set of school reforms—including shorter weeks, relaxed grading and less emphasis on rote learning—that constitute the most sweeping changes to Japan's school system since the end of the second world war.

Fully implemented in 2002, *yutori* was intended to make Japanese classrooms less like stifling academic factories and more like free-range organic farms.

Just under a third of the middle and high school curriculum was dropped and partly replaced by 'integrated studies'—open periods that teachers were meant to fill with horizon-expanding activities, such as trips to nature reserves and old people's homes.

Saturday classes were eliminated and the old evaluation system, in which each pupil was ranked from top performer on down, was scrapped in favour of a less humiliating one (for low achievers) based on absolute scores.

Policymakers hoped to accomplish two things. The first was to eradicate social ills associated with the old, high-pressure system, such as bullying, chronic truancy and suicides. The second was to produce more creative, independent-thinking pupils—and by extension workers—to feed Japan's increasingly globalised, post-industrial economy.

"Japanese had good basic study skills, so the idea was to add the more individualistic things that westerners have on top of that", says Hideki Wada, a psychologist and author of a book critical of the new system.

Mr Wada and others think the attempt to have things both ways has failed. They point to evidence that Japanese pupils are performing less well on international standardised tests, while bullying and the like remain. Ambitious parents are sending their children to more evening cram-school classes, negating the 'breathing room' created by the *yutori* reforms.

Disaffection with the new system has recently spread to business people, as the first of the '*yutori* generation' enter the workforce. Three years ago Sumitomo Metal, a maker of high-tech steel alloys, introduced a remedial science class for new recruits at its factory in Amagasaki, near Osaka. Other companies have similar programmes. "When they join they don't know anything", says Renpei Nakanishi, manager of the Sumitomo plant.

A whole industry of authors and consultants has sprung up to advise executives on dealing with '*yutori* man and woman'. Overpraised and protected from competition at school, this species is said to be lazy and prone to throw fits when criticised. The education ministry, stung by the criticism, is planning a partial rollback of the reforms, while a back-to-basics message on schools helped the once-dominant Liberal Democratic party claw back seats in parliamentary elections in July.

Social panics over education are hardly unique to Japan. But the backlash against *yutori* has been amplified by larger national insecurities. Japan's 20-year economic funk and the rise of its once-backward neighbours China and South Korea, whose Spartan schools resemble pre-*yutori* Japan's, have stung.

"There is a feeling of threat, especially from China", says Takehiko Kariya, a sociology professor at Tokyo University and St. Anthony's College, Oxford. Japanese, he says, are struggling with self-doubt the way Americans did in the 1980s, when they feared a then-ascendant Japan.

Japan's scary demographics lurk in the background. The number of 18-year-olds has fallen from 2m in 1992 to 1.2m in 2008, thinning competition for university places. Ninety-two per cent of applicants to universities and colleges were accepted in 2008, compared with a little over 60 per cent two decades earlier.

"*Yutori* came along at a time when kids no longer had to study anyway", says Mr Wada.

As for the *yutori* generation's attitude to work, larger social changes may explain a lot. Ken Terawaki, a former education ministry official who is one of *yutori*'s rare defenders, says the stiff, outdated management style of many Japanese companies is a poor fit for today's young people.

Past generations were obedient and loyal, he says, because they expected to be rewarded with lifetime job security and steadily rising pay.

But few companies today can make such promises, and young workers see little reason to put in unpaid overtime or spend their leisure hours drinking and golfing with superiors. "*Yutori* education is suited to the 21st century", he says, "but the old men who run Japanese companies have outdated 20th century thinking".

Source: Jonathan Soble in Tokyo, August 30, 2010 (7c-11df-81aa-00144 feabdc0) Email: licensing@ft.com

Reflecting on the nature of education more broadly, taking into account what we found in our research on the PISA discipline and performance dimensions, and also the literature overall pointing towards the importance of (self-) discipline, plus Japan's experience with the *Yutori* education, one might think of the role of the student him-/herself—how are students viewed and treated by the 'system'. At the university level, for example. But school level would not be different in principle. We highlight two distinct outlooks on education for the future, through two lenses and subsequent pedagogical approaches (Baumann et al., 2016):

> **Student as Learner:** This approach is prominent in East Asia where education is part of the overall system of a country with the objective for students to learn facts and figures, skills and knowledge, but equally work ethics are passed on through a focus on strict discipline and academic performance. Education is more aligned with a country's overall objectives and aspirations, and national culture is also instilled in students. Confucian values and manners passed on to children and the youth longer term contribute to maintaining Confucian Dynamism in China, Hong Kong, Japan, Korea, Singapore, and Taiwan. Students have to more actively study the material at hand, and there is a competitive environment with fiercely competitive entry tests to enter elite schools and universities. As evidenced by PISA, strong academic results emerge, and as we have now demonstrated, a focus on strict discipline and academic performance is associated with work ethic.
>
> **Student as Customer:** This approach is more prominent in the Western countries studied here where the student is often viewed as a customer, but much less as a learner where work ethic values have to be instilled. Consequently, there is often less focus on strict discipline and on academic performance, but as also evidenced by PISA, Western countries now rank behind East Asia. Academic material is presented in a more playful way and in easily digestible amounts and formats. Western education systems are often a hybrid of an educational system to pass on knowledge and skills, but equally so, and in some cases by now more so, have become a 'business'. International students are attracted to Western schools and universities, but this may also have led to a more playful approach in pedagogy with fewer challenges in order to attract—rather than deter—students. In such an environment, not only work ethic may be less emphasised, but also national culture is no longer passed on to the next generation in contrast to East Asia where Confucianism is celebrated, practiced, and passed on in educational institutions.

Confucianism was originally designed to bring harmony and structure into society at large, and we have now demonstrated that the Confucian approach to education with high levels of discipline also results in stronger academic performance. Taken together, therefore, a Confucian approach to education does appear to help students to learn better and be more competitive during their adult life. 'Side effects' of Confucian pedagogy also are that students learn about manners, polite communication, and behaviour; develop a strong work ethic; and this makes society more harmonious and prosperous, so there are benefits for society at large beyond economic progression.

The take-home message from our work is very clear: discipline drives academic performance and also competitiveness. Education policy makers and economic policy makers, educators, teachers, and professors may be best advised to take our message to heart and incorporate the new 'taxonomy of discipline dimensions' introduced in our book. This will allow them to educate and inspire the next generations more effectively, 'instil' competitiveness in them and thus make them ready for a world where competitiveness has become key—not just as an overused cliché, but as a very tangible fact of life.

Notes

1. An interview with Lulu Chua-Rubenfeld by Doree Lewak for the *New York Post*: *I Was Raised by Tiger Mom—And It Worked*, 28th March 2018 (source: https://nypost.com/2018/03/28/i-was-raised-by-tiger-mom-and-it-worked/).
2. Induction in our case works as follows: we have our PISA and WEF observations, and through analysing that data we establish patterns to verify our hypotheses (i.e. that discipline drives performance and competitiveness, and that Confucianism has higher discipline standards that drives that higher level of performance and competitiveness), and from that we advance theory on the associations of these key constructs.
3. "China is now home to the best university in Asia, while 72 Chinese universities feature in the *Times Higher Education* World University Rankings, up from 63 last year, making it the fourth most represented nation globally." See: www.timeshighereducation.com/news/world-university-rankings-2019-results-announced.
4. https://en.wikipedia.org/wiki/List_of_countries_by_tertiary_education_attainment

References

Annual Reuters' Ranking of the World's Most Innovative Universities, 2018. Retrieved from https://clarivate.com/blog/news/clarivate-analytics-data-powers-the-annual-reuters-ranking-of-the-worlds-most-innovative-universities/?utm_source=Newsletter&utm_medium=Email&utm_campaign=reutersrankings2018&utm_source=PublonsUsers&utm_campaign=2ef6dee9a6-EMAIL_CAMPAIGN_2018_10_11&utm_medium=email&utm_term=0_d203ec3f11–2ef6dee9a6–137755845

Aunola, Kaisa, Håkan Stattin, and Jari-Erik Nurmi. "Parenting styles and adolescents' achievement strategies." *Journal of Adolescence* 23, no. 2 (2000): 205–222.

Barro, Robert J., and Jong Wha Lee. "International measures of schooling years and schooling quality." *The American Economic Review* 86, no. 2 (1996): 218–223.

Baumann, Chris, Michael Cherry, and Wujin Chu. "Competitive Productivity (CP) at Macro-Meso-Micro levels." *Cross Cultural & Strategic Management* (2019).

Baumann, Chris, Hamin, and Seung Jung Yang. "Work ethic formed by pedagogical approach: Evolution of institutional approach to education and competitiveness." *Asia Pacific Business Review* 22, no. 3 (2016): 374–396.

Baumann, Chris, and Marina Harvey. "Competitiveness vis-à-vis motivation and personality as drivers of academic performance: Introducing the MCP model." *International Journal of Educational Management* 32, no. 1 (2018): 185–202.

Baumann, Chris, and Hana Krskova. "School discipline, school uniforms and academic performance." *International Journal of Educational Management* 30, no. 6 (2016): 1003–1029.

Baumann, Chris, and Iggy Pintado. "Competitive productivity—A new perspective on effective output." *Journal of Institute of Management Services* 57, no. 1 (2013): 9–11.

Baumann, Chris, Rosalie Tung, and Hamin. (2012). "Jade will never become a work of art without being carved: Western versus Chinese attitudes toward discipline in education and society." *Virginia Review of Asian Studies* 10: 1–17.

Baumrind, Diana. "The influence of parenting style on adolescent competence and substance use." *The Journal of Early Adolescence* 11, no. 1 (1991): 56–95.

Chua, Amy. *Battle Hymn of the Tiger Mother*. New York: Bloomsbury Publishing, 2011.

Cleary, Paul (2016). "ANU's chilling discovery: lecture hall boy count drops." *The Australian Online*, 9 February 2016, https://www.theaustralian.com.au/higher-education/anus-chilling-discovering-lecture-hall-body-count-drops/news-story/581137ae7fc2939ff01d768dae3d4c35. Accessed on 15 March 2018.

Deloitte Insights. "From careers to experiences: new pathways." *2018 Global Human Capital Trends*, 2018. Retrieved from https://www2.deloitte.com/insights/us/en/focus/human-capital-trends/2018/building-21st-century-careers.html

Dornbusch, Sanford M., Philip L. Ritter, P. Herbert Leiderman, Donald F. Roberts, and Michael J. Fraleigh. "The relation of parenting style to adolescent school performance." *Child Development* (1987): 1244–1257.

Enhuber, Marisa. "Art, space and technology: How the digitisation and digitalisation of art space affect the consumption of art—A critical approach." *Digital Creativity* 26, no. 2 (2015): 121–137.

Gorbunovs, Aleksandrs, Atis Kapenieks, and Sarma Cakula. "Self-discipline as a key indicator to improve learning outcomes in e-learning environment." *Procedia-Social and Behavioral Sciences* 231 (2016): 256–262.

Hexter, Jimmy, and Jonathan Woetzel. *Operation China: From Strategy to Execution*. Cambridge, MA: Harvard Business Press, 2007.

Juang, Linda P., Desiree Baolin Qin, and Irene J. K. Park. "Deconstructing the myth of the 'tiger mother': An introduction to the special issue on tiger parenting, Asian-heritage families, and child/adolescent well-being." *Asian American Journal of Psychology* 4, no. 1 (2013): 1.

Jung, Kyoung-Rae, Anne Q. Zhou, and Richard M. Lee. "Self-efficacy, self-discipline and academic performance: Testing a context-specific mediation model." *Learning and Individual Differences* 60 (2017): 33–39.

Keller, Katarina R. I. "Investment in primary, secondary, and higher education and the effects on economic growth." *Contemporary Economic Policy* 24, no. 1 (2006): 18–34.

Krskova, Hana, and Chris Baumann. "School discipline, investment, competitiveness and mediating educational performance." *International Journal of Educational Management* 31, no. 3 (2017): 293–319.

Krumsvik, Rune. "Situated learning in the network society and the digitised school." *European Journal of Teacher Education* 32, no. 2 (2009): 167–185.

Leung, Kwok, Sing Lau, and Wai-Lim Lam. "Parenting styles and academic achievement: A cross-cultural study." *Merrill-Palmer Quarterly* 44, no. 2 (1998): 157–172.

Pascale, Richard Tanner, and Anthony G. Athos. "The art of Japanese management." *Business Horizons* 24, no. 6 (1981): 83–85.

Pellerin, Lisa A. "Applying Baumrind's parenting typology to high schools: Toward a middle-range theory of authoritative socialization." *Social Science Research* 34, no. 2 (2005): 283–303.

Proserpio, Luigi, and Dennis A. Gioia. "Teaching the virtual generation." *Academy of Management Learning & Education* 6, no. 1 (2007): 69–80.

Reed, Kayla, James M. Duncan, Mallory Lucier-Greer, Courtney Fixelle, and Anthony J. Ferraro. "Helicopter parenting and emerging adult self-efficacy: Implications for mental and physical health." *Journal of Child and Family Studies* 25, no. 10 (2016): 3136–3149.

Sigelman, Matt. "By the numbers: The job market for data science and analytics." *Burning Glass Technologies*, February 10, 2017.

Shumow, Lee, Deborah Lowe Vandell, and Jill K. Posner. "Harsh, firm, and permissive parenting in low-income families: Relations to children's academic achievement and behavioral adjustment." *Journal of Family Issues* 19, no. 5 (1998): 483–507.

Spera, Christopher. "A review of the relationship among parenting practices, parenting styles, and adolescent school achievement." *Educational Psychology Review* 17, no. 2 (2005): 125–146.

Stadler, Matthias, Miriam Aust, Nicolas Becker, Christoph Niepel, and Samuel Greiff. "Choosing between what you want now and what you want most: Self-control explains academic achievement beyond cognitive ability." *Personality and Individual Differences* 94 (2016): 168–172.

Tung, Rosalie L. "16 the future of East Asian management." In *Managing Across Diverse Cultures in East Asia: Issues and Challenges in a Changing Globalized World*. New York: Routledge, 2013, p. 263.

Tung, Rosalie L., and Chris Baumann. "Comparing the attitudes toward money, material possessions and savings of overseas Chinese vis-à-vis Chinese in China: Convergence, divergence or cross-vergence, vis-à-vis 'one size fits all' human resource management policies and practices." *The International Journal of Human Resource Management* 20, no. 11 (2009): 2382–2401.

Vessman, Ludger, and Eric Hanushek. "The role of education quality in economic growth (Part I)." *Educational Studies* 2 (2007): 86–116.

Viengkham, Doris, Chris Baumann, and Hume Winzar. "Confucianism: Measurement and association with workforce performance." *Cross Cultural & Strategic Management* 25, no. 2 (2018): 337–374.

Wilson, John. "Corporal punishment revisited." *Cambridge Journal of Education* 32, no. 3 (2002): 409–416.

Zhou, Min, and Jennifer Lee. "Hyper-selectivity and the remaking of culture: Understanding the Asian American achievement paradox." *Asian American Journal of Psychology* 8, no. 1 (2017): 7.

Zimmerman, Barry J., and Anastasia Kitsantas. "Comparing students' self-discipline and self-regulation measures and their prediction of academic achievement." *Contemporary Educational Psychology* 39, no. 2 (2014): 145–155.

Epilogue
What Is a Society's Brain For?

Gordon Redding

The clear message from the research reported in this book is that the Confucian heritage provides a context in which teenagers are capable of some of the world's best measured performances derived from school teaching. Distinct contributions include the taxonomies of discipline dimensions, of parent engagement with discipline, and the 'wheel of competitiveness'. Note that the field is school education, and that the book's analysis does not pretend to represent higher education. It does however quite properly suggest implications for societies and economies within a broader framework of analysis than that of schooling. This epilogue points in brief terms to some of the webs of determinacy that might permit or constrain the further exploring of assumptions about how school education contributes to the progress of a society itself. Crucial in this bigger picture is the role of the logical next stage in the process, that of higher education. Even more crucial is the society's form of authority.

The many and varied histories to date of successful societal progress reveal a number of broad and well-founded principles with a bearing on education. In the pre-modern cases the stable coordination of large-scale social systems benefits from the presence of an administrative bureaucracy staffed by a scholar-gentry class held loyal to the leadership. Reliance instead on a land-owning aristocracy eventually runs out of legitimacy. Modern forms of social system that entail very complex coordination of scientific know-how, human skills, finance, system order, and organising capacity, will only work competitively when education spreads to the whole population. Totalitarian control stifles individual initiative and creativity and lessens civic identity. Consequent articles of faith attached to the Asian growth trajectories in recent decades have been that education underpins the growth and stabilises most of the emergent forms of political empowerment.

A book of this kind is fertile of many inquiries that stem from the above principles. It is then appropriate for those looking to the next stages of theorising to take into account the unit of analysis challenge. If one is to make sense of matters at the societal level, one must move on from matters anchored in data about an intermediate level such as the economy, or the education system, or politics, and change conceptual gears upwards. As Ragin (1987) has argued, the societal comparative method rests on seizing a sense of the societal whole. That societal context will be the most relevant determinant of specific influences such as education being amplified or suppressed. In simple terms you cannot compare Singapore and China when it comes to the *outcomes* of school performance because they are Singapore and China.

Complex Adaptive Social Systems

I first consider the nature of societies as complex adaptive systems. On page 170 there is a comment from Brian Atwell that relates to the role of competitiveness in human groups. It suggests that the kind of society built primarily around competition is not one you would want to live in. There would be: a dominant pragmatism; few good deeds; no libraries; no publishing; no conferences; open-ended philosophising would be redundant; public debate constrained. So does collective human evolution work to avoid that mentally blank condition, despite being sometimes stifled inside autocracies of one form or another? If it does so work, then why and how? Is competitiveness an instinct that people normally counterbalance with sociability as Elinor Ostrom (1990) showed? Is it assuaged by being displaced, as for instance into sports, as Patrick Besson (2018) has argued in explaining the immense global fascination with football as a relatively peaceful representation of regulated possessive contest?

Might the Confucian heritage in the context of education induce a perception of competitiveness that stresses individual betterment in the pursuit of socially attributed virtue rather than being biased towards perceptions of winners and losers, the accumulation of the individual betterments then being a societal capacity enhancement? If in the Confucian mindset the meaning of competition reflects a collectivist rather than an individualist worldview, then this carries many implications for societal comparison. And finally might a society be said to have a 'brain' that guides progressive evolution? Are there guidelines to indicate how that larger process works to ensure the steady growth of societal systems as they become more complex?

I suggest that societies do have a metaphorical brain and it is situated largely in its education system, where knowledge is received, created, codified, transmitted, certified, and referred to. Post-infancy that system works in two main stages. Put at its very simplest, school education teaches how to learn; higher education teaches how to think, in other words it adds the crucial overlay of practice in using the taught knowledge. I refer here to formally organised systems of mental preparation for adulthood. There are of course many other parallel learning processes that are less formalised, as richly described in Marvin Konner's (2010) comparative work on the evolution of childhood. But it is principally in teaching how to think for yourself that higher education takes over from early learning. It might then, if encouraged, foster a society's ability to socially re-construct its own reality and to think through its future. This depends on whether the society is designed to take the strain of such a large volume of dispersed and active mental energy. If it is not, then the agenda shifts to the challenges that go with the complexity of modernity, a point I will return to.

The phrase that captures this elusive societal capability is *critical thinking* and this is commonly seen to rest on *scholarship* (Barnett, 2013). The principle of using scholarship to underpin statecraft is visible in ideals such as the 'philosopher king', the mandarin scholar gentry, or the body of Enlightenment philosophy underpinning democracy. But having a society actively using critical thinking means also having a society that encourages constant informed debate. When such debate blends into the worlds of the economy and of politics, there is achieved what Jurgen Habermas (1984) saw as a key catalyst, and termed *communicative action*. This means that a society's key activities are the subject of constant discussion, reconsideration, and possible amendment. When this is widespread a society is equipped mentally to manage its own future and to do so with a motivated population. Simple to state; difficult to achieve; dependent on trust, shared ideals, and freedom of speech.

In ensuring that a society is capable of such thinking, four major education-related considerations come into play. First what kind of inputs arrive from the school experience to the university, including self-discipline. They are interconnected, as Bond and Jing (2019) have shown. They arrive at a faster rate and they never have simple answers. Understanding them becomes more demanding. I will return to these surrounding issues at the conclusion.

The Evolving of Complex Adaptive Systems

All complex adaptive systems that include large numbers of human beings, whether families, tribes, or societies, face the same fundamental kinds of threat. If a social system is to remain capable of surviving, and perhaps in better shape than others, it needs to contain understanding of what new conditions—internal or external—are likely to affect its coherence as a system. When in pre-history the climate changed and their forest habitat became open grassland, early hominids learned to walk, and then later— as the naked ape with sweat glands—to run as hunters. They learned to communicate when their brains grew after they learned fire control and cooking, and so in turn came sociability around hunting and sharing. They evolved to live in groups of around 150 so as to maintain social coherence and defence against other groups competing for resources. They later added more adaptations like trading, urban living, larger-scale systems of identity, and then—quite recently historically—the use of empowerment to deal with rising social complexity. This latter change is worked out differently by society, depending on prehistoric millennia of ecological conditioning, as first argued by Karl Wittfogel (1957) for China, and shown in global terms by the extensive data presented by Christian Welzel (2013). For more recent historical time Steven Pinker (2011) has shown much evidence of societal adaptation towards more complex, more empowered societies.

What are the current threats from change? And with what processes do societies find viable responses to those changes? The word viable in this context carries two meanings; societies need to be able to adjust what they are doing; and they need to retain the willingness of their members to co-operate with the adjustments that may be needed. History suggests (Cardwell, 1972) that the imposing of change without the gaining of adequate co-operativeness may work for a time but it eventually runs out of legitimacy and leads to relative failure.

The ancient survival logics are now more significant today due to a quantum leap in the level of complexity that a modern society has to cope with. The four industrial revolutions, and the new normality of deep globalisation, have added so many new influences to the political challenge of holding a society together that the mental challenge of finding an answer to the cohesion has driven some of them past their philosophical resources. The measure of this challenge is visible in the Middle-Income Trap. A rising 'pre-modern' society trying to get past a 'modern' income per capita achievement of US $15,000 has to be very adaptive indeed. In this it helps if the society is small, and/or is inclined culturally towards instinctive adaptiveness and co-operativeness. Although the Atlantic states tend to have gotten there first, such achievement is not a Western monopoly, as Japan, Singapore, Taiwan, South Korea have shown.

The Idea of Universal Guidelines

A condition of adapting to an increasingly complex set of circumstances is that the society has the capacity to think through how to change while remaining cohesive. The calibrating of a response will inevitably be grounded in a society's cultural understandings of what kind of society fits its civilisational ideal. That is why it needs to use its own brain and not someone else's. *But it must use its brain and not just have it available.* As Kant (1991, p. 1) defined Enlightenment, it is "man's emergence from his self-incurred immaturity. Immaturity is the inability to use one's own understanding without the guidance of another". Which leads to the question of how societies best think through their futures. Are there universal lessons to be learned about the process of such thinking? Beyond that are there universal guidelines about societal progress that such thinking might reveal and that may be relevant not just from studies of the past but for advice about *homo sapiens*' future?

Are There Universal Guidelines?

The question of universal guidelines takes us back to the issue of levels of analysis. What can be said about any single society is conditioned by the fact that its culture will shape how its own formula for progress will evolve. So each society will end up with a distinct character. The American dream is not the same as the Japanese ideal. The French societal formula is very different from the British. East is not West. Accepting that fact, and the societal variety that follows from it, a deeper question can then be entertained. Are there any patterns that still apply across all the varied forms? Are there any underlying universals for human society in general?

The answer is yes, and they are discernible in two sources: across the humanities and social sciences are major respected studies that contain consistent insights and principles for action that apply everywhere;[1] and in the more specific fields of evolutionary studies and complexity theory the same themes become visible.[2] They may be summarised simply here as follows:

As societies evolve they become more complex in their workings.

1. In addition to hierarchy this complexity is dealt with in two ways: interpersonal trust via networks of reciprocal obligation; institutional order underpinning system trust. The mixture of hierarchy, personal, and system trust varies.
2. As the new complexities multiply, a society needs to adapt itself to them by changing to varying degrees what it does. Non-change means stasis.
3. As it changes, the society also needs to remain cohesive so as to preserve the co-operativeness that will allow the changes to work.
4. Such adjustments work better when the thinking that deals with them is spread throughout the society, so as to use fully the society's knowledge and creativity. The effectiveness of such thinking depends on the amount of informed debate and idea-exchange that goes into it, and so the quality of learning that is folded into it. Such societal openness and exchange tends to be legitimated under empowerment, but threatened under autocracy.
5. The moral ideals of the society play a significant part in maintaining the legitimacy that underpins the co-operativeness.

In summary this amounts to *an acquired societal capability for adaptiveness and co-operativeness in stable conditions.*

A Variety of Trajectories

The workings of these principles are visible in many cultures historically. Japan's capability to modernise owed much to the reforms to Tokugawa Confucianism inspired by Ogyu Sorai in the late 1600s. The consequent decentralising of much Japanese administration under strong communal ideals, and a form of Confucian Buddhism, were preparation for the post-Meiji opening and the early modern global search for new societal structures. The flourishing of China in the Sung dynasty rested on the flowering of Neo-Confucian ideas that, for instance, inspired the invention of the mandarinate of intellectuals found by public examination, as the source of societal order. The Republic of Venice dominated much world trade for 400 years after 1400 CE based on political ideals processed in the Renaissance, resting on Greek and Roman classical thinking, but open to influence from other civilisations of the time, including the *mukata'a* structures of the Islamic Ottoman Empire, and those of China. Venice created its own version of these, using scholars to administer the territories of its empire. The great explosion of Atlantic States' wealth and influence after 1820 rested heavily on the scholarship-based ideals of the Enlightenment that underlaid the first industrial revolution, the growth of science, and the emergence of democracy.

In all these and other periods of re-thinking about change and societal progress, the same patterns recur: greater complexity; new forms of order; growing adaptiveness; growing co-operativeness; scholarship and openness in idea-exchange; and moral legitimacy. The concepts of the 'modernisation' process and the Middle-Income Trap are signals that there is a highly significant step change in the handling of escalating complexity, during which some societies change effectively while others struggle. This does not change the universals. Instead it suggests that there may be reasons for them to be especially demanding in some contexts. But that statement may need revising if human evolution takes a new diversion. Within that possibility lies a question: can autocracy sustain the modern condition?

Education as Catalyst

Having suggested some broad parameters for the typical trajectory of societal progress, I now turn back to the issue of education's role as societal brain in guiding people along such a trajectory. Again it is necessary to say that each society will find its own formula at the surface level. But below the surface, if history is any guide, these underlying requirements will still apply: adaptiveness and co-operativeness are not negotiable. So far.

Education as Catalyst Producing Further Catalysts

If the education portion of a society's brain is to contribute to the successful transformation of a society, then it is likely to do so when its ideas and knowledge have a wide influence on its social and economic action. Such influence might be catalytic, providing the stimulus towards re-formulation of what exists. An example would be the fusing of ideas about individual rights, ownership, freedom, competitive logics, and openness that lay behind the British limited liability company created in 1856. Subsequently as both an idea and an institution this interacted with the ideas about steam power, mechanics, etc. and led to quite new forms of enterprise. As economic historian Deidre McCloskey (2016, p. xiii) has stated, "Our riches did not come from piling brick on brick, or bachelor's degree on bachelor's degree, or bank balance on bank balance, but from piling idea on idea".

McCloskey's observation about bachelor's degrees recalls the point made earlier about the brain needing to be used. So how does the society's brain get used? How does it become catalytic? 'It' being of course a collection of individual brains available for thinking, a large component of what would be known as a society's 'human capital'. Before addressing the question specifically, it is necessary to consider the step from school education to higher education, and what the latter might contribute in the maturing of the mental abilities coming through the doors on the first day at university.

Transformation Questions

Personal Transformation

Most students arrive at university with a stock of knowledge that on the whole has been acquired in a highly structured system of learning. They have worked through textbooks, memorised formulae, poetry, facts, and been guided by teachers towards performance in examinations sat by hundreds of thousands. In some schools their individual initiative in thinking may have been encouraged. In some there may have been open debating about issues of principle that call on skills of public speaking, and persuasion. But on the whole, in most countries school performance relies heavily on memorising. In other words in most cases school students are not yet ready to break away from dependence on the thinking of others. In many subjects this may not matter. A child at school is not expected to take a position on one of Newton's *principia*. Much later at the same subject's research frontiers, where new thinking is often crucial, the intellectual independence of an Einstein or Bohr is necessary.

In subjects that serve to shape the nature of societies, informed opinion matters a great deal. Here habits of inquiry, of debate, of persuasive argument are of great value. This is where higher education can take over the responsibility and play its part in the brain work, assuming it is allowed to.

So what are the next processes that school education leads into? And does the working of those processes have influence on the eventual value of what has been achieved by the age of 17? Will the potential of that young knowledge be amplified, left latent, or suppressed? And will that potential be channelled into the society's adaptiveness and co-operativeness, and so contribute to its longer-term quality?

Transforming the School-Leaver Into the Graduate

A great university provides a three or four-year apprenticeship in critical thinking; in other words thinking for yourself, knowing the subject you are thinking about, being used to debating your position against others, and adopting principled guidelines for future thinking, perhaps with moral content. An added qualitative feature is behaviour of a polite and rational nature, allowing for the tolerance of disagreement and the option of compromise. Your opponent is still 'your honourable friend'.

Not every university meets these ideals as so many are now under constraint from two sources: the rising costs of providing such individual stimulus; and the presence in some countries of blockages to free speech (Redding, Drew and Crump, 2019). Universities under the latter pressure become 'hollow' (Whitley, 2019), in other words they lose the heart of what may have been their original scholarship-based mission. Their graduates may have knowledge, but many are deprived of the instincts surrounding learning and personal curiosity across many fields. A university is called that because it deals with a *universum*, not only job training.

Against such a background, two major higher education contributions still remain, regardless of the constraints that may affect them. Students can acquire habits of learning that wean them away from dependence on the taught lesson and provide them with room to expand their minds and become confident in their accumulating understanding. In consort with this can go a maturing in social relations along with new forms of personal independence, of reciprocities, and of sensitivity to wider issues of principle, including duty to community. It is these two influences of achieved understanding combined with a social conscience that foster the workings of critical thinking. This then in turn, when used, underpins a society's ability to cope effectively with change.

Transforming the Society

Schmuel Eisenstadt (1965) in his theory of societal development wrote of certain 'transformative capacities' needed to make change effective, i.e. producing a desired outcome while retaining social cohesion. Such transformative capacities might be interpreted as processes, systems of meaning, or societal influences such as helpful institutions acting to support both adaptation and social cohesion. The contribution of education here may be summarised as having three elements: forms of scholarship-based knowledge; the injection into the society of educated understanding and habits of open civil debate and communicative action; fostering a societal culture with a moral core in which incentives for adaptiveness can flow from the application of knowledge, for instance with risk-taking entrepreneurs who behave decently.

In the workings of society what education as whole contributes may then be thought of as follows:

Scholarship as Contribution

1. The use of scholarship and criticality through socialised habits (learning, debate, tolerance, rationality, openness, politeness, etc).
2. Socialised learning habits (perception, introspection, observation, etc).
3. Pragmatic skill use (technical and political enacting of ideals).
4. Motivation to know.

Shared Critical Thinking

5. Debate and idea-exchange as a basis for social action.
6. Freedom from coercion.
7. Common goods responsibility.
8. Professionalisation and expert opinion
9. Educated respectful argumentation.

Shared Moral Ideals

10. Enacting of socialised virtues including within entrepreneurship.
11. Open tolerant knowledge diffusion and public debate.
12. Respect for applied knowledge.

Keeping up the Learning Momentum?

How a government looks at a body of knowledge vested in a cohort of graduates depends on how it sees what is going to be done with that knowledge. This question is of less significance in school education but it is of high significance in the relations between graduates and governments. The issue rests on the question of who is in charge of the knowledge's use. This depends on the society's architecture of power.

Across a large range of subjects of study there is close alignment between government and graduates. This is most clear in the sciences where the direct use of technical and scientific knowledge keeps the national economy running. At the other end of the spectrum in the Arts and Humanities, much may be taught that stimulates the graduate to be a critical thinker about his or her society. The influence of this may be heightened if habits of openness in debate and ideals of public responsibility have also been acquired at university. A tension may then arise between freedom of speech and a state concern to maintain predictable order. A common reaction in states where that applies is to restrict academic freedom and as a result to induce 'hollow' universities. When present such constraints often extend into controls of religious expression, of press freedom, and of academic freedom.

Two Scenarios and Some Observations

Scenario 1

This society rests on a civilisational ideal that allocates dominant authority to a central power. This permits the society to remain cohesive. Traditional forms of stable administration evolve based on extremes of this central power, but with extensive controlled decentralisation of local decision power tightly constrained within a codified ideological framework, yet still traditionally including much educated thinking. Much social order and social welfare rests within family units. As a result individual identities are family centred. Under competition for scarce resources the social units are competitive with each other apart from personalistic extensions of reciprocal bonding. Morality evolves around themes of paternalism and personalism in a context of insecurity, but expresses limited civic duty despite retaining an overarching civilisational identity. In terms of initiative and free thought the structure oscillates historically between periods of opening and closing. In periods of opening it suffers from the effects of the communal moral void as self-serving meets no counterforce. The society is however capable, especially in periods of openness and empowerment, of economic efflorescence benefitting heavily from the interpreting of imported knowledge.

Scenario 2

This society is comparatively small and although also shaped by cultural ideals of paternalism and personalism, and affected by insecurity, has consciously followed a path of politically empowering citizens and encouraging openness. Foreign influences have played a significant part. It has also consciously bonded with sources of advanced technical and industrial knowledge. Its economy has grown under government guidance but not control, and its entrepreneurial dynamism remains shaped by global competitive forces. As an open society it witnesses much debate.

Observations

As this is an epilogue, what follows now is a set of conjectures that together outline a future research agenda. They are set against the polar opposites symbolised in the two scenarios. There is evidence for all the propositions, but it would take another book to present it. Instead I leave them for consideration as parts of the answer to the question: how does school education contribute to societal progress?

The issues raised earlier lead us to see how that product of a society's thinking capacity associated with school education may make its contribution to the subsequent societal dynamics. The questions raised were: what kind of inputs are brought from the school experience? If carried through into university learning, how can that larger contribution assist a society's progress? Is this contribution affected by political and economic factors? And is societal complexity rising to a point where a society's thinking capacity will meet higher demands on its flexibility, openness, and moral core?

Inputs From School

Across both of the above scenarios the school experience is likely to differ only marginally, as the shared heritage as far as learning is concerned would instil rote learning, dependence on the teacher, high diligence, and competitive striving. Although innovative teaching is available to stress individual curiosity and creativity, it is not the norm in the shared culture, even though aspirations for—and experience of—university study abroad, may be influencing its rise.

Can Universities Influence Societal Progress?

In states where authority is imposed, it is normal for the political hierarchy to protect its claimed legitimacy by policing debate on that topic. This has great advantages for stability and may well be necessary at large scale or in conditions of societal stress, as with widespread corruption, but it is not conducive to societal adaptiveness or to the inner motivations of widespread co-operativeness. This is because societal change policy becomes a monopoly of a dominant elite. In those circumstances common syndromes are restrictions of academic freedom, syllabus control, and bias towards the technical and scientific subject fields. Universities in such circumstances are hollowed out, and their potential for scholarship narrowly channelled. The society is then affected in two ways: graduates are not exposed to open debate on matters of societal import; and the catalytic role of higher education in the wider societal exchanges of knowledge is reduced to the fields of applied technology.

Also in such a context, professionalism is not practiced within autonomous bodies having policy impact, but as a state extension. So too business behaviour is located in a surrounding context of meaning in which the market is within the state, rather than the state within the market, so political priorities dominate (Zheng and Huang, 2018). Coercion is implicitly attached to surveillance. Communicative action is muted, as is also civil society and by extension civic consciousness.

In other states where open debate of societal issues is tolerated and even encouraged, then the volume of ideas in open circulation is likely to be higher in ratio, and the thinkers working on complex issues are in ratio more numerous, more widely informed, and less constrained by orthodoxy. They are also more likely to be able to bring in insights and experiences from other societies. A middle class is normally autonomous and influential and engages in extensive communicative action. Professions are also independent, and civic identity can be fostered where state welfare responsibility is exercised and informed empowerment encouraged.

Rising Complexity as Societal Challenge

The modern economy (across the Middle-Income Trap) is very much more complex than the pre-modern. It is entered usually via a transition from relation-based order to rule-based order (Li, 2009). Rule-basing brings a layer of stable institutions that become, in Max Boisot's terms 'zones of stability' where people can find predictable and reliable sources of understanding, as with an audited professional accounting system. As these stabilities grow they support more and more complex exchange and wean the society away from reliance on personal relations for the guaranteeing of trust. To have this layer of new order in place requires large resources of professional skill in such fields. Although such skills in terms of knowing rules and procedures are widely available from a rote-learning process, for the most demanding fields of professional practice, as e.g. in law, public administration, forensic accounting business, large-project engineering, and the higher ranks of professionalism, the exercise of principled individual judgment becomes strategic. The more the education system encourages critical thinking and open debate the more likely it is that such skills will be available.

Much of the handling of societal complexity in modern conditions is achieved with the emergence of a bourgeois class who live and work in the world of coordinated action and exchange. Historically they have tended to take over responsibility for much social order within that arena, with such bodies as Chambers of Commerce or guilds, industry standards institutions, hospital trusts, etc. As McCloskey (2006, 2010, 2016) has shown in great detail, most economic growth and societal progress can be traced to the energies of various bourgeois groups acting as entrepreneurs, but also adding the crucial contribution of ideals of virtue and societal good. When the virtue fails, the dynamo slows down. Two observations are relevant here: successful bourgeois have normally been heavily involved in the interflows between scientific invention and business application; and large numbers of them have been leaders in setting standards of moral conduct, often expressing great respect for learning. A possible tension between political control and business interests may affect a society's moral culture as well as its economy.

Epilogue

It is clear that tracing the patterns of determinacy between school exam results and societal progress takes one through a thicket of intervening influences. And while the correlation between education and societal progress is robustly convincing, there is much else in the equation that plays a part in success and failure. And there are features that will block progress.

Of all the features that control the flow of benevolent influence, one stands out above all and it is the architecture of power. This might take the form of religious power as in Islam, it might be political power as under Communism, it might be market power having lost its moral compass as now becoming a concern in many Western societies. But in all these contexts it is at least conceivable that people could think their way through to a formula better than their current one.

In such thinking it is necessary to recall that although each society will find its own formula, they are nevertheless all bound to follow the laws of societal evolution that say a society must be always ready to adapt; it must in adapting pay attention to keeping its people co-operative; that can only be achieved in new conditions of complexity by engaging the collective brain in critical thinking and so releasing the motivation of that widespread intelligence. This is education's ultimate rationale.

Gordon Redding is an Adjunct Professor of Asian Business and Comparative Management, Institut Européen d'Administration des Affaires (INSEAD), Professor Emeritus, University of Hong Kong, Fellow, The Head Foundation, Singapore, Conjoint Professor of Asian Business, University of Newcastle, New South Wales, MA (Cambridge), PhD (Manchester), D.Econ h.c. (Stockholm SSE). Redding worked for 24 years at the University of Hong Kong, where he founded and directed the HKU Business School. For ten years he was a Director of the Wharton International Forum. For 20 years he was honorary secretary of the Association of Deans of SE Asian Graduate Schools of Management. He has published 15 books and 100 articles, including the *Spirit of Chinese Capitalism* (1990), *The Future of Chinese Capitalism* (2007), *The Hidden Form of Capital*, and *The Oxford Handbook of Asian Business Systems*. He has recently co-edited *The Oxford Handbook of Higher*

Education Systems and University Management. He has consulted with HSBC, Cathay Pacific, Hutchison Whampoa, Mandarin Oriental Hotel Group, Bank Mandiri, Incofood, BHP Billiton, Daimler Chrysler, and Christie's.

Notes

1. A few examples are Smith (1776), Kant (1991), Weber (1964), Eisenstadt (1965), Habermas (1984), Durkheim (1984), Mokyr (2017), North (2005), McCloskey (2006, 2010, 2016), Nussbaum (2010), Fukuyama (2014), Himmelfarb (2004), Gellner (1992), Sen (2006), Berger (1988), Ostrom (1990), and Polanyi (1944).
2. E.g. Boisot (1995), Nicolis and Prigogine (1989), Kauffman (1995), Ball (2004), Black (2014), Baldwin (2016).

References

Baldwin, R. *The Great Convergence: Information Technology and the New Globalization*. Cambridge, MA: Belknap Press, 2016.

Ball, P. *Critical Mass: How One Thing Leads to Another*. London: Heinemann, 2004.

Barnett, R. *Imagining the University*. London: Routledge, 2013.

Berger, P. L. "An East Asian development model?" In Peter L. Berger and Hsing-Huang M. Hsiao (Eds.), *In Search of an East Asian Development Model*. Transaction Books. New York: Transaction Publications, 1988, 3–23.

Besson, P. *Le Milieu de Terrain*. Paris: Grasset, 2018.

Black, J. *The Power of Knowledge: How Information and Technology Made the Modern World*. New Haven: Yale University Press, 2014.

Boisot, M. *Information Space*. London: Routledge, 1995.

Bond, M. H., and Y. Jing. "Socializing human capital for twenty-first century educational goals: suggestive empirical findings from multinational research." Ch.3. In Redding, Drew and Crump (Eds.), 2019.

Cardwell, D. S. L. *Turning Points in Western Technology*. New York: Neale Watson Science History Publications, 1972.

Durkheim, E. *The Division of Labour in Society*. New York: The Free Press, 1984 (originally 1893).

Eisenstadt, S. N. "Transformation of social, political and cultural orders in Modernization." *American Sociological Review* 30, no. 5 (1965): 659–673.

Fukuyama, F. *Political Order and Political Decay: From the Industrial Revolution to the Globalization of Democracy*. London: Profile Books, 2014.

Gellner, E. *Reason and Culture*. Oxford: Blackwell, 1992.

Habermas, J. *The Theory of Communicative Action: Volume 1. Reason and the Rationalisation of Society*. Boston, MA: Beacon Press, 1984.

Himmelfarb, G. *The Roads to Modernity*. New York: Alfred A. Knopf, 2004.

Kant, I. *What Is Enlightenment?* London: Penguin, 1991.

Kauffman, S. *At Home in the Universe*. New York: Oxford University Press, 1995.

Konner, M. *The Evolution of Childhood: Relationships, Emotion, Mind*. Cambridge, MA: Belknap Press, 2010.

Li, S. M. *Managing International Business in Relation-based Versus Rule-based Countries*. New York: Business Expert Press, 2009.

McCloskey, D. N. *The Bourgeois Virtues: Ethics for an Age of Commerce*. Chicago: University of Chicago Press, 2006.

McCloskey, D. N. *Bourgeois Dignity: Why Economics Can't Explain the Modern World*. Chicago: University of Chicago Press, 2010.

McCloskey, D. N. *Bourgeois Equality*. Chicago: University of Chicago Press, 2016.

Mokyr, J. *A Culture of Growth: The Origins of the Modern Economy*. Princeton: Princeton University Press, 2017.

Nicolis, G., and I. Prigogine. *Exploring Complexity*. New York: W. H. Freeman, 1989.

North, D. C. *Understanding the Process of Economic Change*. Princeton: Princeton University Press, 2005.

Nussbaum, M. C. *Not for Profit: Why Democracy Needs the Humanities*. Princeton, NJ: Princeton University Press, 2010.

Ostrom, E. *Governing the Commons: The Evolution of Institutions for Collective Action*. Cambridge: Cambridge University Press, 1990.

Pinker, S. *The Better Angels of Our Nature*. London: Penguin, 2011.

Polanyi, K. *The Great Transformation*. Boston: Beacon Press, 1944.

Ragin, C. C. *The Comparative Method*. Berkeley, CA: University of California Press, 1987.

Redding, G., A. Drew, and S. Crump, eds. *The Oxford Handbook of Higher Education Systems and University Management*. Oxford: Oxford University Press, 2019.

Sen, A. *Identity and Violence: The Illusion of Destiny*. New York: Norton, 2006.

Smith, A. *The Wealth of Nations*. London: Strahan and Cadell, 1776.

Weber, M. *The Theory of Social and Economic Organization*. New York: The Free Press, 1964.

Welzel, C. *Freedom Rising*. Cambridge: Cambridge University Press, 2013.

Whitley, R. "Changing the nature and role of universities: The effects of funding and governance reforms on universities as accountable actors." Ch.4. In Redding, Drew and Crump (Eds.), 2019.

Wittfogel, K. A. *Oriental Despotism: A Comparative View of Total Power*. New Haven: Yale University Press, 1957.

Zheng Y. N., and Y. J. Huang. *Market in State: The Political Economy of Domination in China*. Cambridge: Cambridge University Press, 2018.

Author Biographies

Chris Baumann is an Associate Professor at Macquarie University, Sydney, a Visiting Professor at Seoul National University (SNU) in South Korea, and a Visiting Associate Professor at Osaka University in Japan; formerly also at Aarhus University in Denmark. His research is on the 3 Cs:

- Competitiveness;
- Confucianism;
- Customer loyalty (share of wallet).

Baumann received his doctorate from Macquarie University after postgraduate and undergraduate studies in Canada (MBA from Simon Fraser University, SFU) and Switzerland. He has been awarded for excellence in his research and teaching, including from the Carrick Institute of Education for enthusiastic approach to education, and from the Academy of International Business (AIB) as outstanding reviewer. He is also the recipient of Emerald Literati Awards and a best paper award from The Western Decision Sciences Institute (WDSI) for his research.

He has published in leading international journals and introduced new ways of looking at things, or concepts: Competitive Productivity (CP), Brand Competitiveness, Latecomer Brand, Premium Generic Brand (PGB), and 'country of origin of service staff' (COSS) effect. For cross-cultural and international business (IB) research, he introduced (with Hume Winzar) the ReVaMB model (Relative Values and Moderated Behaviour) as a framework for study. Baumann, Winzar, and Tony Fang (Stockholm Business School) also introduced 'Inter-Ocular Testing (IOT)' to avoid 错觉 (Cuòjué, or wrong impression). Baumann is passionate about Inter-Ocular Testing (IOT) rather than relying on traditional statistical mean/association testing alone.

He has extensive teaching experience worldwide: in Canada, Denmark, Hong Kong, South Korea, Singapore, and of course Australia. Not least as a result of his exposure to a variety of dissimilar approaches to management, pedagogy, and life in general, he has developed a deep interest in cross-cultural and cross-national comparison of performance and competitiveness, an interest in East Asian wisdom such as Confucianism, Taoism, Legalism, and Buddhism and their associations with strategy, management, and performance. His passion is to understand better the cross-cultural perspectives on education and training; he wants to further explore how discipline, motivation, personality, culture, and performance all relate.

Hume Winzar is an Associate Professor at Macquarie University, Sydney, and director of the degree in Business Analytics. He is co-author of two bestselling textbooks on marketing research (Cengage) and consumer behaviour (Oxford University Press). Current research interests include the contextual effects of culture on consumer choice, customer analytics, and complex systems analysis applied to markets. Together with Chris Baumann, Hume developed the ReVaMB model. Like Baumann, Winzar is sceptical of the value of traditional null-hypothesis statistical tests, preferring Inter-Ocular Tests (IOT) and Bayesian thinking. Winzar has a passion (and talent for) statistical testing far beyond the usual quantitative researcher. With a quest for knowledge, he explores and explores, and explores. . . .

Doris Viengkham was a doctoral candidate in the Faculty of Business and Economics (FBE) at Macquarie University, Sydney, at the time of writing. Her dissertation focusses on the values-behaviour nexus in East Asia at the individual level, through an application of novel concepts, the role of context, and experimental designs. Specifically, her research is interested in the interplay of Eastern traditional philosophies and economic ideologies across these societies, to understand their impact on work-related behaviours under different conditions. Viengkham's recent work, co-authored with Baumann and Winzar, explores the various aspects of Confucian values as they relate to employee performance, further demonstrating the applicability of the CDC framework presented in this book within an organisational context. She is similarly interested in the development of Competitive Productivity, or CP, a new concept combining competitiveness and productivity.

Index

ability: academic 54, 224; perceived 54
absenteeism 121
Absolute Advantage Trade 34
academic performance 38
academic success 68, 71, 75, 105, 108, 201
acclimatising 72
accountability 99, 139
achievement motivation 48, 53, 128–129, 144
achievement pressure 24, 129
achievement scores 149, 170
action-dispositional property 65
adaptations 11, 137, 139, 234–235, 240
adaptiveness 235–237, 239–240, 242
adolescence 22, 45–46, 50, 88, 143, 145, 196, 228–229
adulthood 55, 69, 104, 113, 208, 212, 233
advancements 38–39, 170, 203
affection 69, 212
after-school tutor 22
Airbnb 40
alternative causal directions 156–157
altruism 171
American: culture 201; dominance 220; dream 236; education system 140; imagination 200; Ivy League 207; schools 76; students 99; workers 41
analysis: longitudinal 149, 153; multivariate 51, 93, 121
ancestors 10, 72
ancient survival logics 235
anecdotal evidence 61, 199
Annual Reuters' Ranking 207, 228
anxiety 130, 212
applied knowledge 240

approaches 16, 19, 23–24, 62, 103–106, 120–121, 139, 141, 199–200, 203, 205, 211–212, 216, 218, 227; authoritarian 19, 73, 206, 222; authoritative 19, 22, 24, 205, 210; balanced 105, 107; chalk and talk 23; crueller 109; disciplined learning 7, 17, 200, 207, 211–212, 214, 221; educational 74; explicit 16; harsh 105; less-disciplined 212; motivational 53; pedagogic 149; strict versus fair disciplinarian 22, 76, 200; tiger 104; unsupportive 104
arrived late 53, 122
artificial intelligence 39–40
Asian achievement 200
Asian American 89, 197, 201, 207–209; achievement paradox 209, 231; students 209
Asian business 244
Asian century 220–221
Asian classroom 132
Asian crisis 40
Asian culture 208–209
Asian families 104
Asian growth trajectories 232
Asian-heritage families 104, 143, 200, 229; parenting 5, 69, 72, 104, 200–201
Asian immigrant groups 73, 167, 209
Asian Miracle 11–12, 38–39
Asian students 70, 73, 76, 103, 130, 208
Asian universities 207
aspirations 52, 138, 211, 227, 242
association: direct 5, 148; negative 60; positive 57, 96, 157
attendance 207; improved 78; low 207; poor 207; required class 207